STAR WARS®
DARK TIMES

VOLUME SIX

FIRE CARRIER

D1200712

THE RISE OF THE EMPIRE

From 1,000 to 0 years before the Battle of Yavin

After the seeming final defeat of the Sith, the Republic enters a state of complacency.
In the waning years of the Republic, the Senate rife with corruption, the ambitious
Senator Palpatine causes himself to be elected Supreme Chancellor.
This is the era of the prequel trilogy.

The events in this story take place a few months after the
events in *Star Wars:* Episode III—*Revenge of the Sith.*

STAR WARS®
DARK TIMES

VOLUME SIX

FIRE CARRIER

Script
RANDY STRADLEY

Art
GABRIEL GUZMAN

Colors
GARRY HENDERSON

Lettering
MICHAEL HEISLER

Cover Art
DOUGLAS WHEATLEY

DARK HORSE BOOKS   LUCAS BOOKS

President and Publisher
MIKE RICHARDSON

Collection Designer
JIMMY PRESLER

Editor
DAVE MARSHALL

Assistant Editor
FREDDYE LINS

Neil Hankerson **Executive Vice President** • Tom Weddle **Chief Financial Officer** • Randy Stradley **Vice President of Publishing** • Michael Martens **Vice President of Book Trade Sales** • Scott Allie **Editor in Chief** • Matt Parkinson **Vice President of Marketing** • David Scroggy **Vice President of Product Development** • Dale LaFountain **Vice President of Information Technology** • Darlene Vogel **Senior Director of Print, Design, and Production** • Ken Lizzi **General Counsel** • Davey Estrada **Editorial Director** • Chris Warner **Senior Books Editor** • Diana Schutz **Executive Editor** • Cary Grazzini **Director of Print and Development** • Lia Ribacchi **Art Director** • Cara Niece **Director of Scheduling** • Tim Wiesch **Director of International Licensing** • Mark Bernardi **Director of Digital Publishing**

Special thanks to Jennifer Heddle, Leland Chee, Troy Alders, Carol Roeder, Jann Moorhead, and David Anderman at Lucas Licensing.

STAR WARS: DARK TIMES Volume Six—Fire Carrier

This volume collects issues one through five of the Dark Horse comic-book series
Star Wars: Dark Times—Fire Carrier.

Published by Dark Horse Books, a division of Dark Horse Comics, Inc.
10956 SE Main Street, Milwaukie, OR 97222

DarkHorse.com| StarWars.com

International Licensing: 503-905-2377
To find a comics shop in your area, call the Comic Shop Locator Service
toll-free at 1-888-266-4226

Library of Congress Cataloging-in-Publication Data

Stradley, Randy, 1956-
Star Wars, Dark times. Volume six, Fire carrier / script, Randy Stradley ; art, Gabriel Guzman ; colors, Garry Henderson ; letters, Michael Heisler ; cover art, Douglas Wheatley.
pages cm
Summary: "In a galaxy suddenly hunting Jedi, Master K'Kruhk is on the run with a group of young Padawans. Crash landing on an Imperial-run planet, they stumble upon an evil greater than they could have imagined"-- Provided by publisher.
ISBN 978-1-61655-173-5
1. Graphic novels. I. Guzman, Gabriel, illustrator. II. Wheatley, Douglas, cover artist. III. Title. IV. Title: Fire carrier.
PZ7.7.S76St 2013
741.5'973--dc23
2013015048

First printing: September 2013
ISBN 978-1-61655-173-5

1 3 5 7 9 10 8 6 4 2
Printed in China

DURING THE DEVASTATION OF ORDER 66, when clone troopers everywhere turned on their Jedi generals, Jedi Master K'Kruhk narrowly escaped with a group of younglings on a damaged shuttle.

Unsure of the reason for the clone troopers' new anti-Jedi orders, K'Kruhk tried simply to get the younglings away . . . But when they encountered space pirates, the Padawans were again in danger. This time, however, Master K'Kruhk allowed his anger to take part in saving the Padawans.

Now, traveling in the pirates' ship, the Jedi and the younglings are looking for a safe haven. They have all been through so much, and the future remains clouded . . .

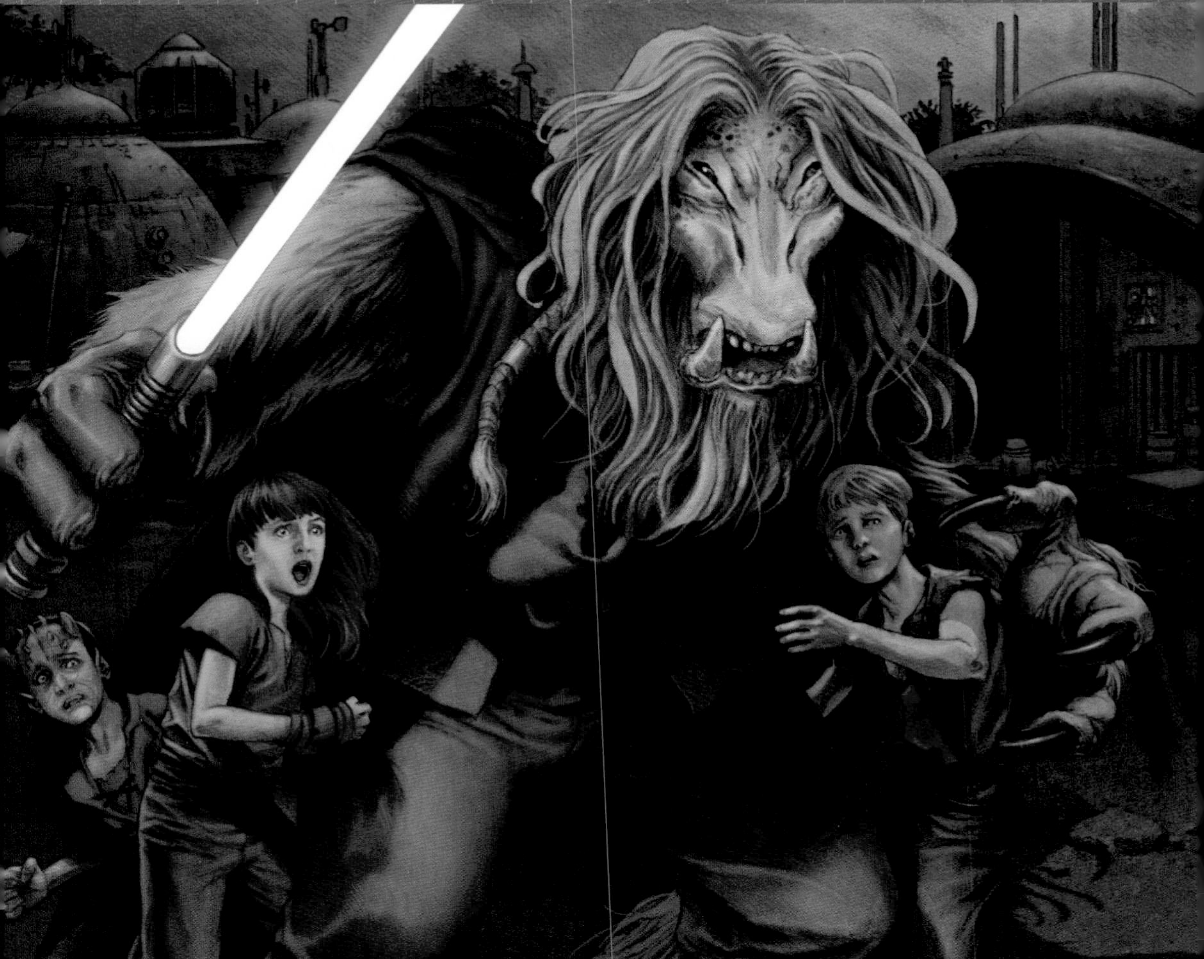

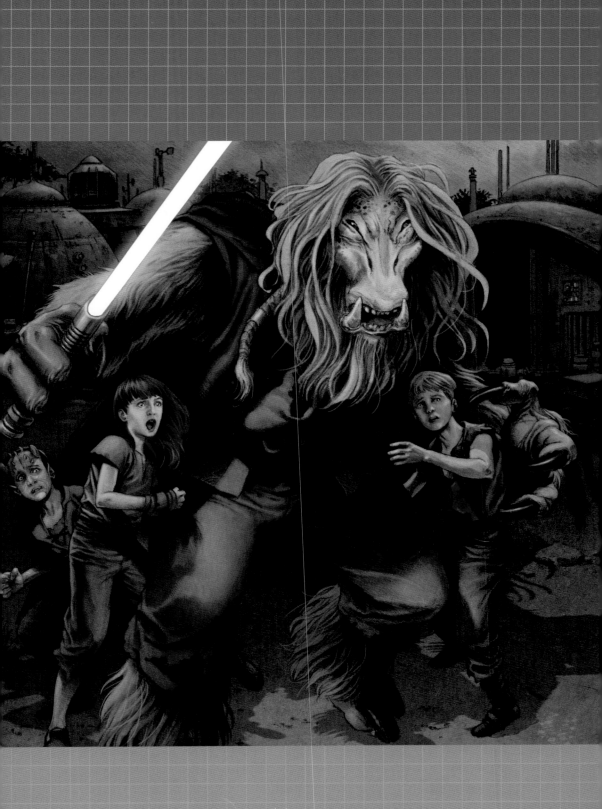

Art by
DOUGLAS WHEATLEY

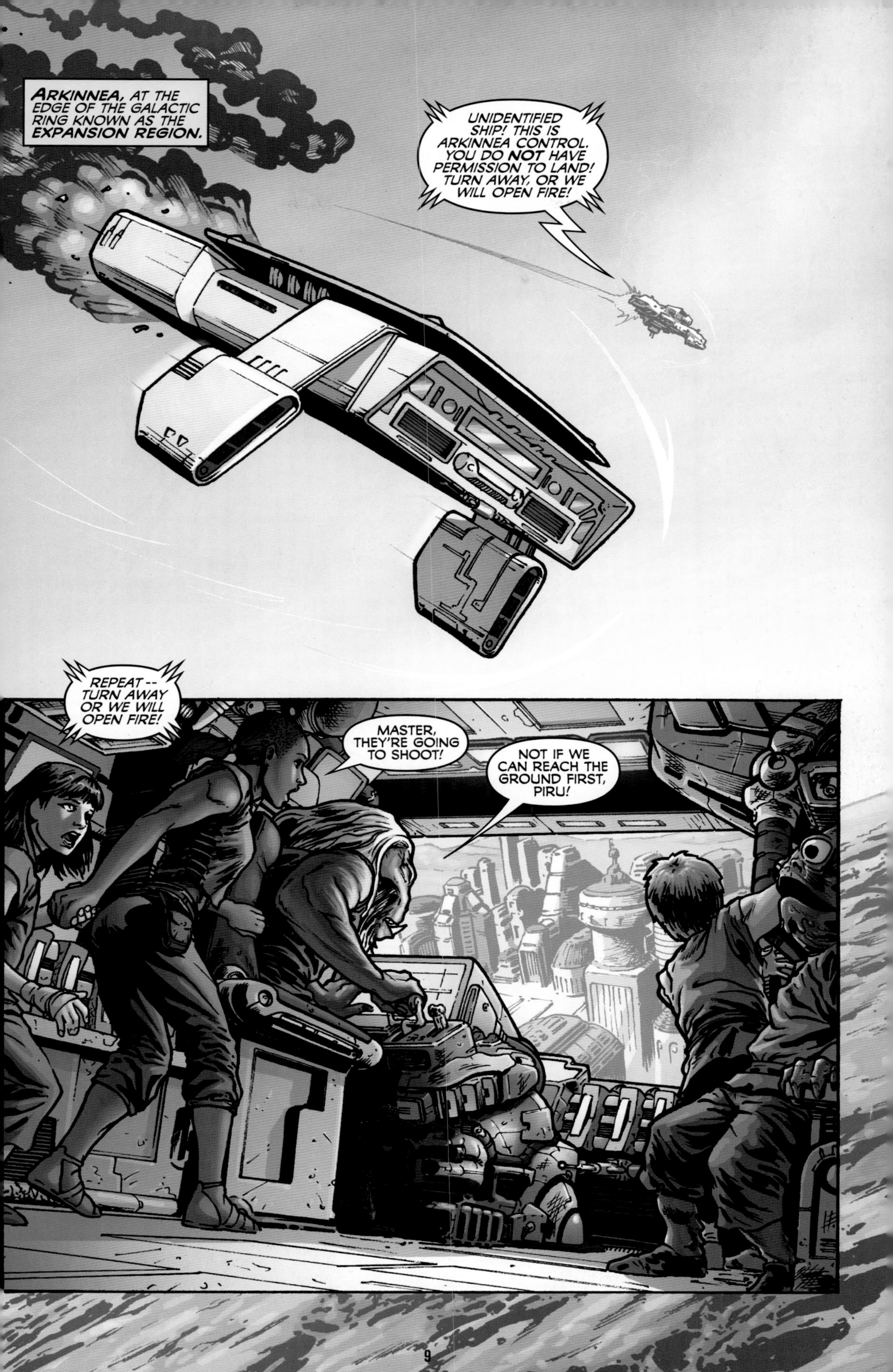
ARKINNEA, AT THE EDGE OF THE GALACTIC RING KNOWN AS THE EXPANSION REGION.
UNIDENTIFIED SHIP! THIS IS ARKINNEA CONTROL. YOU DO NOT HAVE PERMISSION TO LAND! TURN AWAY, OR WE WILL OPEN FIRE!
REPEAT -- TURN AWAY OR WE WILL OPEN FIRE!
MASTER, THEY'RE GOING TO SHOOT!
NOT IF WE CAN REACH THE GROUND FIRST, PIRU!

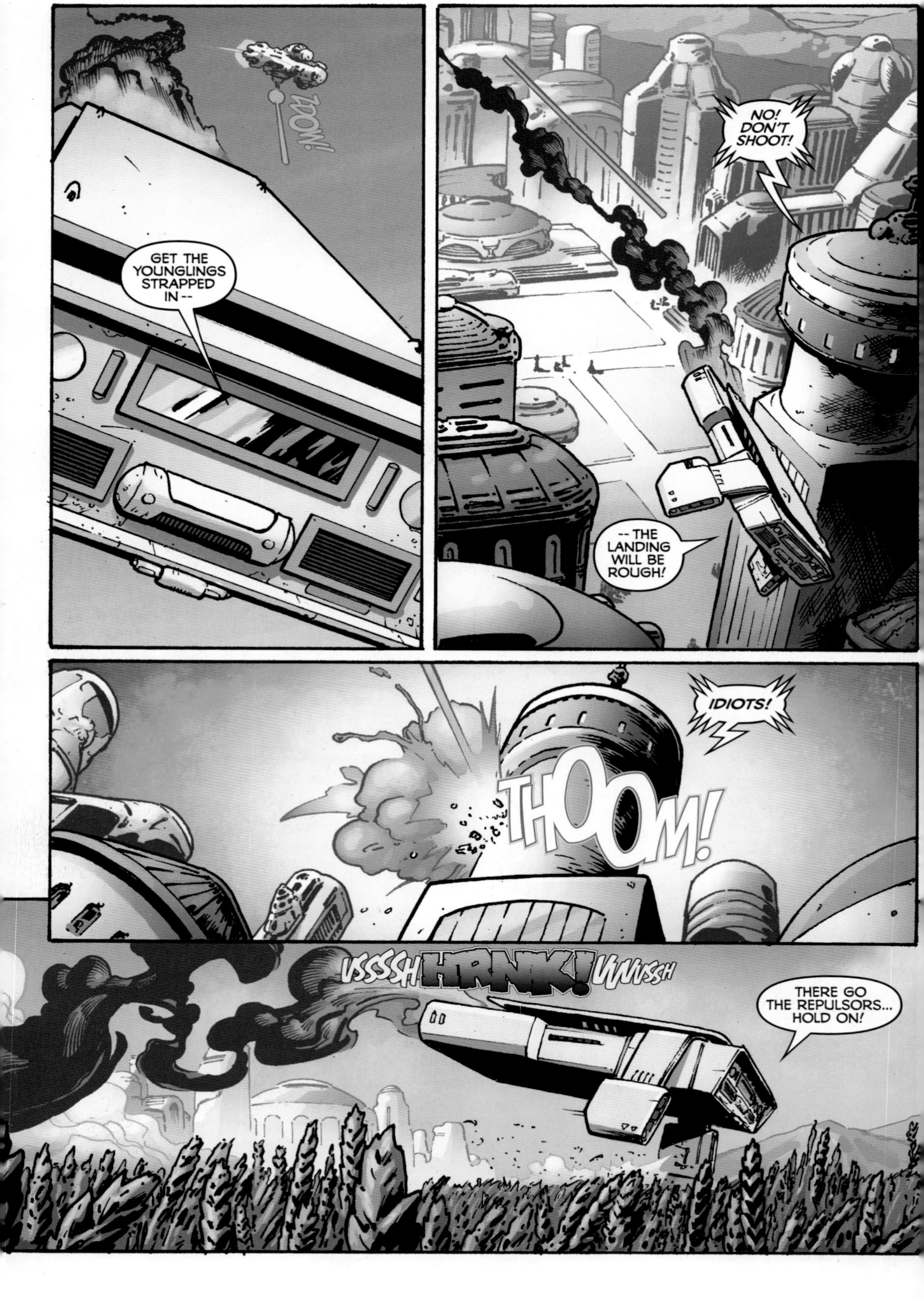
TDOW!
GET THE YOUNGLINGS STRAPPED IN --
NO! DON'T SHOOT!
-- THE LANDING WILL BE ROUGH!
IDIOTS!
THOOM!
VSSSSH HRNK! VVVVSSH
THERE GO THE REPULSORS... HOLD ON!

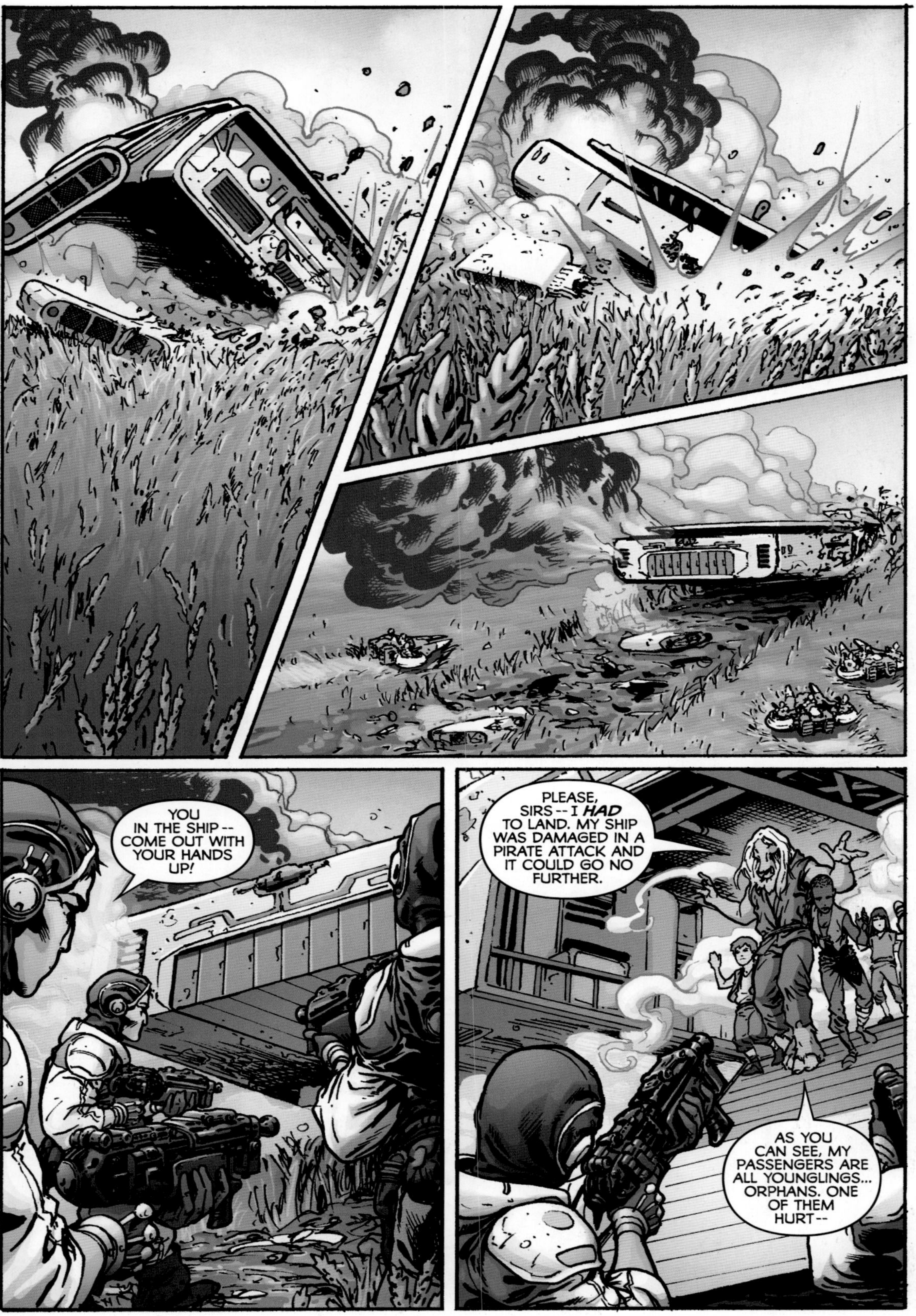
YOU IN THE SHIP -- COME OUT WITH YOUR HANDS UP!
PLEASE, SIRS -- I HAD TO LAND. MY SHIP WAS DAMAGED IN A PIRATE ATTACK AND IT COULD GO NO FURTHER.
AS YOU CAN SEE, MY PASSENGERS ARE ALL YOUNGLINGS... ORPHANS. ONE OF THEM HURT--

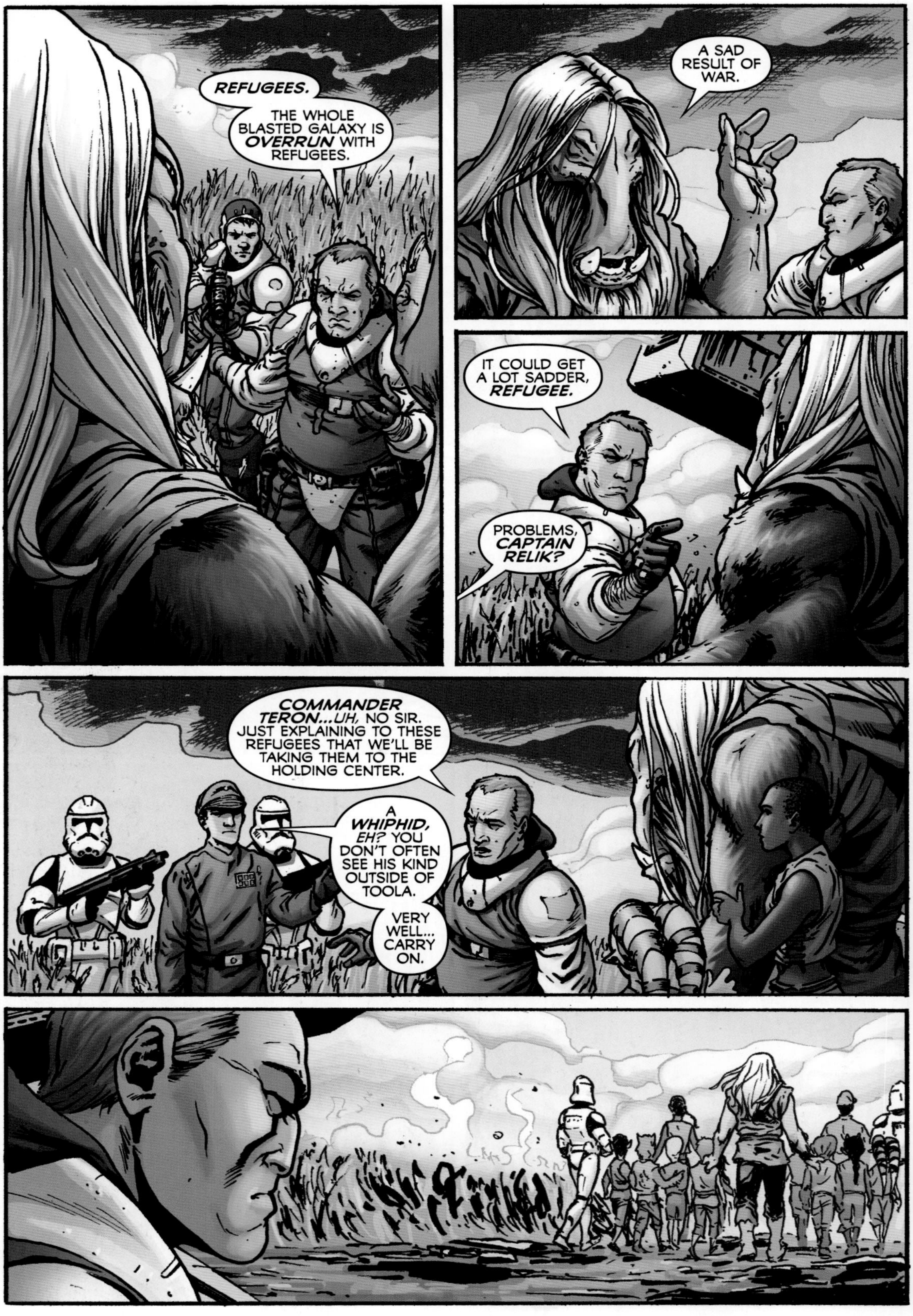
REFUGEES.
THE WHOLE BLASTED GALAXY IS OVERRUN WITH REFUGEES.
A SAD RESULT OF WAR.
IT COULD GET A LOT SADDER, REFUGEE.
PROBLEMS, CAPTAIN RELIK?
COMMANDER TERON... UH, NO SIR. JUST EXPLAINING TO THESE REFUGEES THAT WE'LL BE TAKING THEM TO THE HOLDING CENTER.
A WHIPHID, EH? YOU DON'T OFTEN SEE HIS KIND OUTSIDE OF TOOLA.
VERY WELL... CARRY ON.

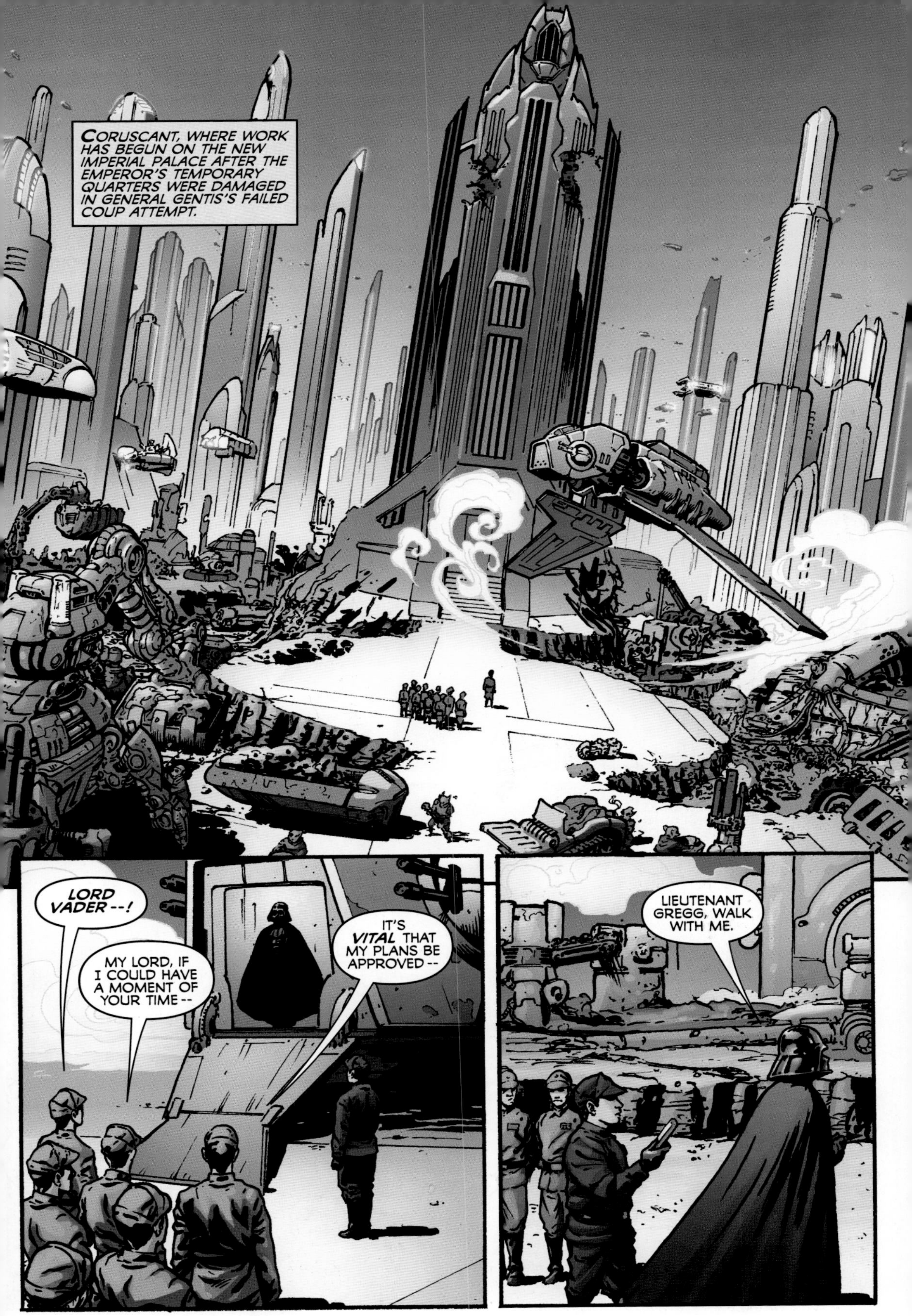
CORUSCANT, WHERE WORK HAS BEGUN ON THE NEW IMPERIAL PALACE AFTER THE EMPEROR'S TEMPORARY QUARTERS WERE DAMAGED IN GENERAL GENTIS'S FAILED COUP ATTEMPT.
LORD VADER --!
MY LORD, IF I COULD HAVE A MOMENT OF YOUR TIME --
IT'S VITAL THAT MY PLANS BE APPROVED --
LIEUTENANT GREGG, WALK WITH ME.

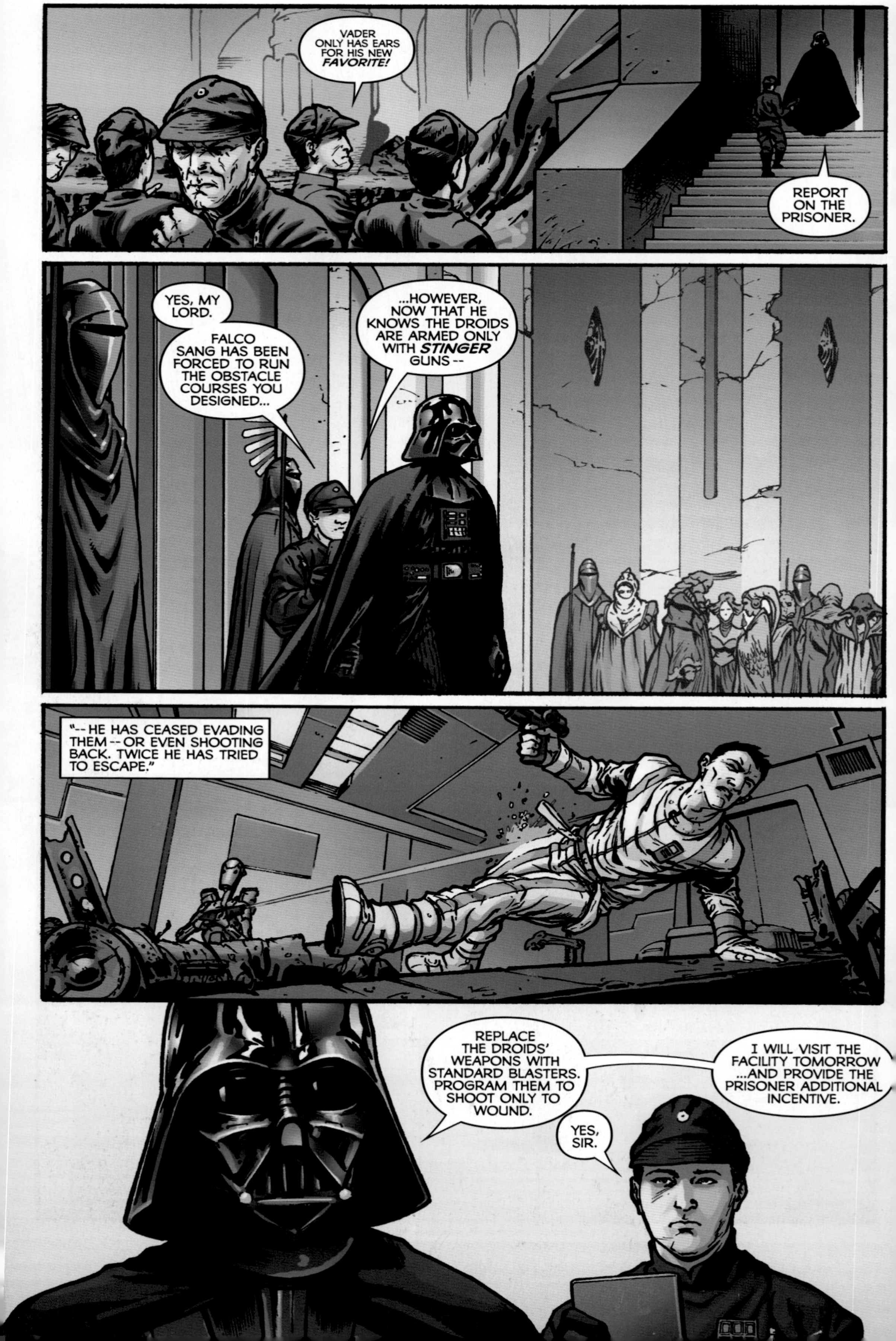
VADER ONLY HAS EARS FOR HIS NEW *FAVORITE!*
REPORT ON THE PRISONER.
YES, MY LORD.
FALCO SANG HAS BEEN FORCED TO RUN THE OBSTACLE COURSES YOU DESIGNED...
...HOWEVER, NOW THAT HE KNOWS THE DROIDS ARE ARMED ONLY WITH *STINGER* GUNS --
"-- HE HAS CEASED EVADING THEM -- OR EVEN SHOOTING BACK. TWICE HE HAS TRIED TO ESCAPE."
REPLACE THE DROIDS' WEAPONS WITH STANDARD BLASTERS. PROGRAM THEM TO SHOOT ONLY TO WOUND.
I WILL VISIT THE FACILITY TOMORROW ...AND PROVIDE THE PRISONER ADDITIONAL INCENTIVE.
YES, SIR.

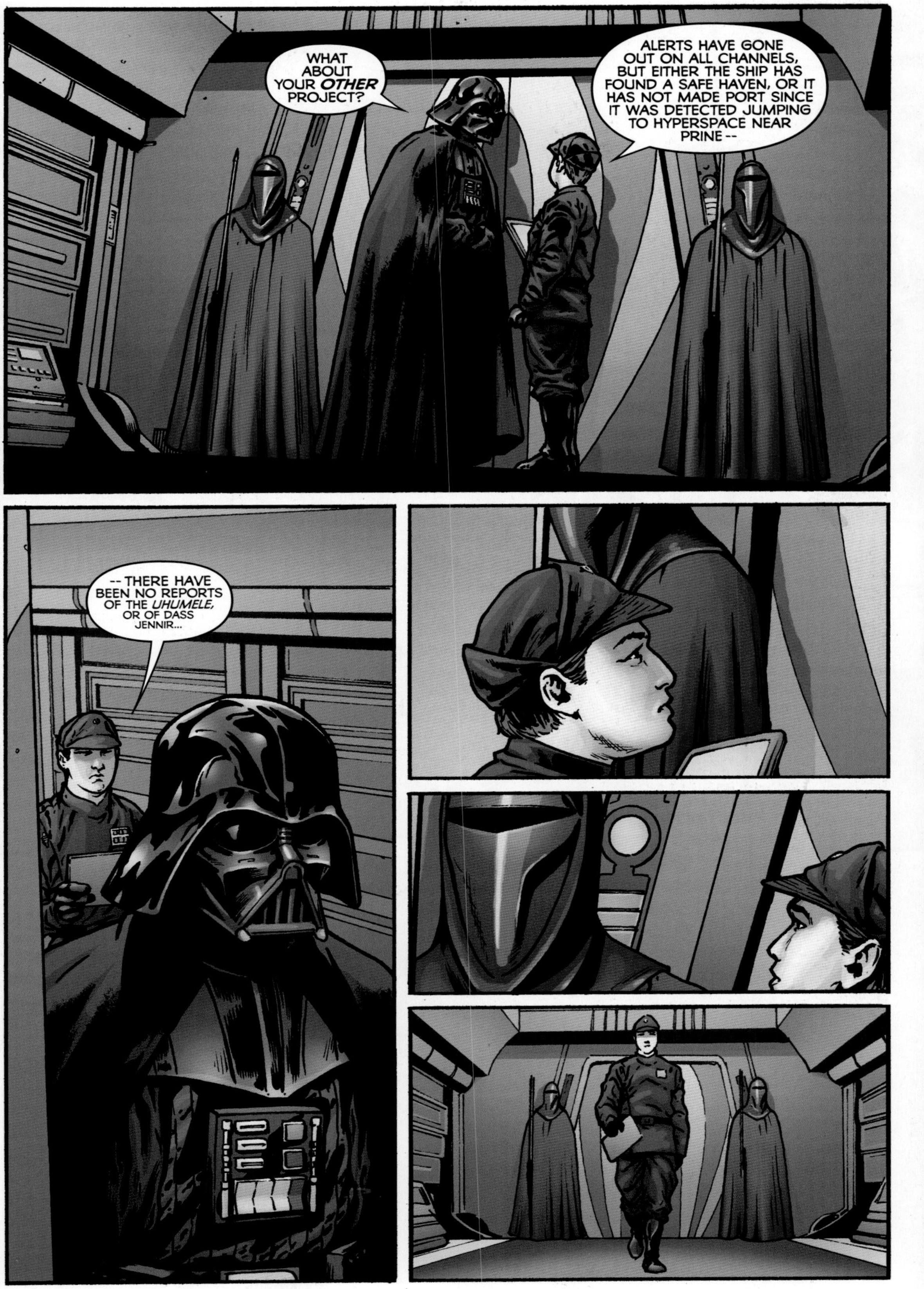
WHAT ABOUT YOUR *OTHER* PROJECT?
ALERTS HAVE GONE OUT ON ALL CHANNELS, BUT EITHER THE SHIP HAS FOUND A SAFE HAVEN, OR IT HAS NOT MADE PORT SINCE IT WAS DETECTED JUMPING TO HYPERSPACE NEAR PRINE --
-- THERE HAVE BEEN NO REPORTS OF THE *UHUMELE,* OR OF DASS JENNIR...

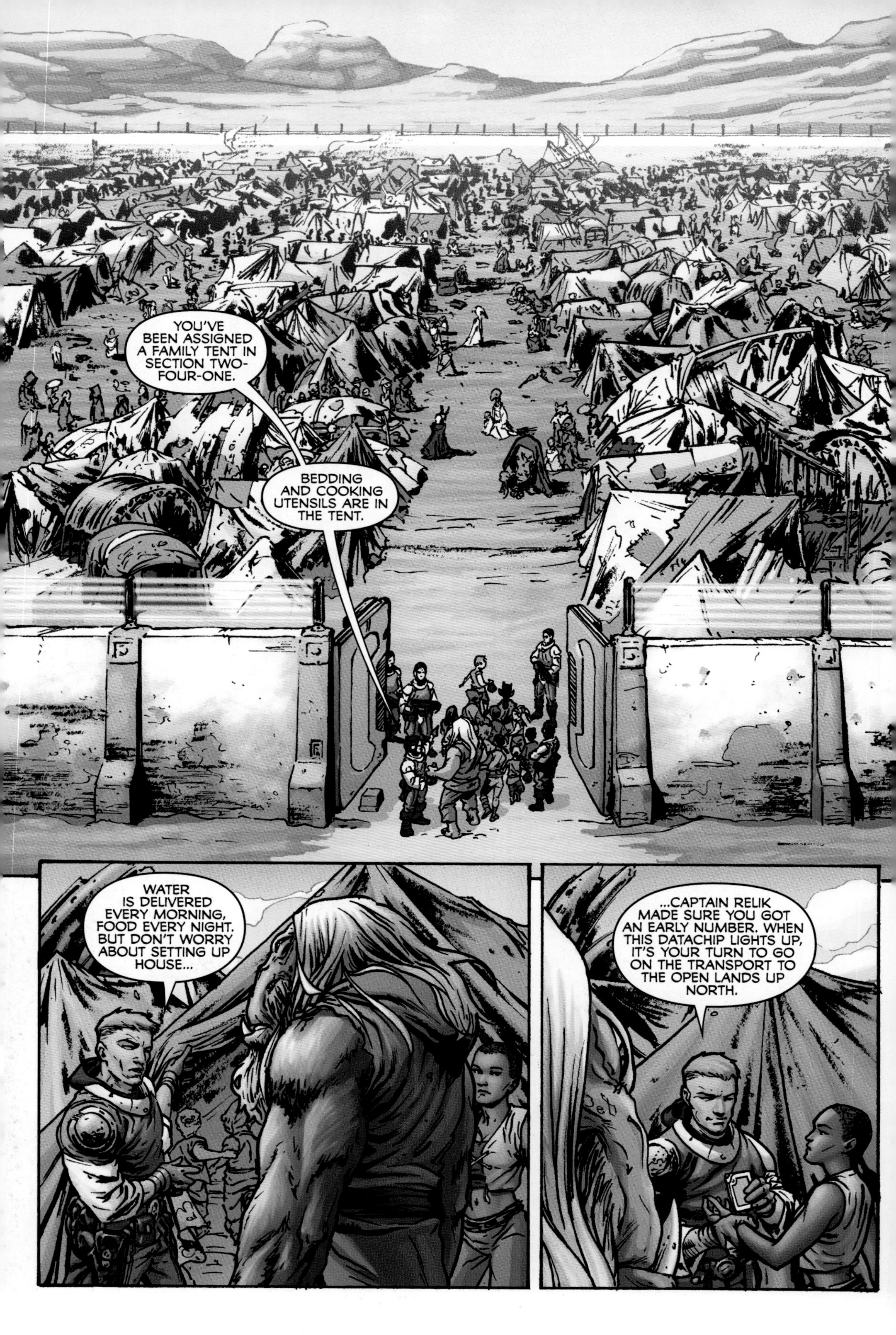
YOU'VE BEEN ASSIGNED A FAMILY TENT IN SECTION TWO-FOUR-ONE.
BEDDING AND COOKING UTENSILS ARE IN THE TENT.
WATER IS DELIVERED EVERY MORNING, FOOD EVERY NIGHT. BUT DON'T WORRY ABOUT SETTING UP HOUSE...
...CAPTAIN RELIK MADE SURE YOU GOT AN EARLY NUMBER. WHEN THIS DATACHIP LIGHTS UP, IT'S YOUR TURN TO GO ON THE TRANSPORT TO THE OPEN LANDS UP NORTH.

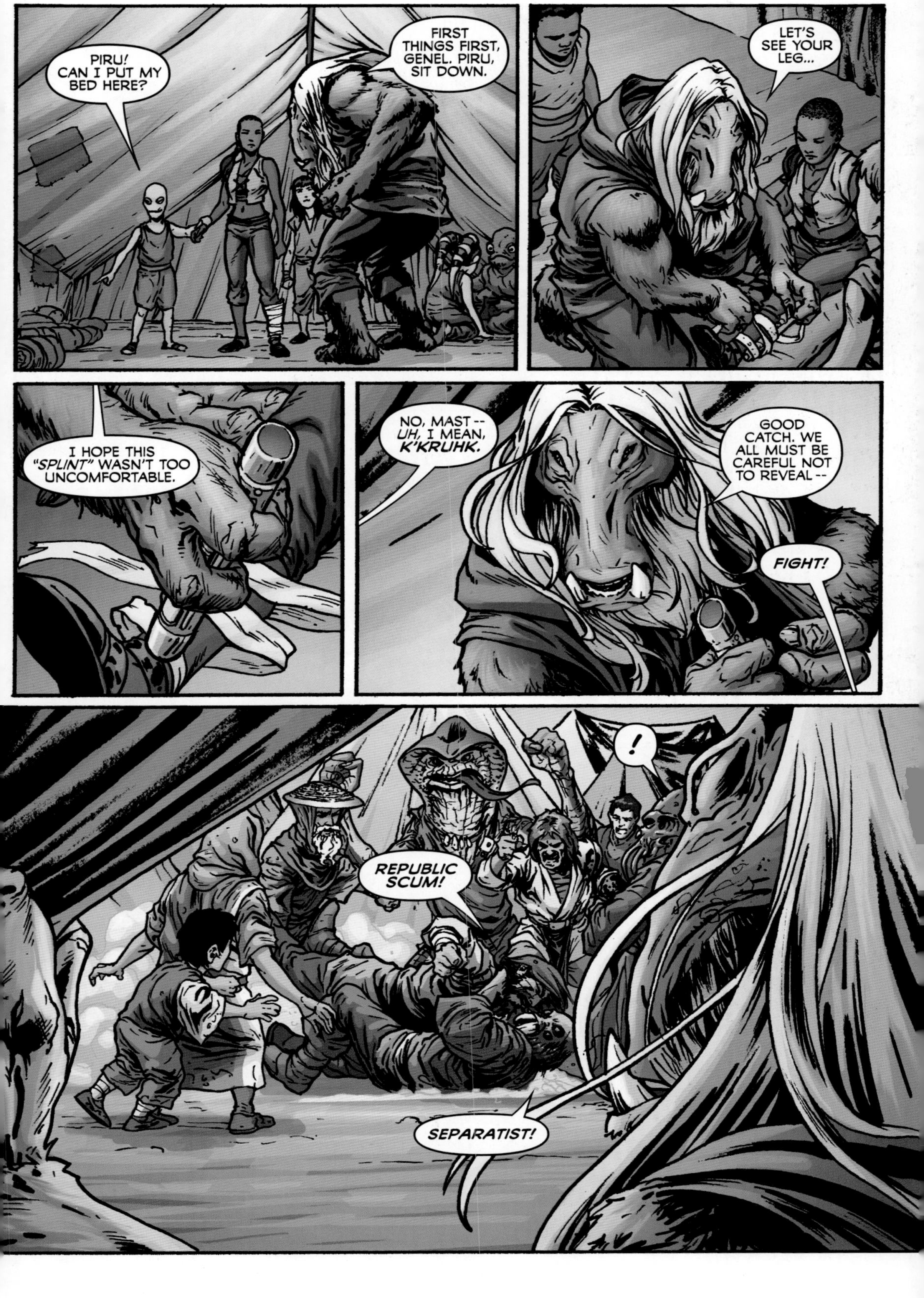
PIRU! CAN I PUT MY BED HERE?
FIRST THINGS FIRST, GENEL. PIRU, SIT DOWN.
LET'S SEE YOUR LEG...
I HOPE THIS "SPLINT" WASN'T TOO UNCOMFORTABLE.
NO, MAST -- UH, I MEAN, K'KRUHK.
GOOD CATCH. WE ALL MUST BE CAREFUL NOT TO REVEAL --
FIGHT!
!
REPUBLIC SCUM!
SEPARATIST!

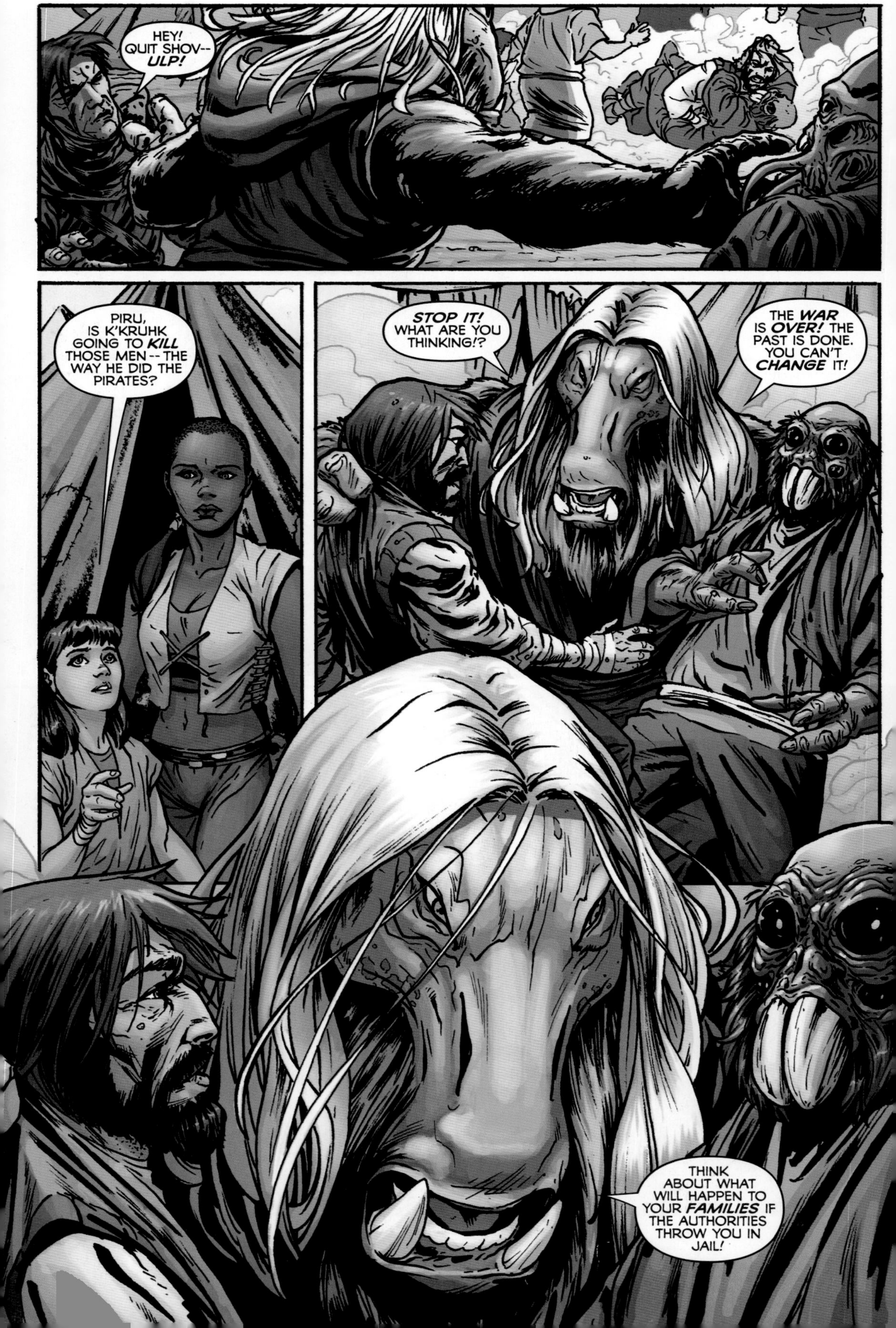
HEY! QUIT SHOV-- ULP!
PIRU, IS K'KRUHK GOING TO KILL THOSE MEN -- THE WAY HE DID THE PIRATES?
STOP IT! WHAT ARE YOU THINKING!?
THE WAR IS OVER! THE PAST IS DONE. YOU CAN'T CHANGE IT!
THINK ABOUT WHAT WILL HAPPEN TO YOUR FAMILIES IF THE AUTHORITIES THROW YOU IN JAIL!

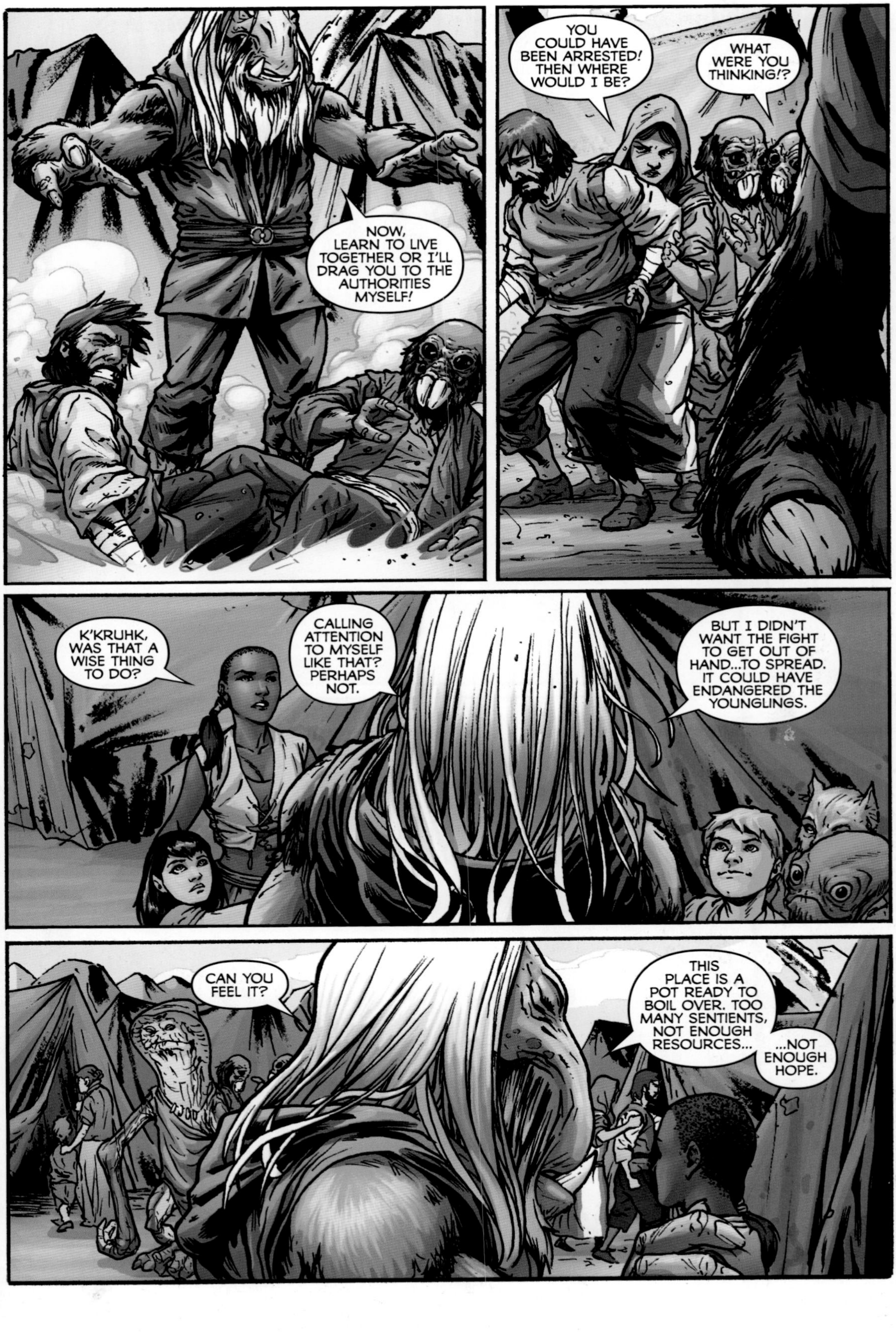
NOW, LEARN TO LIVE TOGETHER OR I'LL DRAG YOU TO THE AUTHORITIES MYSELF!
YOU COULD HAVE BEEN ARRESTED! THEN WHERE WOULD I BE?
WHAT WERE YOU THINKING!?
K'KRUHK, WAS THAT A WISE THING TO DO?
CALLING ATTENTION TO MYSELF LIKE THAT? PERHAPS NOT.
BUT I DIDN'T WANT THE FIGHT TO GET OUT OF HAND...TO SPREAD. IT COULD HAVE ENDANGERED THE YOUNGLINGS.
CAN YOU FEEL IT?
THIS PLACE IS A POT READY TO BOIL OVER. TOO MANY SENTIENTS, NOT ENOUGH RESOURCES...
...NOT ENOUGH HOPE.

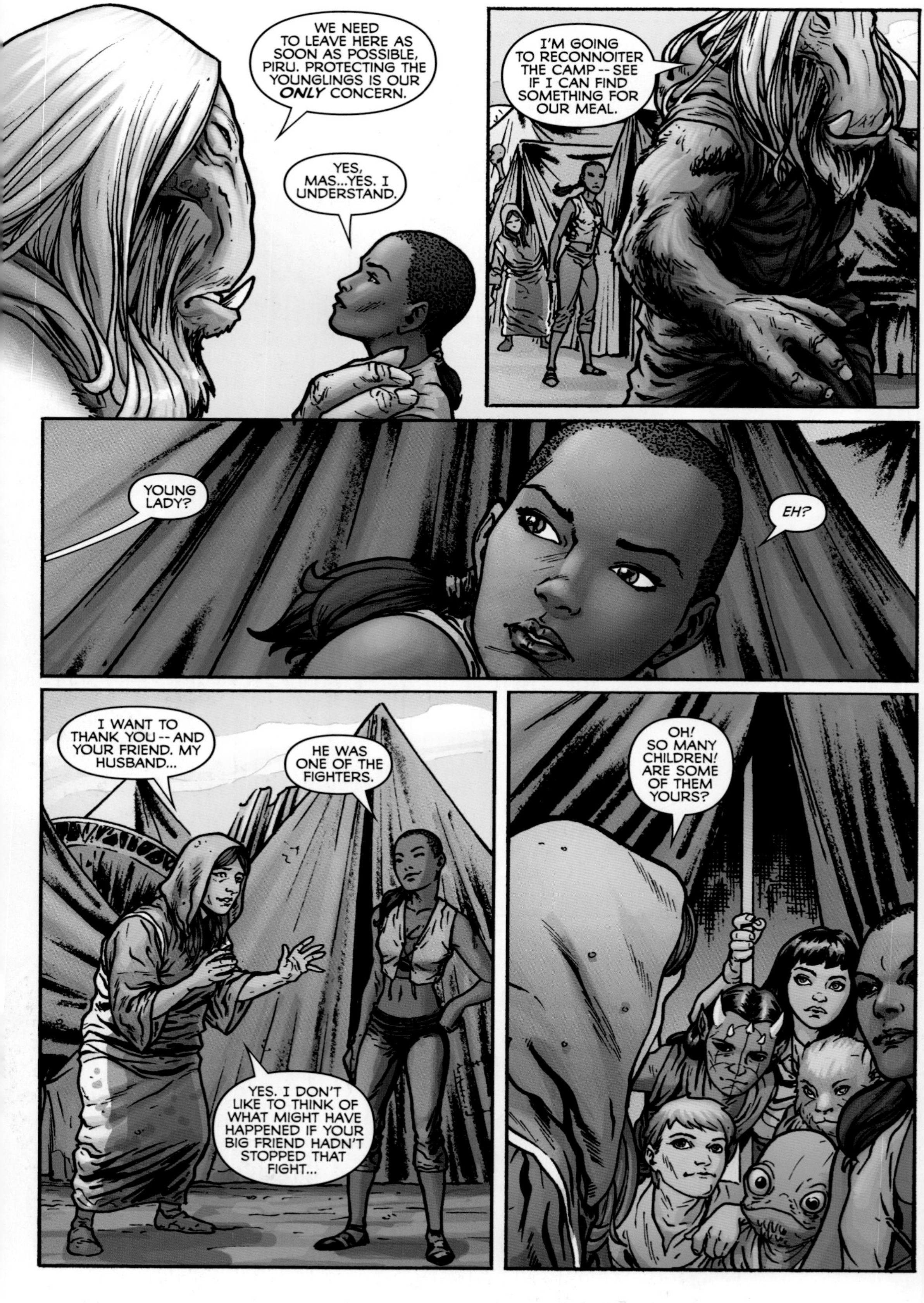
WE NEED TO LEAVE HERE AS SOON AS POSSIBLE, PIRU. PROTECTING THE YOUNGLINGS IS OUR ONLY CONCERN.
YES, MAS...YES. I UNDERSTAND.
I'M GOING TO RECONNOITER THE CAMP -- SEE IF I CAN FIND SOMETHING FOR OUR MEAL.
YOUNG LADY?
EH?
I WANT TO THANK YOU -- AND YOUR FRIEND. MY HUSBAND...
HE WAS ONE OF THE FIGHTERS.
YES. I DON'T LIKE TO THINK OF WHAT MIGHT HAVE HAPPENED IF YOUR BIG FRIEND HADN'T STOPPED THAT FIGHT...
OH! SO MANY CHILDREN! ARE SOME OF THEM YOURS?

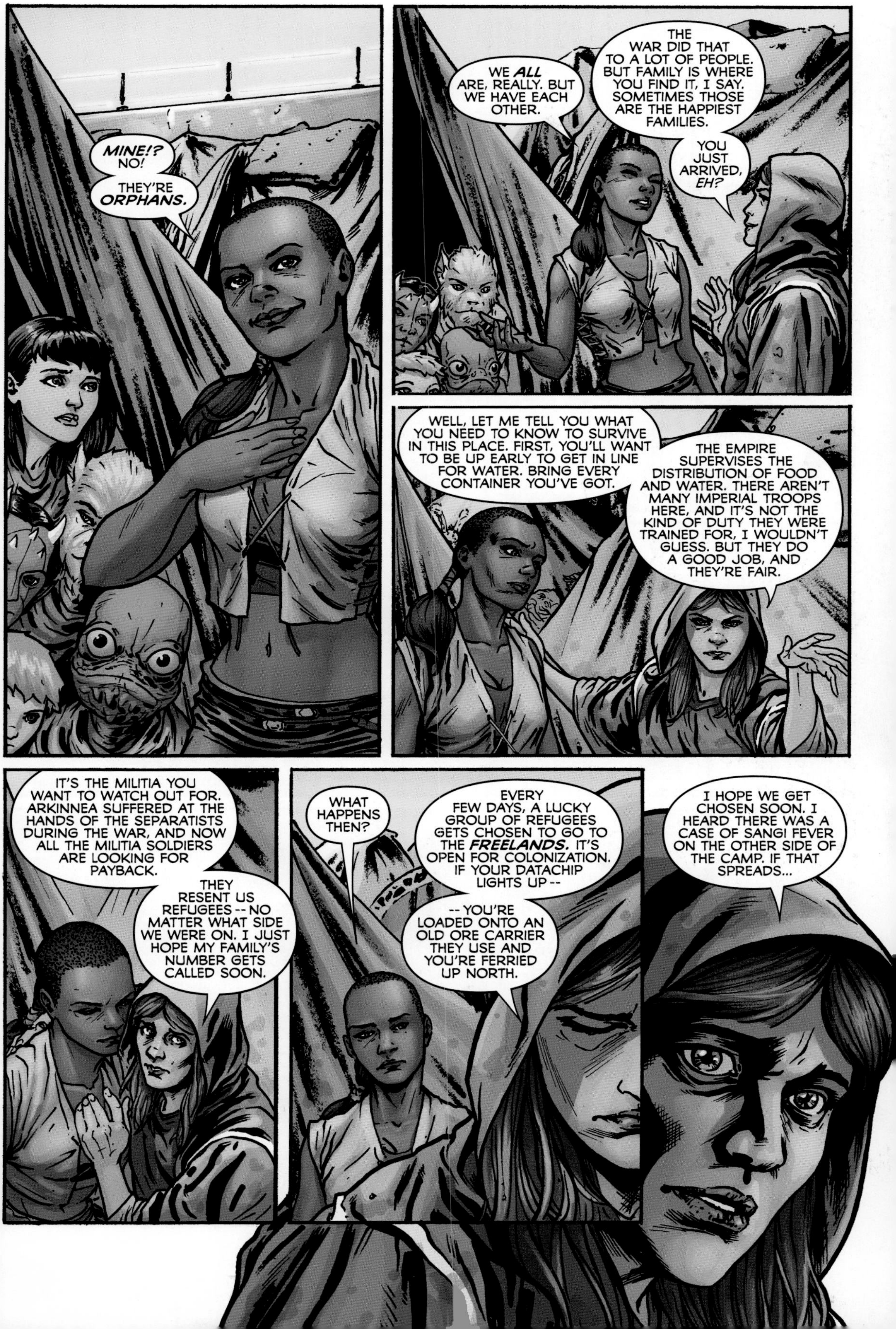
MINE!? NO!
THEY'RE ORPHANS.
WE ALL ARE, REALLY. BUT WE HAVE EACH OTHER.
THE WAR DID THAT TO A LOT OF PEOPLE. BUT FAMILY IS WHERE YOU FIND IT, I SAY. SOMETIMES THOSE ARE THE HAPPIEST FAMILIES.
YOU JUST ARRIVED, EH?
WELL, LET ME TELL YOU WHAT YOU NEED TO KNOW TO SURVIVE IN THIS PLACE. FIRST, YOU'LL WANT TO BE UP EARLY TO GET IN LINE FOR WATER. BRING EVERY CONTAINER YOU'VE GOT.
THE EMPIRE SUPERVISES THE DISTRIBUTION OF FOOD AND WATER. THERE AREN'T MANY IMPERIAL TROOPS HERE, AND IT'S NOT THE KIND OF DUTY THEY WERE TRAINED FOR, I WOULDN'T GUESS. BUT THEY DO A GOOD JOB, AND THEY'RE FAIR.
IT'S THE MILITIA YOU WANT TO WATCH OUT FOR. ARKINNEA SUFFERED AT THE HANDS OF THE SEPARATISTS DURING THE WAR, AND NOW ALL THE MILITIA SOLDIERS ARE LOOKING FOR PAYBACK.
THEY RESENT US REFUGEES -- NO MATTER WHAT SIDE WE WERE ON. I JUST HOPE MY FAMILY'S NUMBER GETS CALLED SOON.
WHAT HAPPENS THEN?
EVERY FEW DAYS, A LUCKY GROUP OF REFUGEES GETS CHOSEN TO GO TO THE FREELANDS. IT'S OPEN FOR COLONIZATION. IF YOUR DATACHIP LIGHTS UP --
-- YOU'RE LOADED ONTO AN OLD ORE CARRIER THEY USE AND YOU'RE FERRIED UP NORTH.
I HOPE WE GET CHOSEN SOON. I HEARD THERE WAS A CASE OF SANGI FEVER ON THE OTHER SIDE OF THE CAMP. IF THAT SPREADS...

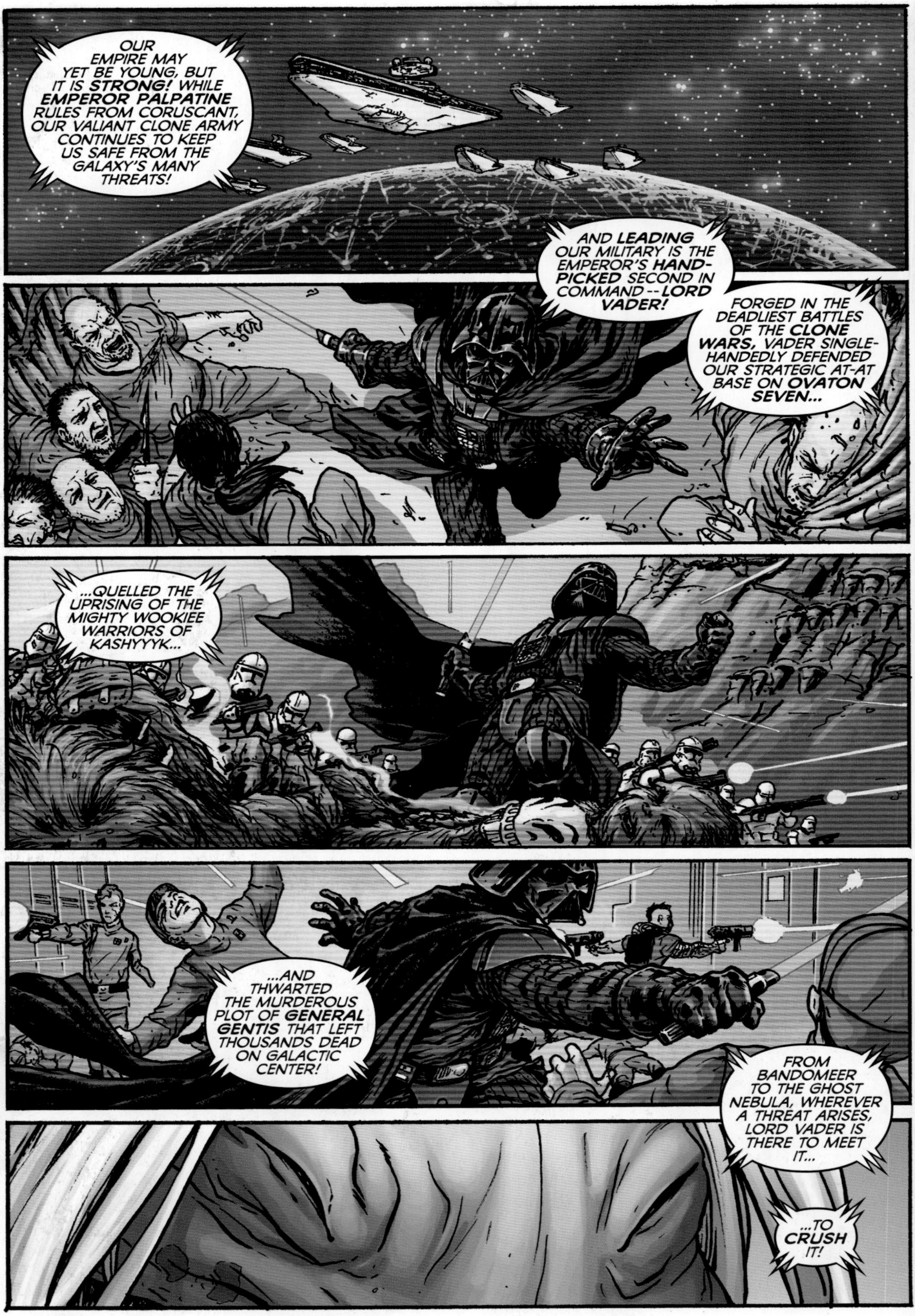
OUR EMPIRE MAY YET BE YOUNG, BUT IT IS STRONG! WHILE EMPEROR PALPATINE RULES FROM CORUSCANT, OUR VALIANT CLONE ARMY CONTINUES TO KEEP US SAFE FROM THE GALAXY'S MANY THREATS!
AND LEADING OUR MILITARY IS THE EMPEROR'S HAND-PICKED SECOND IN COMMAND--LORD VADER!
FORGED IN THE DEADLIEST BATTLES OF THE CLONE WARS, VADER SINGLE-HANDEDLY DEFENDED OUR STRATEGIC AT-AT BASE ON OVATON SEVEN...
...QUELLED THE UPRISING OF THE MIGHTY WOOKIEE WARRIORS OF KASHYYYK...
...AND THWARTED THE MURDEROUS PLOT OF GENERAL GENTIS THAT LEFT THOUSANDS DEAD ON GALACTIC CENTER!
FROM BANDOMEER TO THE GHOST NEBULA, WHEREVER A THREAT ARISES, LORD VADER IS THERE TO MEET IT...
...TO CRUSH IT!

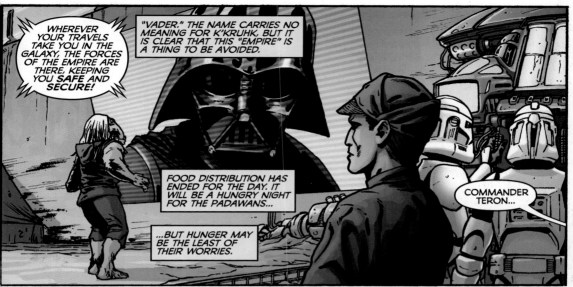

WHEREVER YOUR TRAVELS TAKE YOU IN THE GALAXY, THE FORCES OF THE EMPIRE ARE THERE, KEEPING YOU *SAFE* AND *SECURE!*

"VADER." THE NAME CARRIES NO MEANING FOR K'KRUHK, BUT IT IS CLEAR THAT THIS "EMPIRE" IS A THING TO BE AVOIDED.

FOOD DISTRIBUTION HAS ENDED FOR THE DAY. IT WILL BE A HUNGRY NIGHT FOR THE PADAWANS...

...BUT HUNGER MAY BE THE LEAST OF THEIR WORRIES.

COMMANDER TERON...

CAPTAIN RELIK.

A *TOOLAN!* WHAT NEXT, *EH?* THE SEPARATIST SCUM --

I AM WELL AWARE OF YOUR FEELING TOWARD THE SEPARATISTS, CAPTAIN...

...BUT THESE SENTIENTS WERE NOT ALL SEPARATISTS. AND THOSE WHO WERE ARE NOT *JUST* OUR DEFEATED FOES, BUT NOW *CITIZENS* OF THE *EMPIRE.*

AS SUCH THEY ARE DESERVING OF OUR RESPECT AND COMPASSION.

COMPASSION?

WHERE WAS THE SEPARATISTS' *COMPASSION* WHEN THEIR DROID ARMIES OVERRAN ARKINNEA, I ASK YOU?

I DON'T MIND SAYIN' IT, COMMANDER -- I CAN'T WAIT 'TILL *ALL* OF THESE OFF-WORLDERS ARE GONE!

AT LEAST THERE IS PLENTY OF OPEN LAND IN THE NORTH FOR THEM TO SETTLE.

YES, SIR. AT LEAST THERE'S *THAT...*

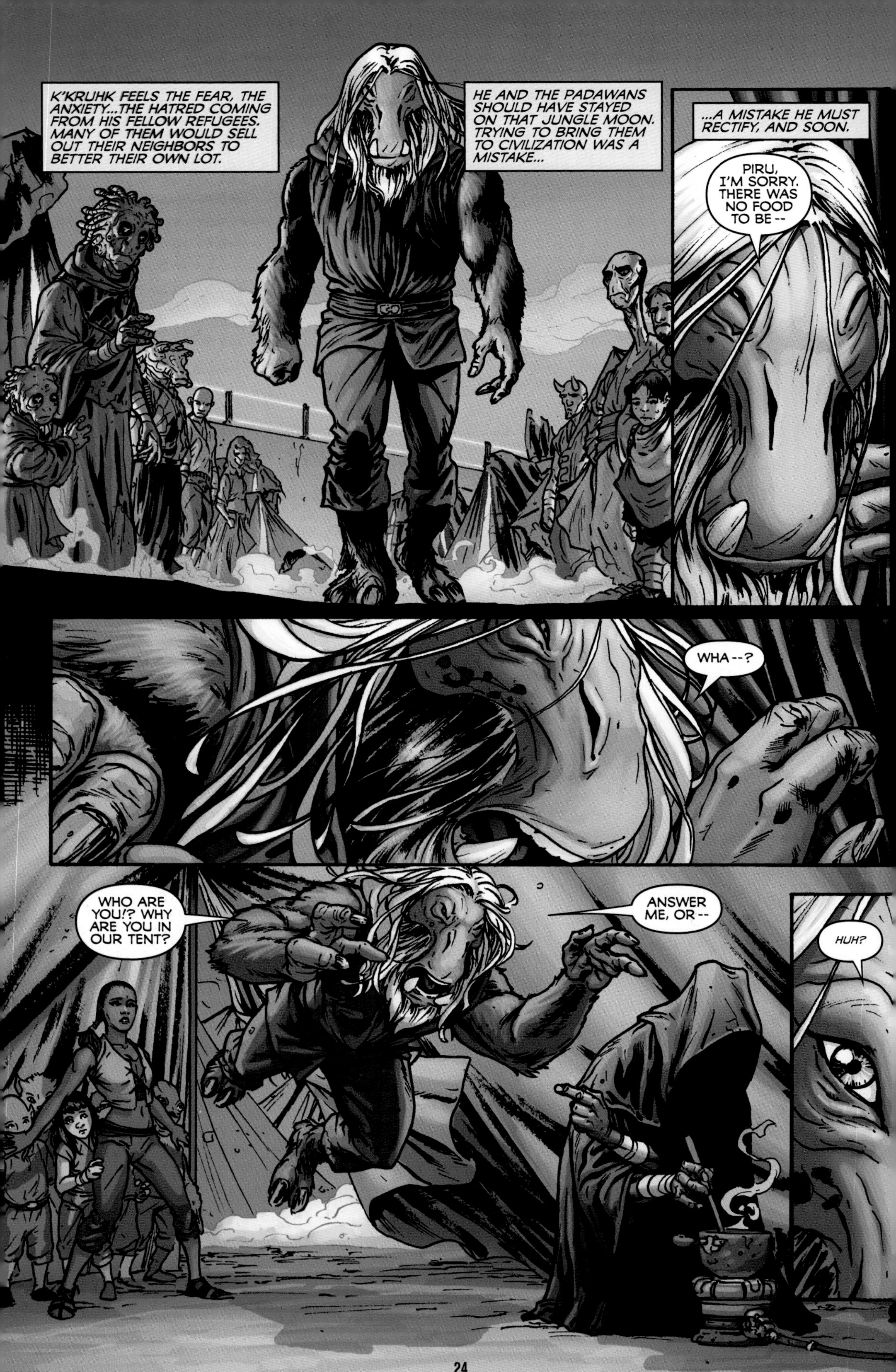
K'KRUHK FEELS THE FEAR, THE ANXIETY...THE HATRED COMING FROM HIS FELLOW REFUGEES. MANY OF THEM WOULD SELL OUT THEIR NEIGHBORS TO BETTER THEIR OWN LOT.
HE AND THE PADAWANS SHOULD HAVE STAYED ON THAT JUNGLE MOON. TRYING TO BRING THEM TO CIVILIZATION WAS A MISTAKE...
...A MISTAKE HE MUST RECTIFY, AND SOON.
PIRU, I'M SORRY. THERE WAS NO FOOD TO BE --
WHA --?
WHO ARE YOU!? WHY ARE YOU IN OUR TENT?
ANSWER ME, OR --
HUH?

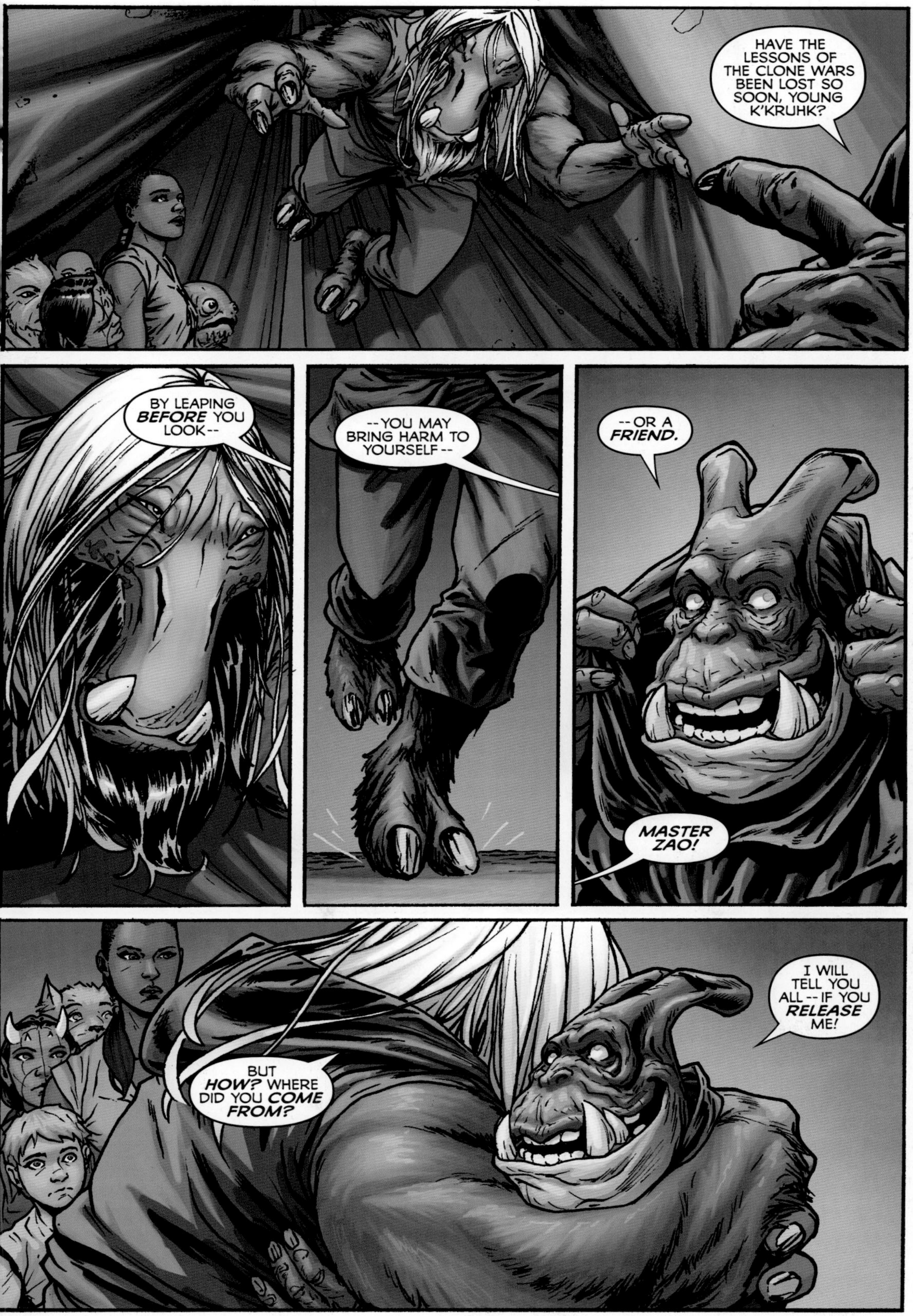
HAVE THE LESSONS OF THE CLONE WARS BEEN LOST SO SOON, YOUNG K'KRUHK?
BY LEAPING *BEFORE* YOU LOOK--
--YOU MAY BRING HARM TO YOURSELF--
--OR A *FRIEND.*
MASTER ZAO!
BUT *HOW?* WHERE DID YOU *COME FROM?*
I WILL TELL YOU ALL--IF YOU *RELEASE* ME!

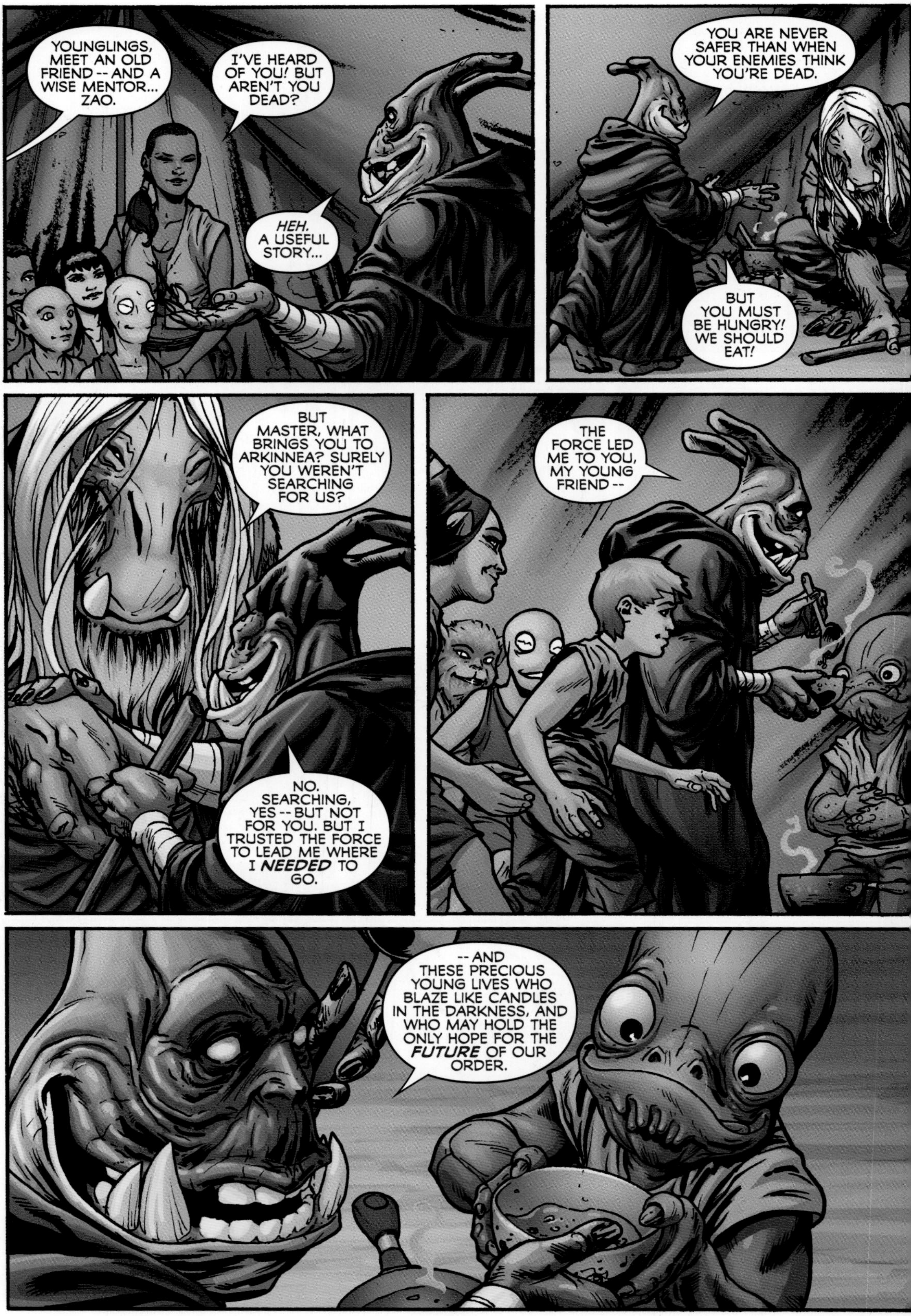
YOUNGLINGS, MEET AN OLD FRIEND -- AND A WISE MENTOR... ZAO.
I'VE HEARD OF YOU! BUT AREN'T YOU DEAD?
HEH. A USEFUL STORY...
YOU ARE NEVER SAFER THAN WHEN YOUR ENEMIES THINK YOU'RE DEAD.
BUT YOU MUST BE HUNGRY! WE SHOULD EAT!
BUT MASTER, WHAT BRINGS YOU TO ARKINNEA? SURELY YOU WEREN'T SEARCHING FOR US?
NO. SEARCHING, YES -- BUT NOT FOR YOU. BUT I TRUSTED THE FORCE TO LEAD ME WHERE I ***NEEDED*** TO GO.
THE FORCE LED ME TO YOU, MY YOUNG FRIEND --
-- AND THESE PRECIOUS YOUNG LIVES WHO BLAZE LIKE CANDLES IN THE DARKNESS, AND WHO MAY HOLD THE ONLY HOPE FOR THE ***FUTURE*** OF OUR ORDER.

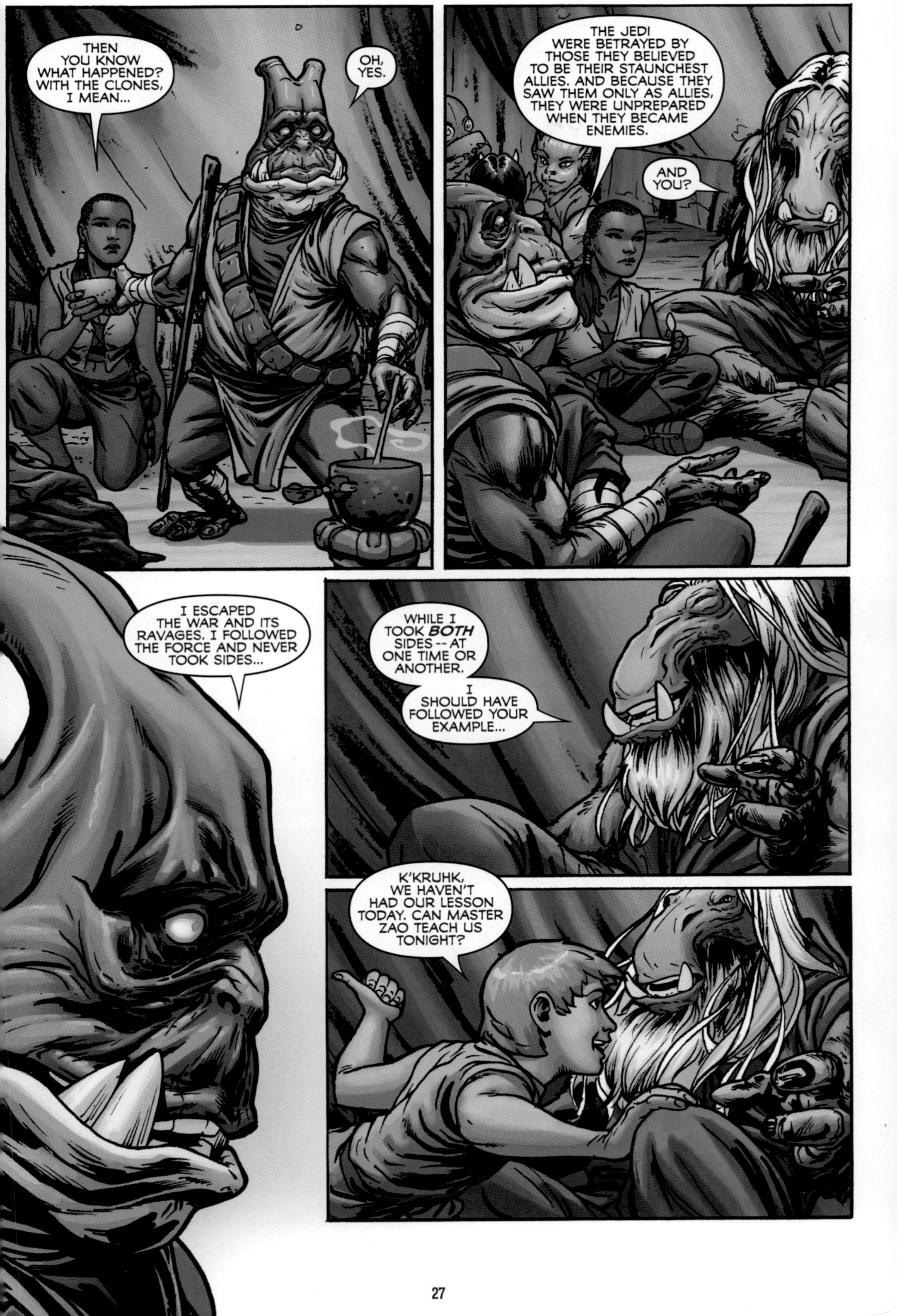
THEN YOU KNOW WHAT HAPPENED? WITH THE CLONES, I MEAN...
OH, YES.
THE JEDI WERE BETRAYED BY THOSE THEY BELIEVED TO BE THEIR STAUNCHEST ALLIES. AND BECAUSE THEY SAW THEM ONLY AS ALLIES, THEY WERE UNPREPARED WHEN THEY BECAME ENEMIES.
AND YOU?
I ESCAPED THE WAR AND ITS RAVAGES. I FOLLOWED THE FORCE AND NEVER TOOK SIDES...
WHILE I TOOK *BOTH* SIDES -- AT ONE TIME OR ANOTHER.
I SHOULD HAVE FOLLOWED YOUR EXAMPLE...
K'KRUHK, WE HAVEN'T HAD OUR LESSON TODAY. CAN MASTER ZAO TEACH US TONIGHT?

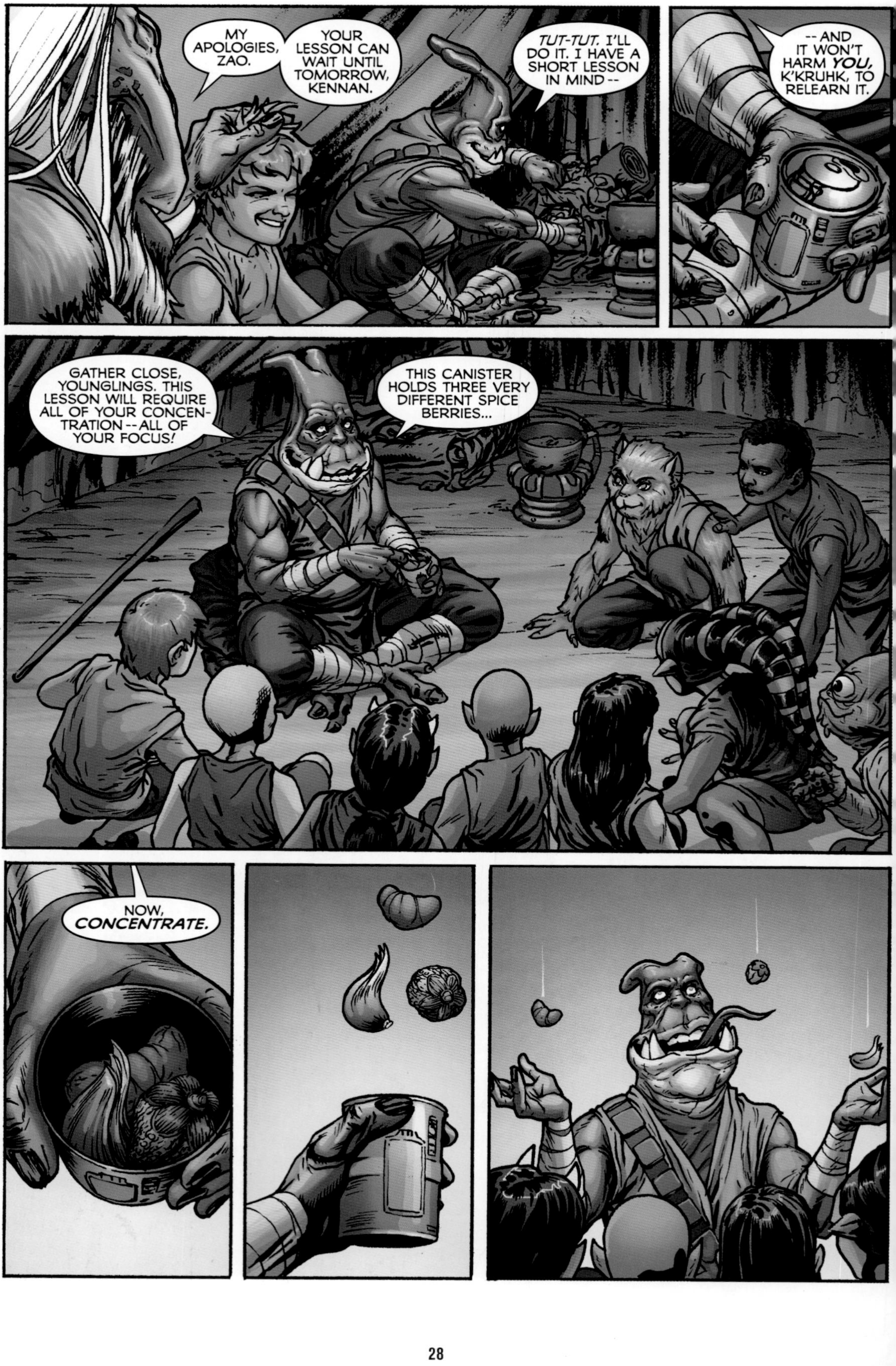
MY APOLOGIES, ZAO.
YOUR LESSON CAN WAIT UNTIL TOMORROW, KENNAN.
TUT-TUT. I'LL DO IT. I HAVE A SHORT LESSON IN MIND --
-- AND IT WON'T HARM YOU, K'KRUHK, TO RELEARN IT.
GATHER CLOSE, YOUNGLINGS. THIS LESSON WILL REQUIRE ALL OF YOUR CONCENTRATION -- ALL OF YOUR FOCUS!
THIS CANISTER HOLDS THREE VERY DIFFERENT SPICE BERRIES...
NOW, CONCENTRATE.

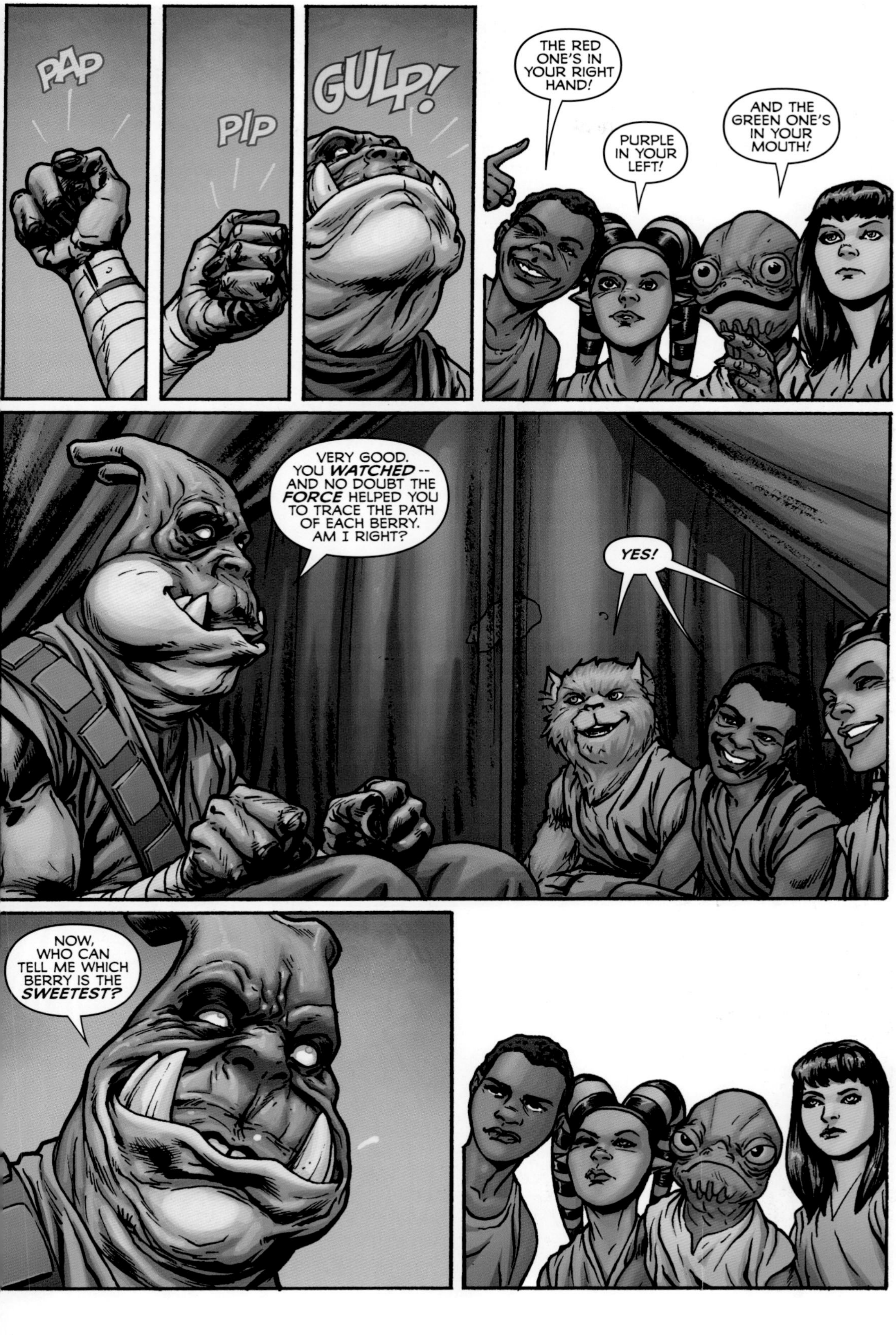
PAP
PIP
GULP!
THE RED ONE'S IN YOUR RIGHT HAND!
PURPLE IN YOUR LEFT!
AND THE GREEN ONE'S IN YOUR MOUTH!
VERY GOOD. YOU *WATCHED* -- AND NO DOUBT THE *FORCE* HELPED YOU TO TRACE THE PATH OF EACH BERRY. AM I RIGHT?
YES!
NOW, WHO CAN TELL ME WHICH BERRY IS THE *SWEETEST?*

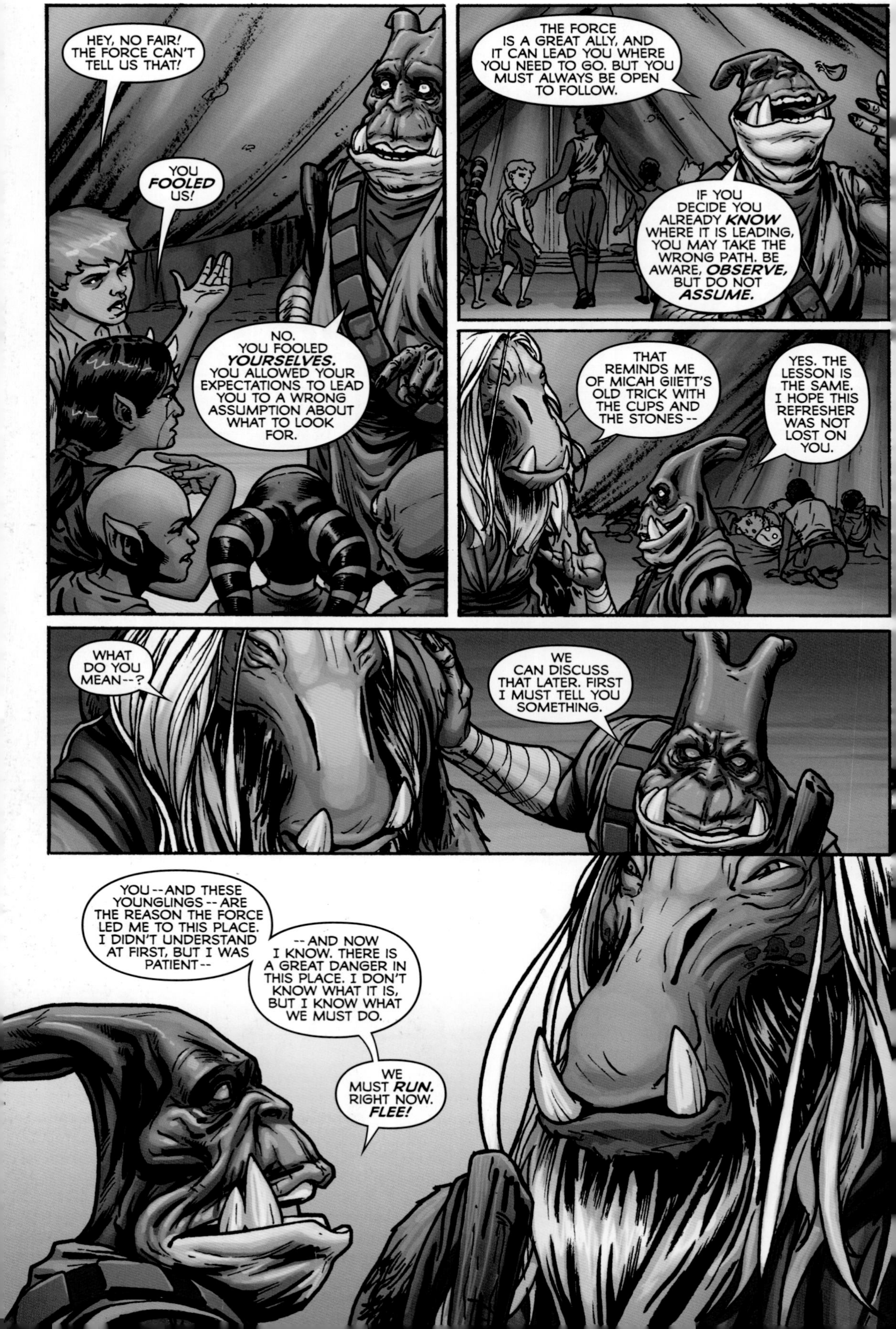
HEY, NO FAIR! THE FORCE CAN'T TELL US THAT!
YOU FOOLED US!
NO. YOU FOOLED YOURSELVES. YOU ALLOWED YOUR EXPECTATIONS TO LEAD YOU TO A WRONG ASSUMPTION ABOUT WHAT TO LOOK FOR.
THE FORCE IS A GREAT ALLY, AND IT CAN LEAD YOU WHERE YOU NEED TO GO. BUT YOU MUST ALWAYS BE OPEN TO FOLLOW.
IF YOU DECIDE YOU ALREADY KNOW WHERE IT IS LEADING, YOU MAY TAKE THE WRONG PATH. BE AWARE, OBSERVE, BUT DO NOT ASSUME.
THAT REMINDS ME OF MICAH GIIETT'S OLD TRICK WITH THE CUPS AND THE STONES--
YES. THE LESSON IS THE SAME. I HOPE THIS REFRESHER WAS NOT LOST ON YOU.
WHAT DO YOU MEAN--?
WE CAN DISCUSS THAT LATER. FIRST I MUST TELL YOU SOMETHING.
YOU--AND THESE YOUNGLINGS--ARE THE REASON THE FORCE LED ME TO THIS PLACE. I DIDN'T UNDERSTAND AT FIRST, BUT I WAS PATIENT--
--AND NOW I KNOW. THERE IS A GREAT DANGER IN THIS PLACE. I DON'T KNOW WHAT IT IS, BUT I KNOW WHAT WE MUST DO.
WE MUST RUN. RIGHT NOW. FLEE!

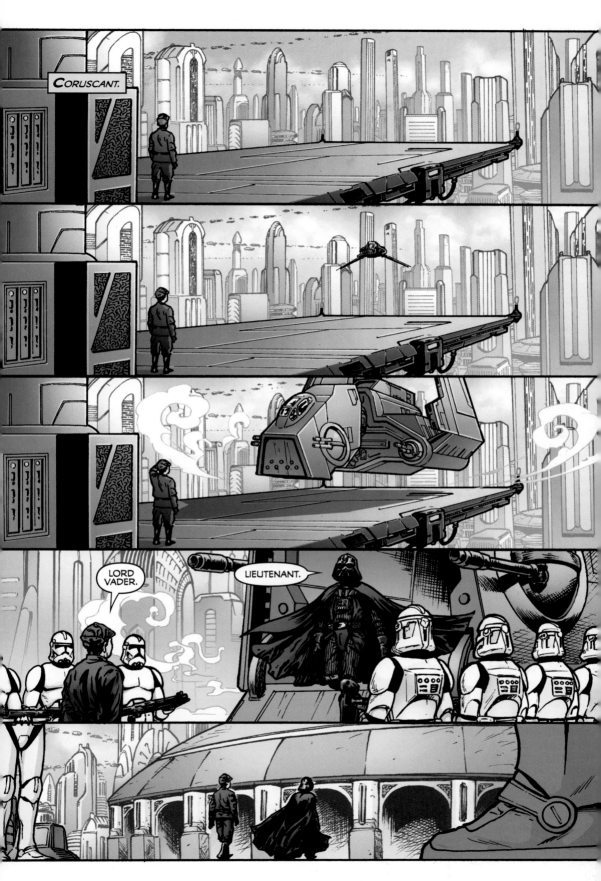

CORUSCANT.

LORD VADER.

LIEUTENANT.

31

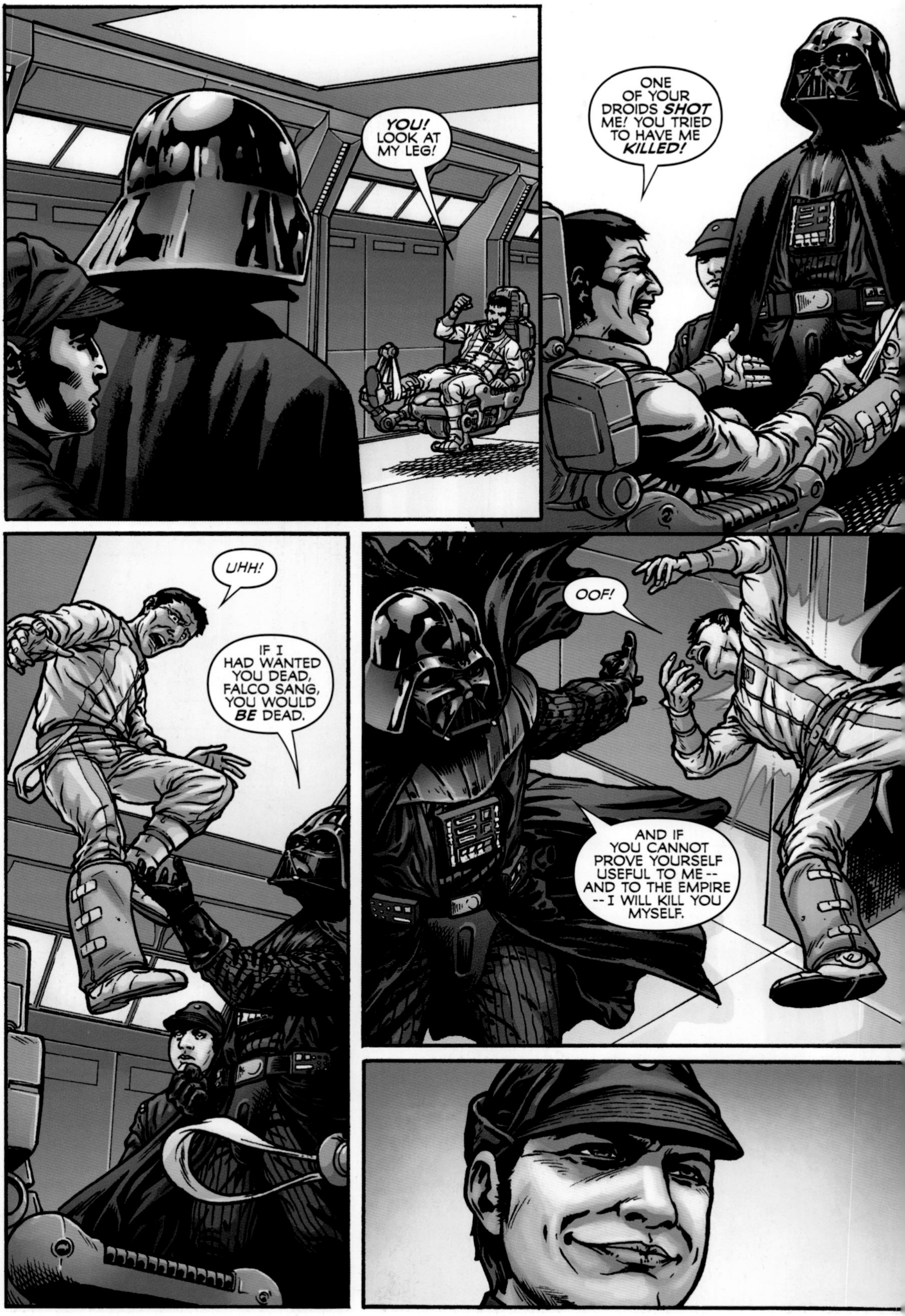
YOU! LOOK AT MY LEG!
ONE OF YOUR DROIDS SHOT ME! YOU TRIED TO HAVE ME KILLED!
UHH!
IF I HAD WANTED YOU DEAD, FALCO SANG, YOU WOULD BE DEAD.
OOF!
AND IF YOU CANNOT PROVE YOURSELF USEFUL TO ME -- AND TO THE EMPIRE -- I WILL KILL YOU MYSELF.

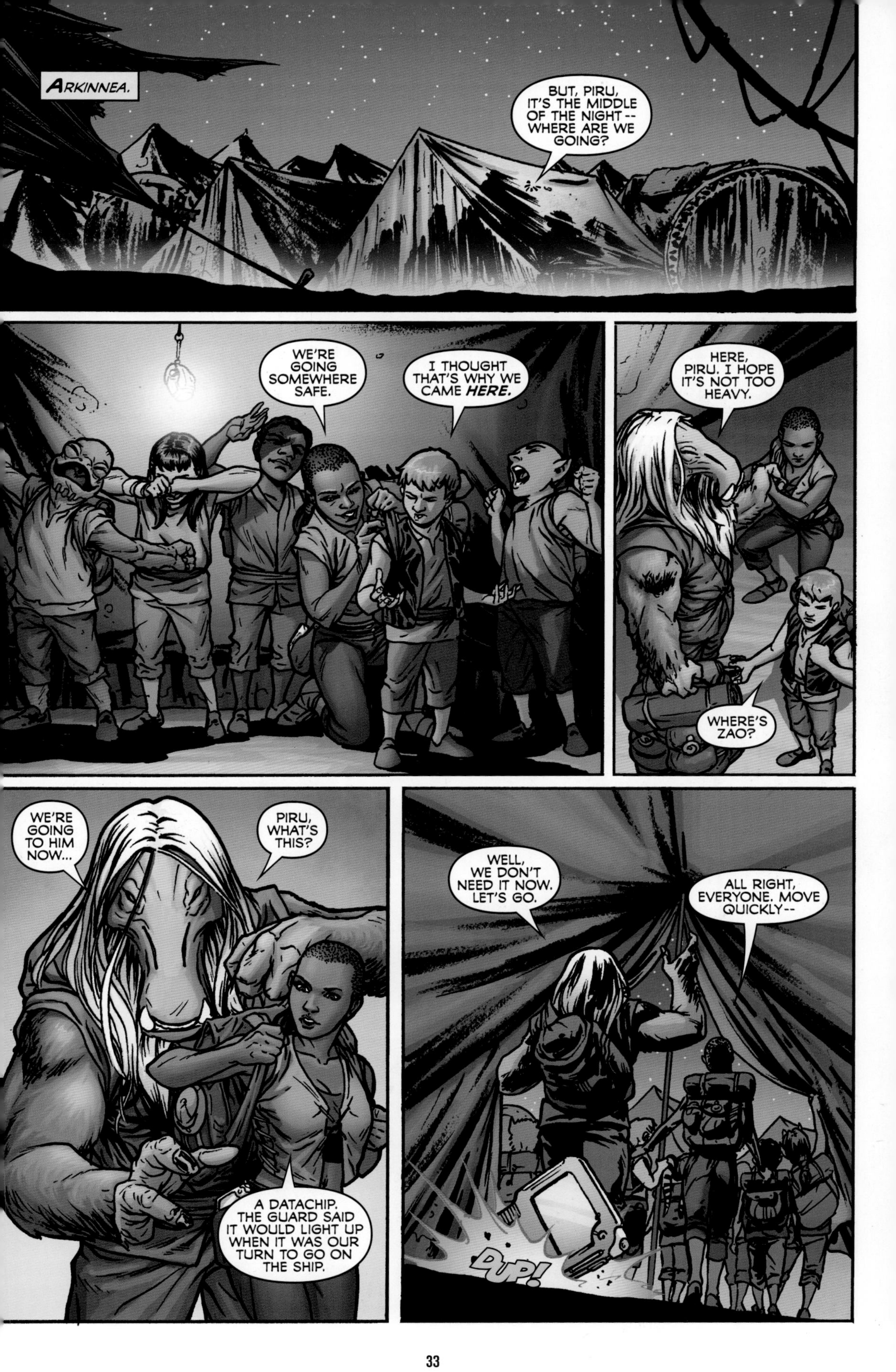
ARKINNEA.
BUT, PIRU, IT'S THE MIDDLE OF THE NIGHT -- WHERE ARE WE GOING?
WE'RE GOING SOMEWHERE SAFE.
I THOUGHT THAT'S WHY WE CAME HERE.
HERE, PIRU. I HOPE IT'S NOT TOO HEAVY.
WHERE'S ZAO?
WE'RE GOING TO HIM NOW...
PIRU, WHAT'S THIS?
A DATACHIP. THE GUARD SAID IT WOULD LIGHT UP WHEN IT WAS OUR TURN TO GO ON THE SHIP.
WELL, WE DON'T NEED IT NOW. LET'S GO.
ALL RIGHT, EVERYONE. MOVE QUICKLY--
DUP!

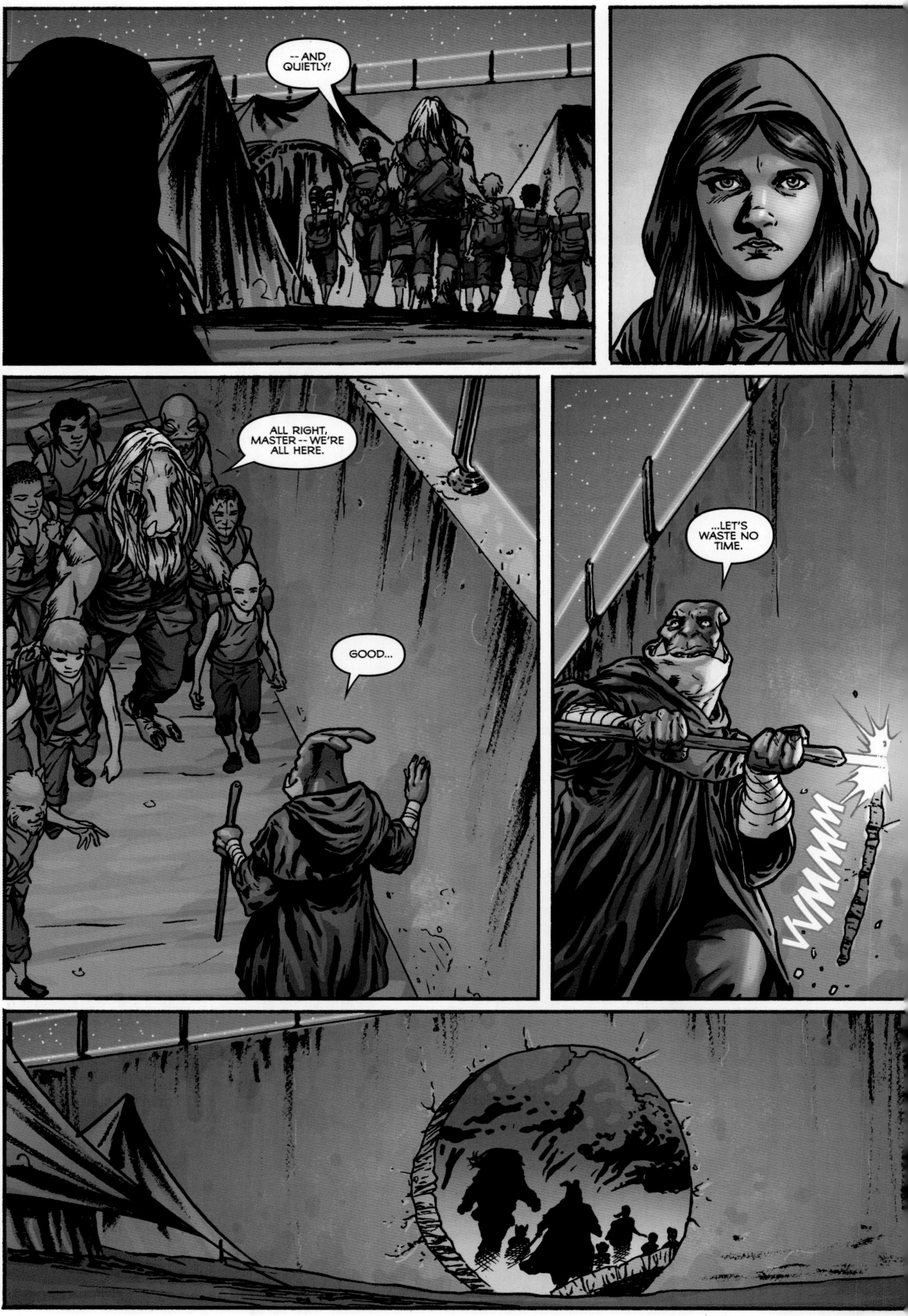
-- AND QUIETLY!
ALL RIGHT, MASTER -- WE'RE ALL HERE.
GOOD...
...LET'S WASTE NO TIME.
VWMMM

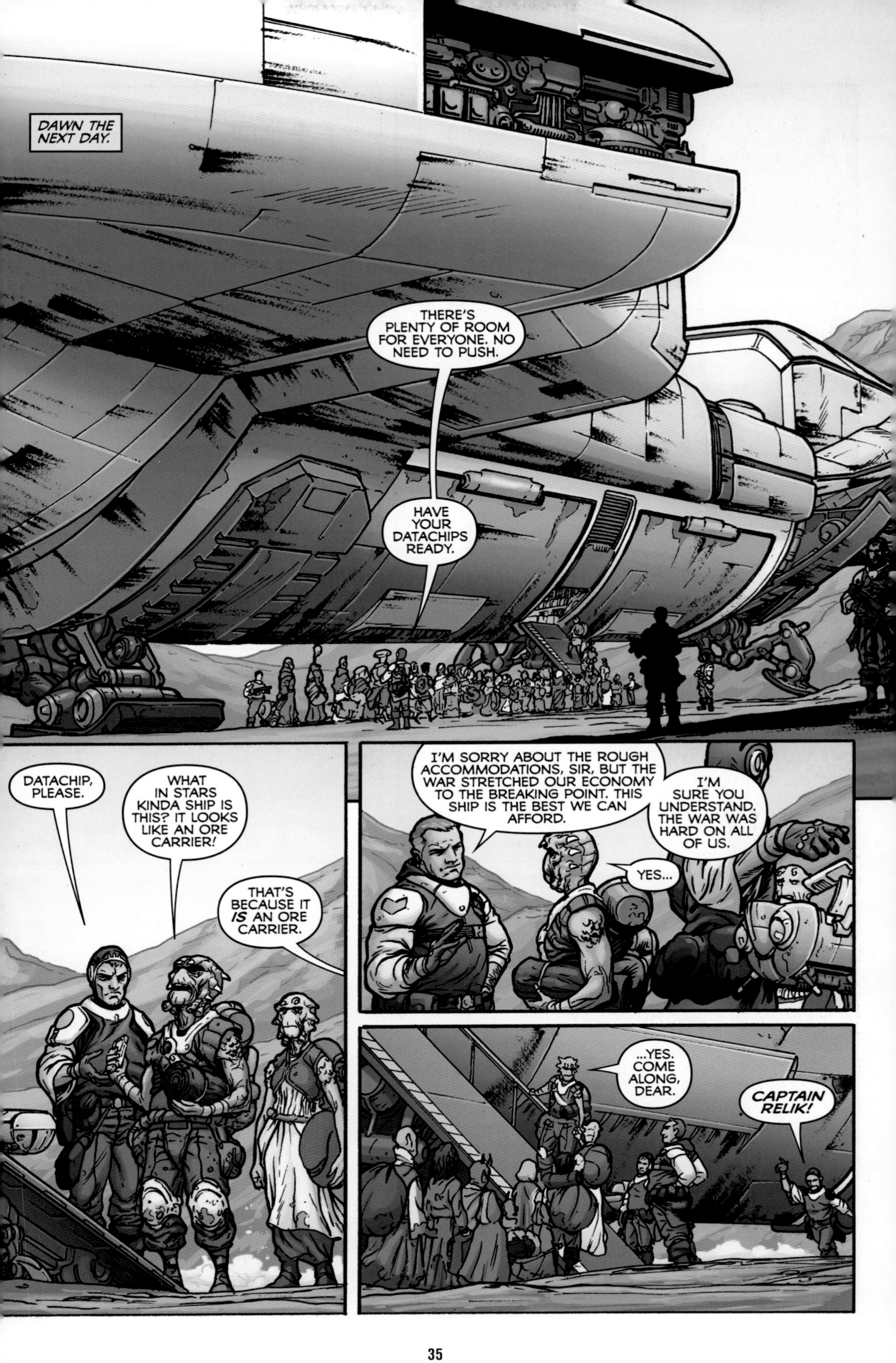
DAWN THE NEXT DAY.
THERE'S PLENTY OF ROOM FOR EVERYONE. NO NEED TO PUSH.
HAVE YOUR DATACHIPS READY.
DATACHIP, PLEASE.
WHAT IN STARS KINDA SHIP IS THIS? IT LOOKS LIKE AN ORE CARRIER!
THAT'S BECAUSE IT *IS* AN ORE CARRIER.
I'M SORRY ABOUT THE ROUGH ACCOMMODATIONS, SIR, BUT THE WAR STRETCHED OUR ECONOMY TO THE BREAKING POINT. THIS SHIP IS THE BEST WE CAN AFFORD.
YES...
I'M SURE YOU UNDERSTAND. THE WAR WAS HARD ON ALL OF US.
...YES. COME ALONG, DEAR.
CAPTAIN RELIK!

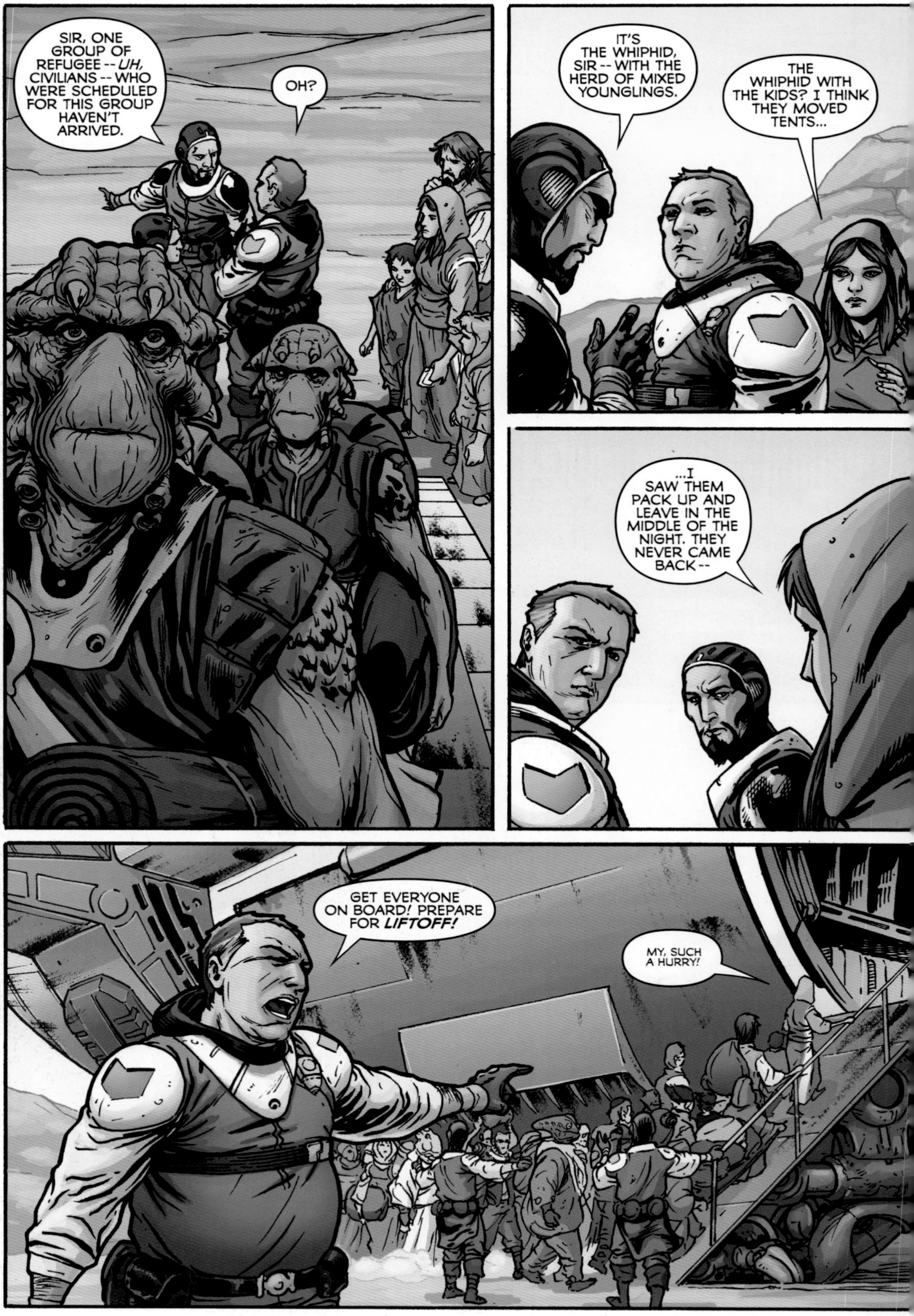
SIR, ONE GROUP OF REFUGEE -- *UH,* CIVILIANS -- WHO WERE SCHEDULED FOR THIS GROUP HAVEN'T ARRIVED.
OH?
IT'S THE WHIPHID, SIR -- WITH THE HERD OF MIXED YOUNGLINGS.
THE WHIPHID WITH THE KIDS? I THINK THEY MOVED TENTS...
...I SAW THEM PACK UP AND LEAVE IN THE MIDDLE OF THE NIGHT. THEY NEVER CAME BACK --
GET EVERYONE ON BOARD! PREPARE FOR *LIFTOFF!*
MY, SUCH A HURRY!

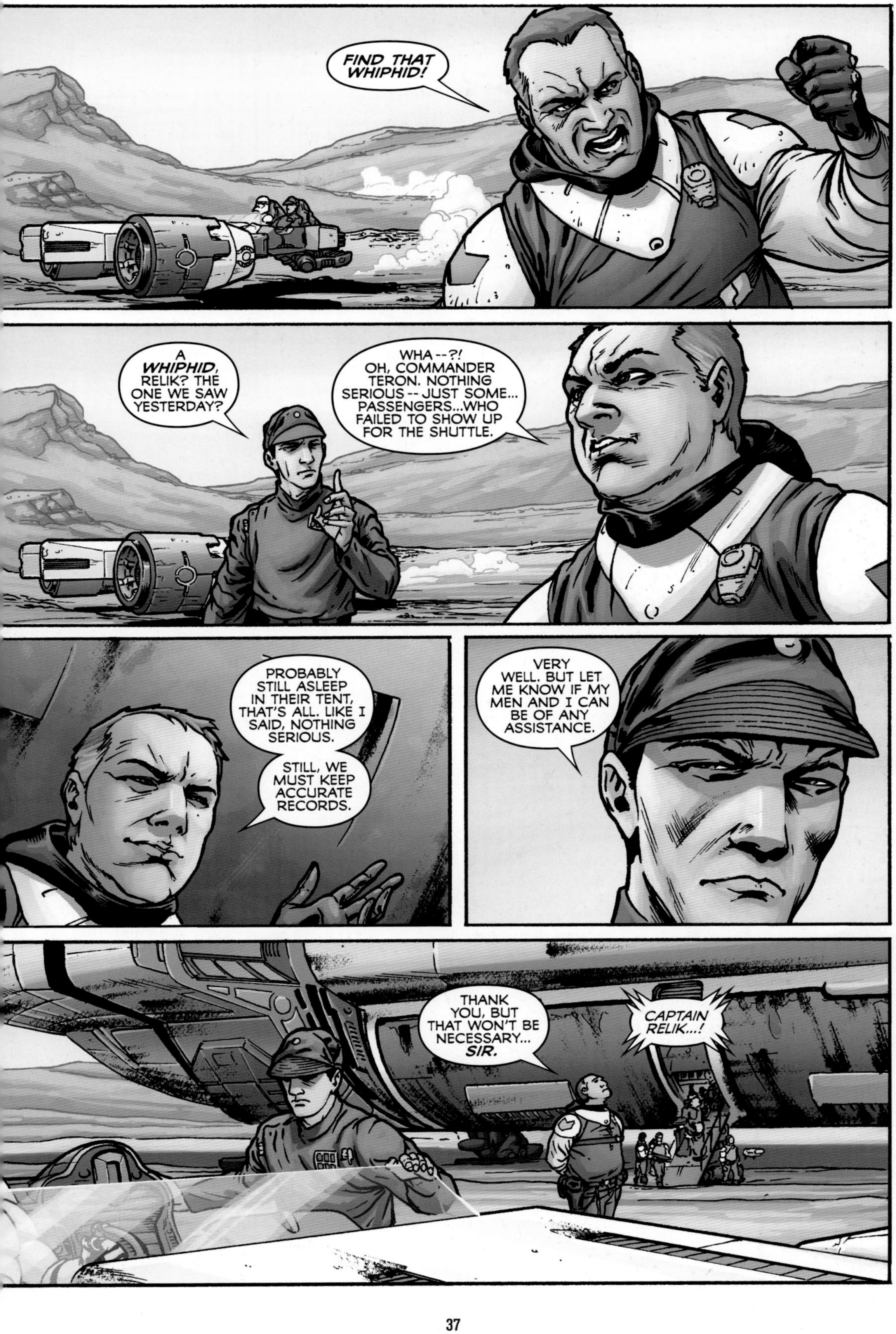
FIND THAT WHIPHID!
A WHIPHID, RELIK? THE ONE WE SAW YESTERDAY?
WHA--?! OH, COMMANDER TERON. NOTHING SERIOUS--JUST SOME... PASSENGERS...WHO FAILED TO SHOW UP FOR THE SHUTTLE.
PROBABLY STILL ASLEEP IN THEIR TENT, THAT'S ALL. LIKE I SAID, NOTHING SERIOUS.
STILL, WE MUST KEEP ACCURATE RECORDS.
VERY WELL. BUT LET ME KNOW IF MY MEN AND I CAN BE OF ANY ASSISTANCE.
THANK YOU, BUT THAT WON'T BE NECESSARY... SIR.
CAPTAIN RELIK...!

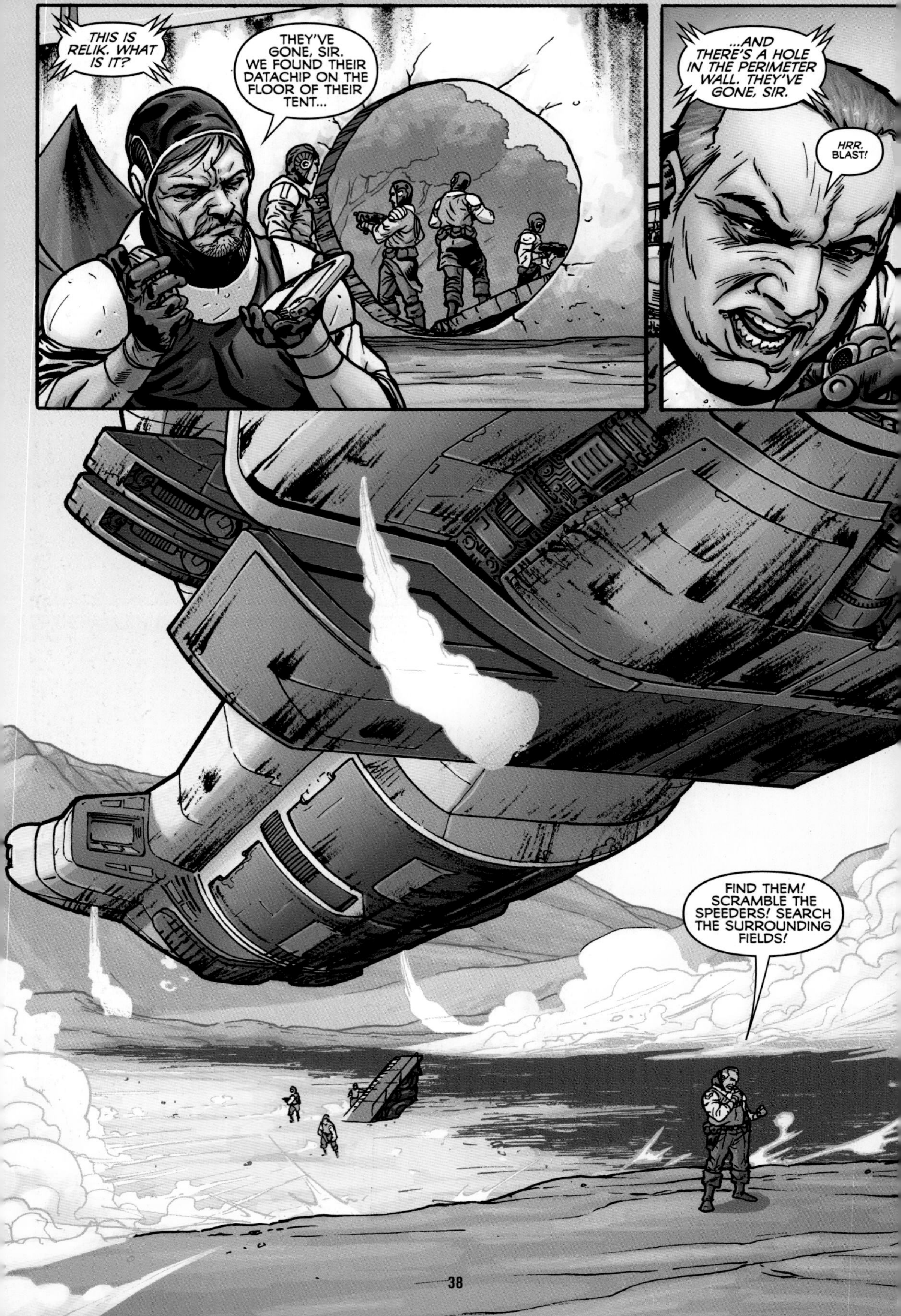
THIS IS RELIK. WHAT IS IT?
THEY'VE GONE, SIR. WE FOUND THEIR DATACHIP ON THE FLOOR OF THEIR TENT...
...AND THERE'S A HOLE IN THE PERIMETER WALL. THEY'VE GONE, SIR.
HRR. BLAST!
FIND THEM! SCRAMBLE THE SPEEDERS! SEARCH THE SURROUNDING FIELDS!

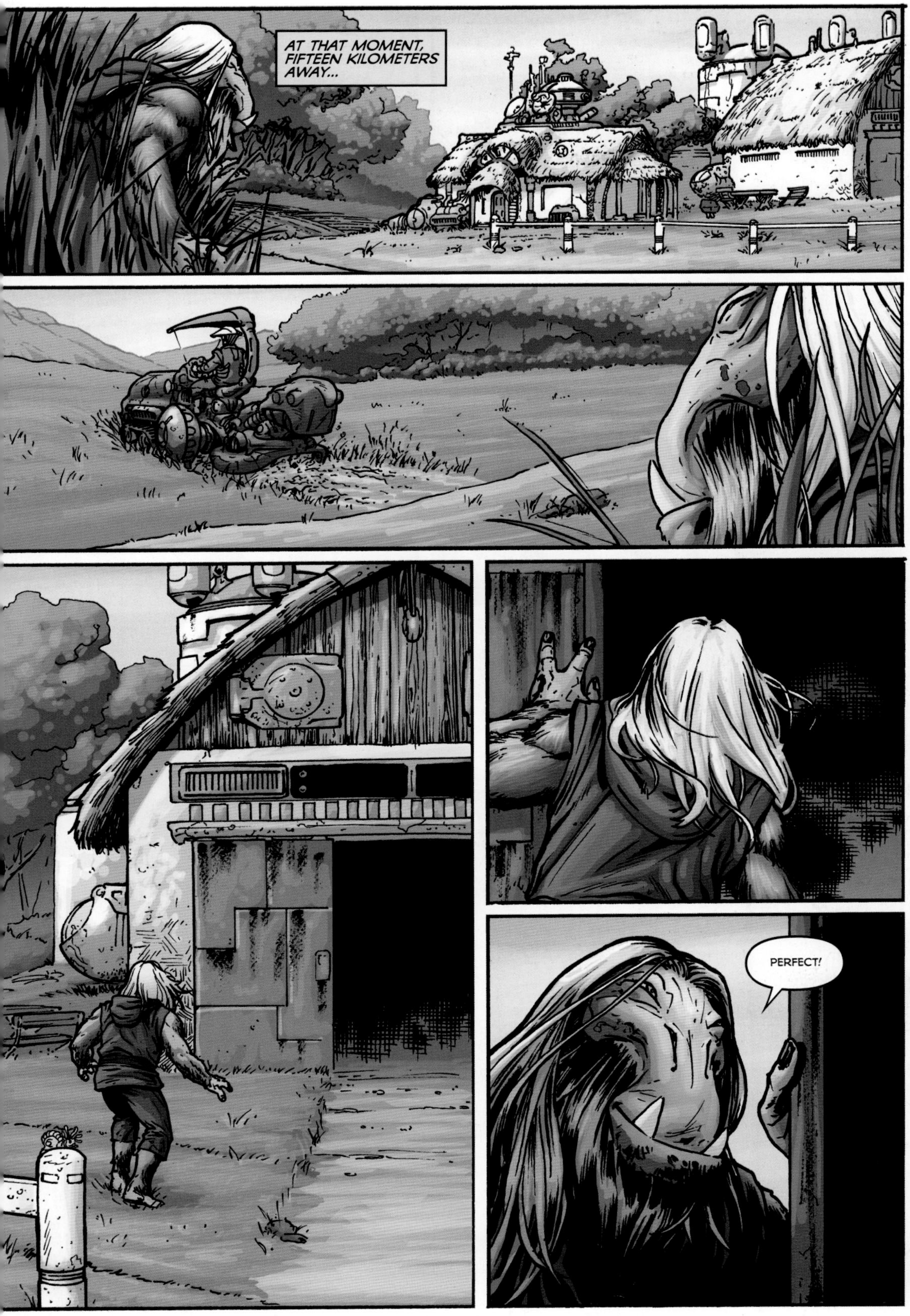
AT THAT MOMENT, FIFTEEN KILOMETERS AWAY...
PERFECT!

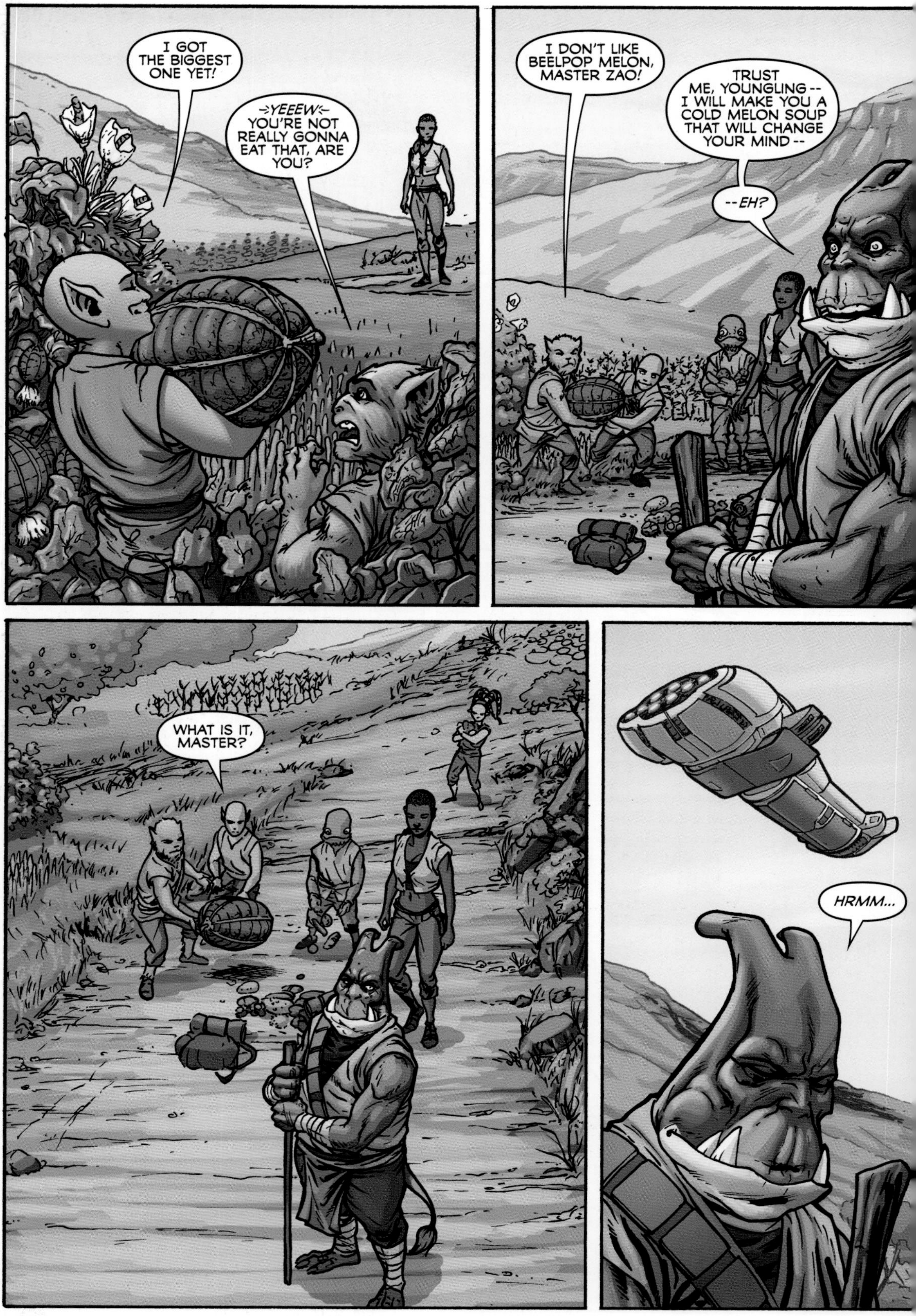
I GOT THE BIGGEST ONE YET!
-YEEEW- YOU'RE NOT REALLY GONNA EAT THAT, ARE YOU?
I DON'T LIKE BEELPOP MELON, MASTER ZAO!
TRUST ME, YOUNGLING -- I WILL MAKE YOU A COLD MELON SOUP THAT WILL CHANGE YOUR MIND --
--EH?
WHAT IS IT, MASTER?
HRMM...

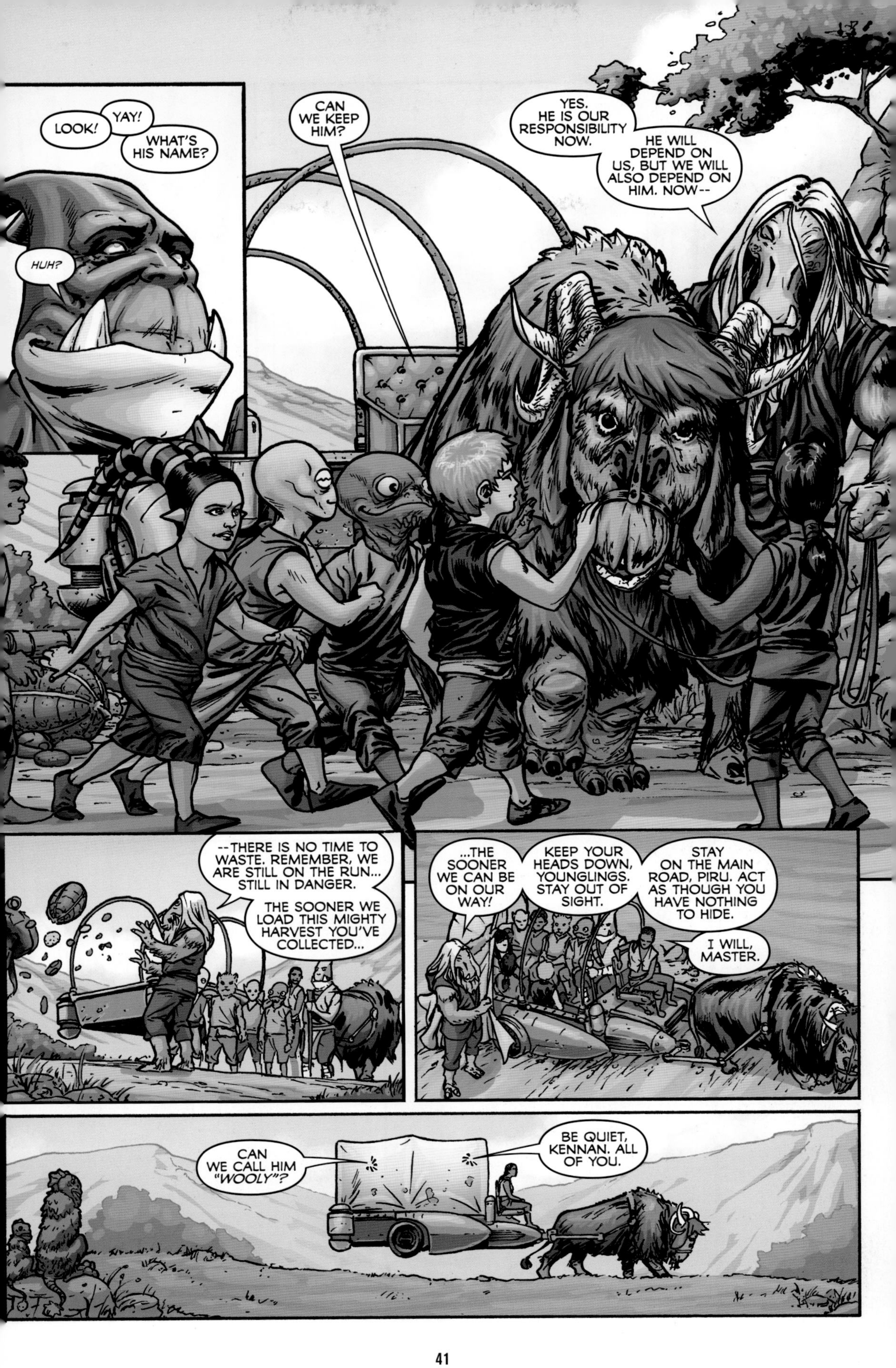
LOOK!
YAY!
WHAT'S HIS NAME?
HUH?
CAN WE KEEP HIM?
YES. HE IS OUR RESPONSIBILITY NOW.
HE WILL DEPEND ON US, BUT WE WILL ALSO DEPEND ON HIM. NOW--
--THERE IS NO TIME TO WASTE. REMEMBER, WE ARE STILL ON THE RUN... STILL IN DANGER.
THE SOONER WE LOAD THIS MIGHTY HARVEST YOU'VE COLLECTED...
...THE SOONER WE CAN BE ON OUR WAY!
KEEP YOUR HEADS DOWN, YOUNGLINGS. STAY OUT OF SIGHT.
STAY ON THE MAIN ROAD, PIRU. ACT AS THOUGH YOU HAVE NOTHING TO HIDE.
I WILL, MASTER.
CAN WE CALL HIM *"WOOLY"*?
BE QUIET, KENNAN. ALL OF YOU.

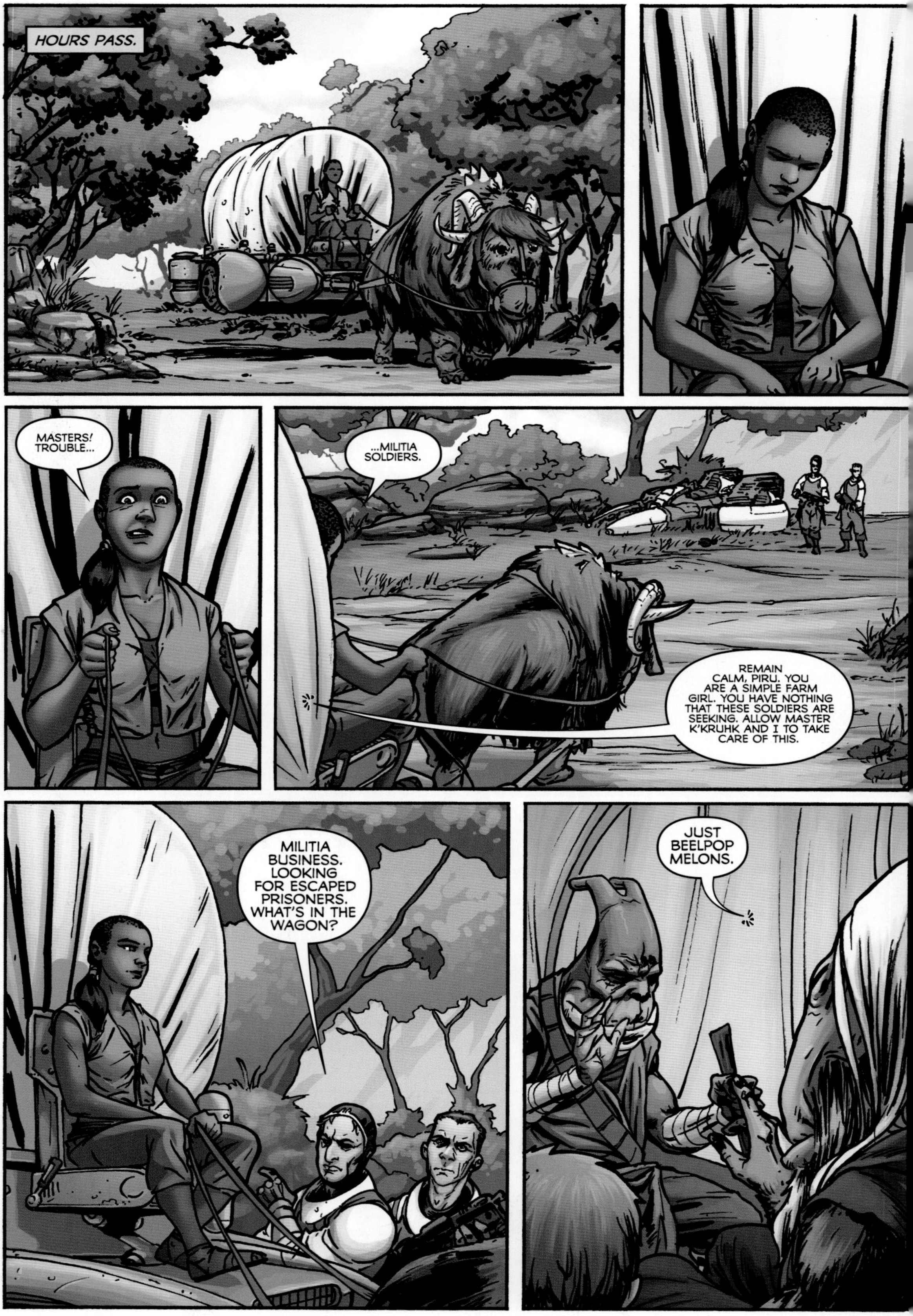
HOURS PASS.
MASTERS! TROUBLE...
...MILITIA SOLDIERS.
REMAIN CALM, PIRU. YOU ARE A SIMPLE FARM GIRL. YOU HAVE NOTHING THAT THESE SOLDIERS ARE SEEKING. ALLOW MASTER K'KRUHK AND I TO TAKE CARE OF THIS.
MILITIA BUSINESS. LOOKING FOR ESCAPED PRISONERS. WHAT'S IN THE WAGON?
JUST BEELPOP MELONS.

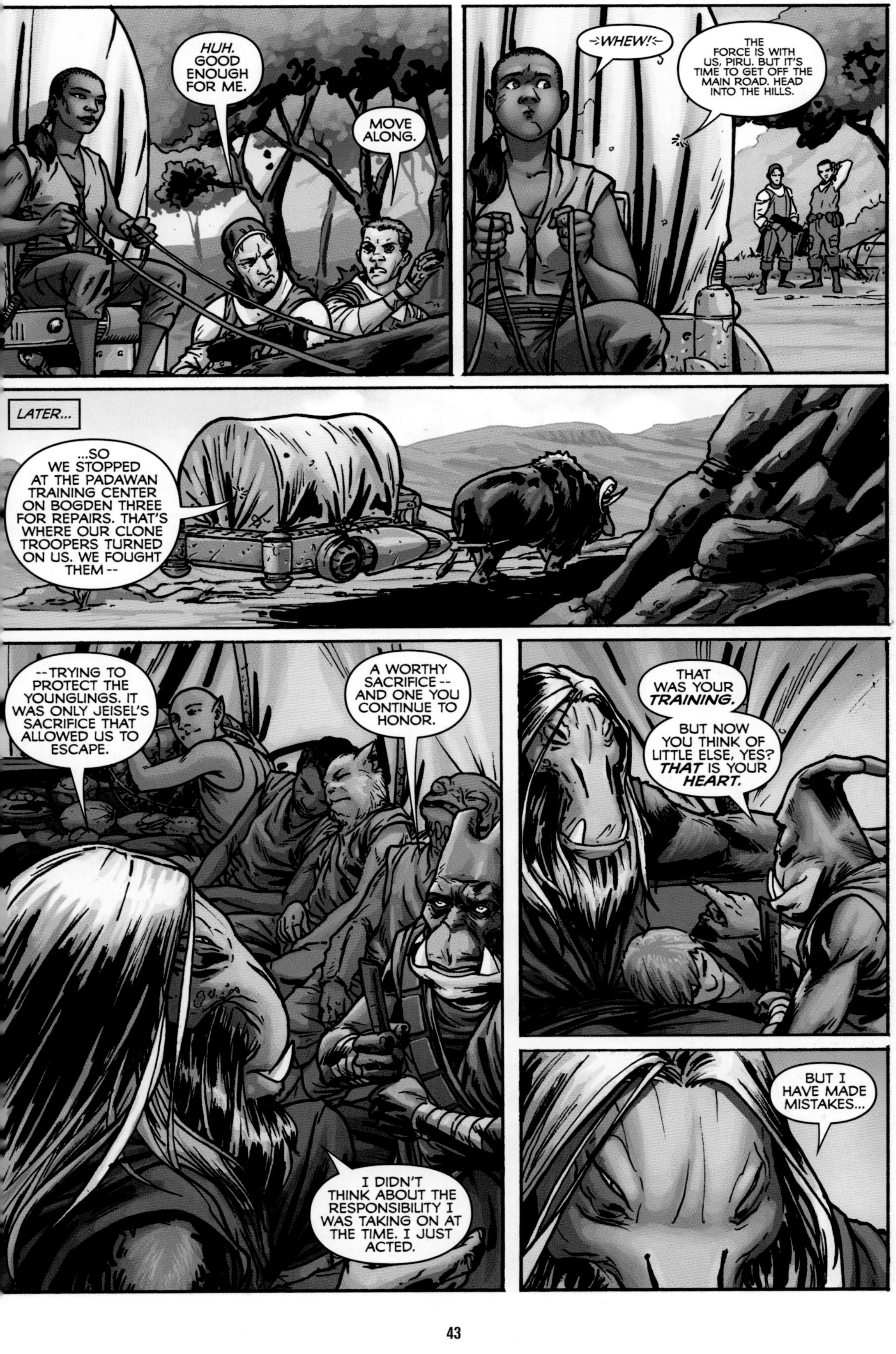
HUH. GOOD ENOUGH FOR ME.
MOVE ALONG.
-WHEW!-
THE FORCE IS WITH US, PIRU. BUT IT'S TIME TO GET OFF THE MAIN ROAD. HEAD INTO THE HILLS.
LATER...
...SO WE STOPPED AT THE PADAWAN TRAINING CENTER ON BOGDEN THREE FOR REPAIRS. THAT'S WHERE OUR CLONE TROOPERS TURNED ON US. WE FOUGHT THEM --
--TRYING TO PROTECT THE YOUNGLINGS. IT WAS ONLY JEISEL'S SACRIFICE THAT ALLOWED US TO ESCAPE.
A WORTHY SACRIFICE -- AND ONE YOU CONTINUE TO HONOR.
I DIDN'T THINK ABOUT THE RESPONSIBILITY I WAS TAKING ON AT THE TIME. I JUST ACTED.
THAT WAS YOUR TRAINING.
BUT NOW YOU THINK OF LITTLE ELSE, YES? THAT IS YOUR HEART.
BUT I HAVE MADE MISTAKES...

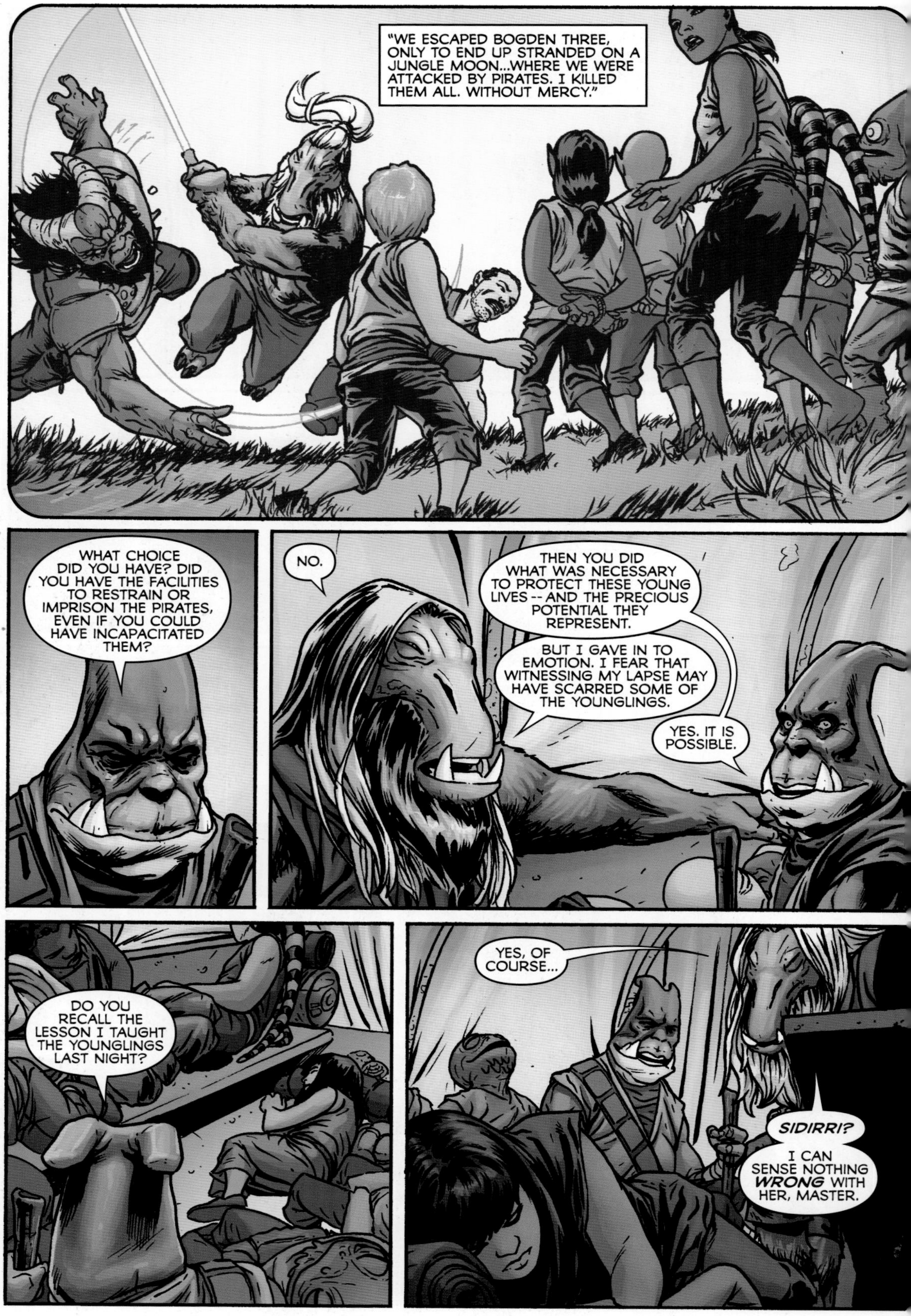
"WE ESCAPED BOGDEN THREE, ONLY TO END UP STRANDED ON A JUNGLE MOON...WHERE WE WERE ATTACKED BY PIRATES. I KILLED THEM ALL. WITHOUT MERCY."
WHAT CHOICE DID YOU HAVE? DID YOU HAVE THE FACILITIES TO RESTRAIN OR IMPRISON THE PIRATES, EVEN IF YOU COULD HAVE INCAPACITATED THEM?
NO.
THEN YOU DID WHAT WAS NECESSARY TO PROTECT THESE YOUNG LIVES -- AND THE PRECIOUS POTENTIAL THEY REPRESENT.
BUT I GAVE IN TO EMOTION. I FEAR THAT WITNESSING MY LAPSE MAY HAVE SCARRED SOME OF THE YOUNGLINGS.
YES. IT IS POSSIBLE.
DO YOU RECALL THE LESSON I TAUGHT THE YOUNGLINGS LAST NIGHT?
YES, OF COURSE...
SIDIRRI?
I CAN SENSE NOTHING ***WRONG*** WITH HER, MASTER.

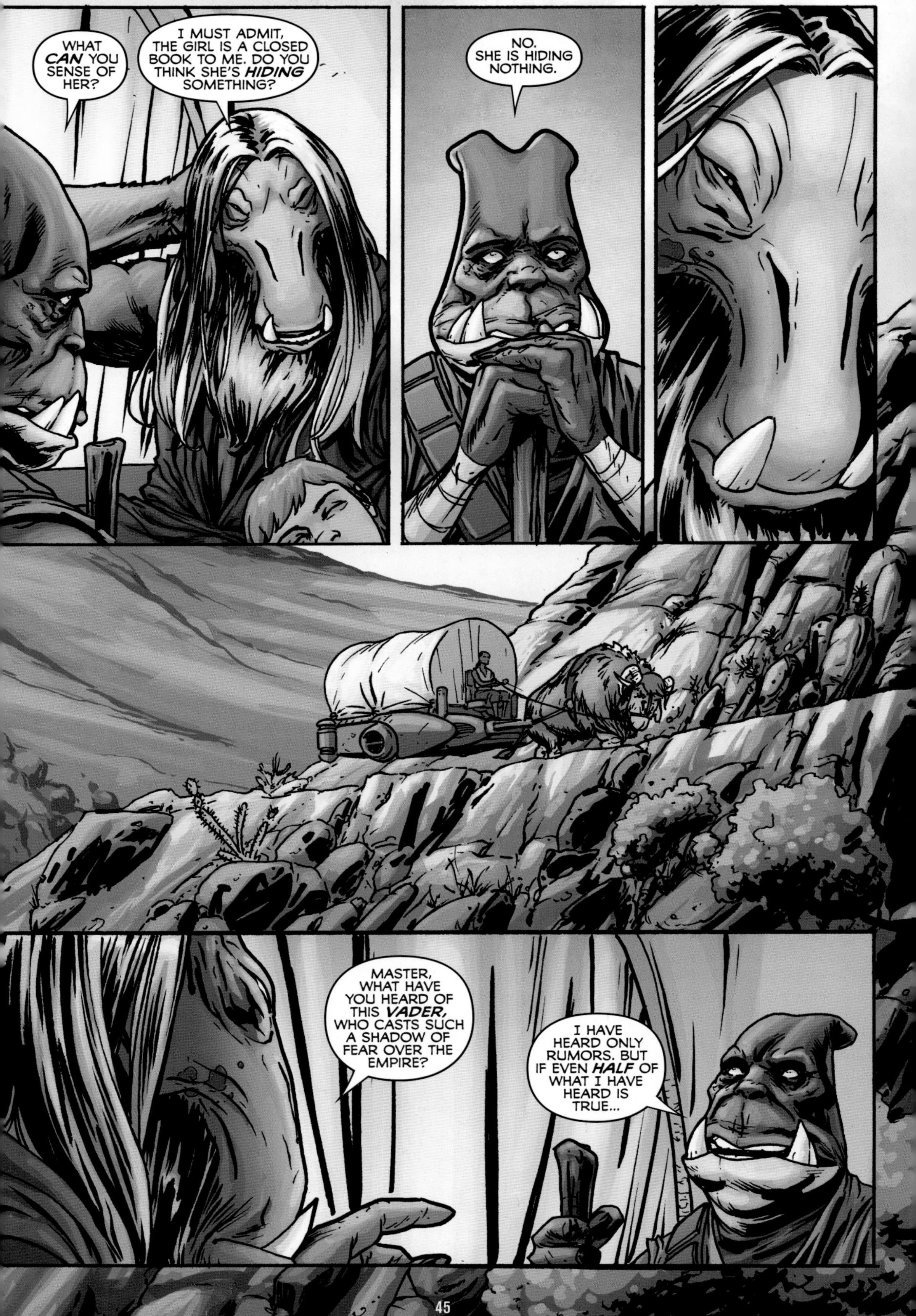

WHAT *CAN* YOU SENSE OF HER?
I MUST ADMIT, THE GIRL IS A CLOSED BOOK TO ME. DO YOU THINK SHE'S *HIDING* SOMETHING?
NO. SHE IS HIDING NOTHING.
MASTER, WHAT HAVE YOU HEARD OF THIS *VADER,* WHO CASTS SUCH A SHADOW OF FEAR OVER THE EMPIRE?
I HAVE HEARD ONLY RUMORS. BUT IF EVEN *HALF* OF WHAT I HAVE HEARD IS TRUE...

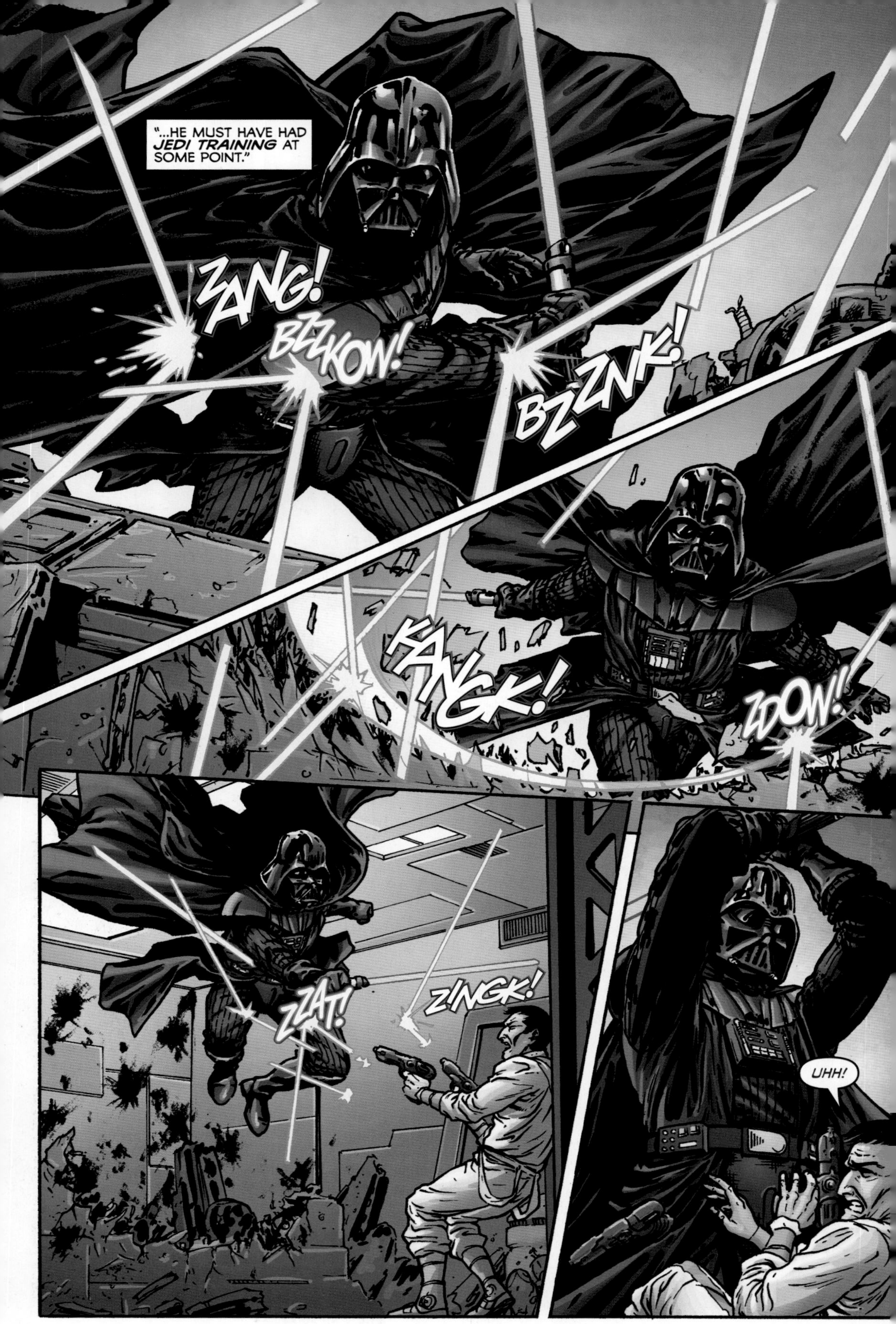
"...HE MUST HAVE HAD *JEDI TRAINING* AT SOME POINT."
ZANG!
BZZKOW!
BZZZNK!
KANGK!
ZDOW!
ZZZAT!
ZINGK!
UHH!

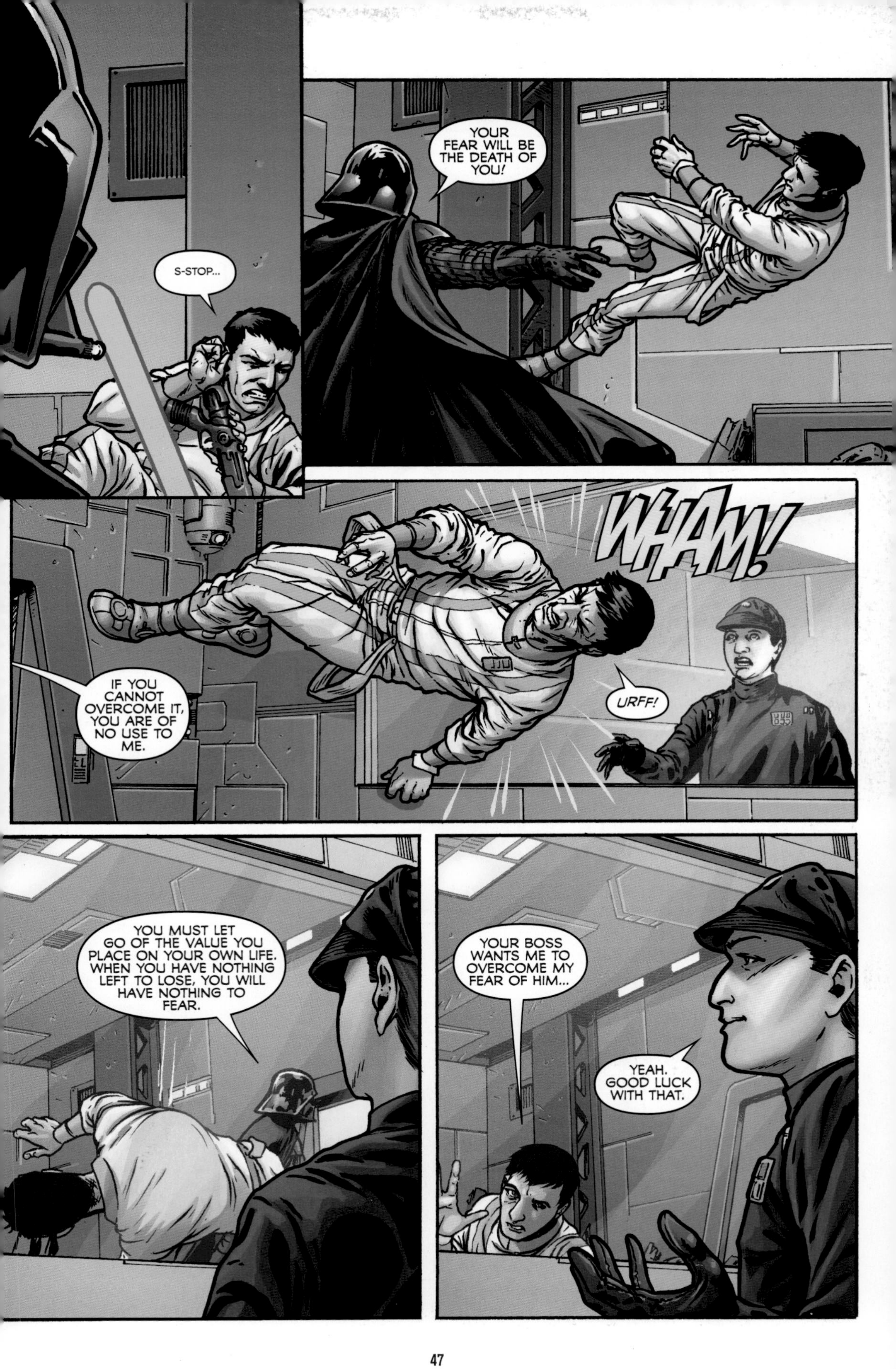
S-STOP...
YOUR FEAR WILL BE THE DEATH OF YOU!
WHAM!
IF YOU CANNOT OVERCOME IT, YOU ARE OF NO USE TO ME.
URFF!
YOU MUST LET GO OF THE VALUE YOU PLACE ON YOUR OWN LIFE. WHEN YOU HAVE NOTHING LEFT TO LOSE, YOU WILL HAVE NOTHING TO FEAR.
YOUR BOSS WANTS ME TO OVERCOME MY FEAR OF HIM...
YEAH. GOOD LUCK WITH THAT.

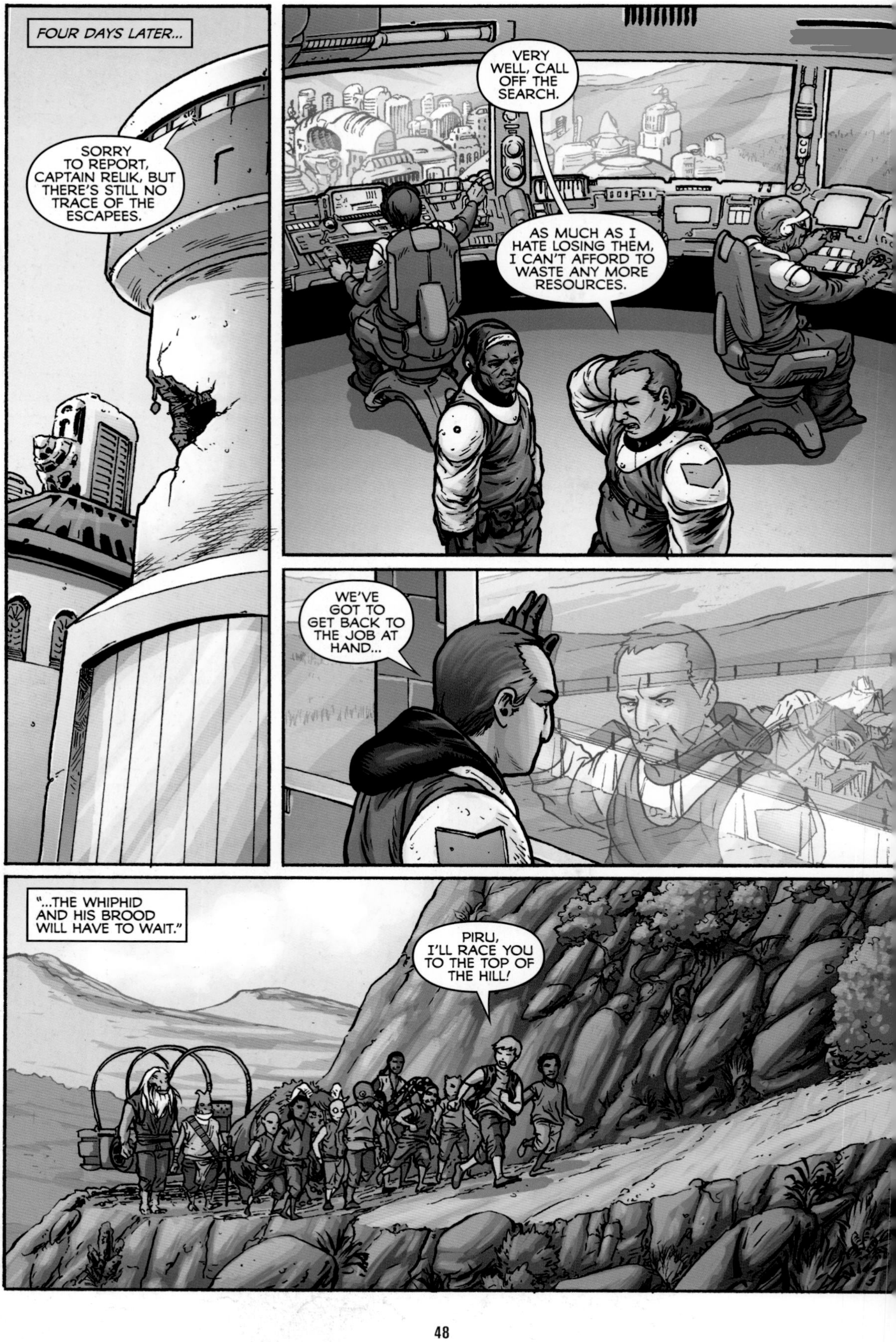
FOUR DAYS LATER...
SORRY TO REPORT, CAPTAIN RELIK, BUT THERE'S STILL NO TRACE OF THE ESCAPEES.
VERY WELL, CALL OFF THE SEARCH.
AS MUCH AS I HATE LOSING THEM, I CAN'T AFFORD TO WASTE ANY MORE RESOURCES.
WE'VE GOT TO GET BACK TO THE JOB AT HAND...
"...THE WHIPHID AND HIS BROOD WILL HAVE TO WAIT."
PIRU, I'LL RACE YOU TO THE TOP OF THE HILL!

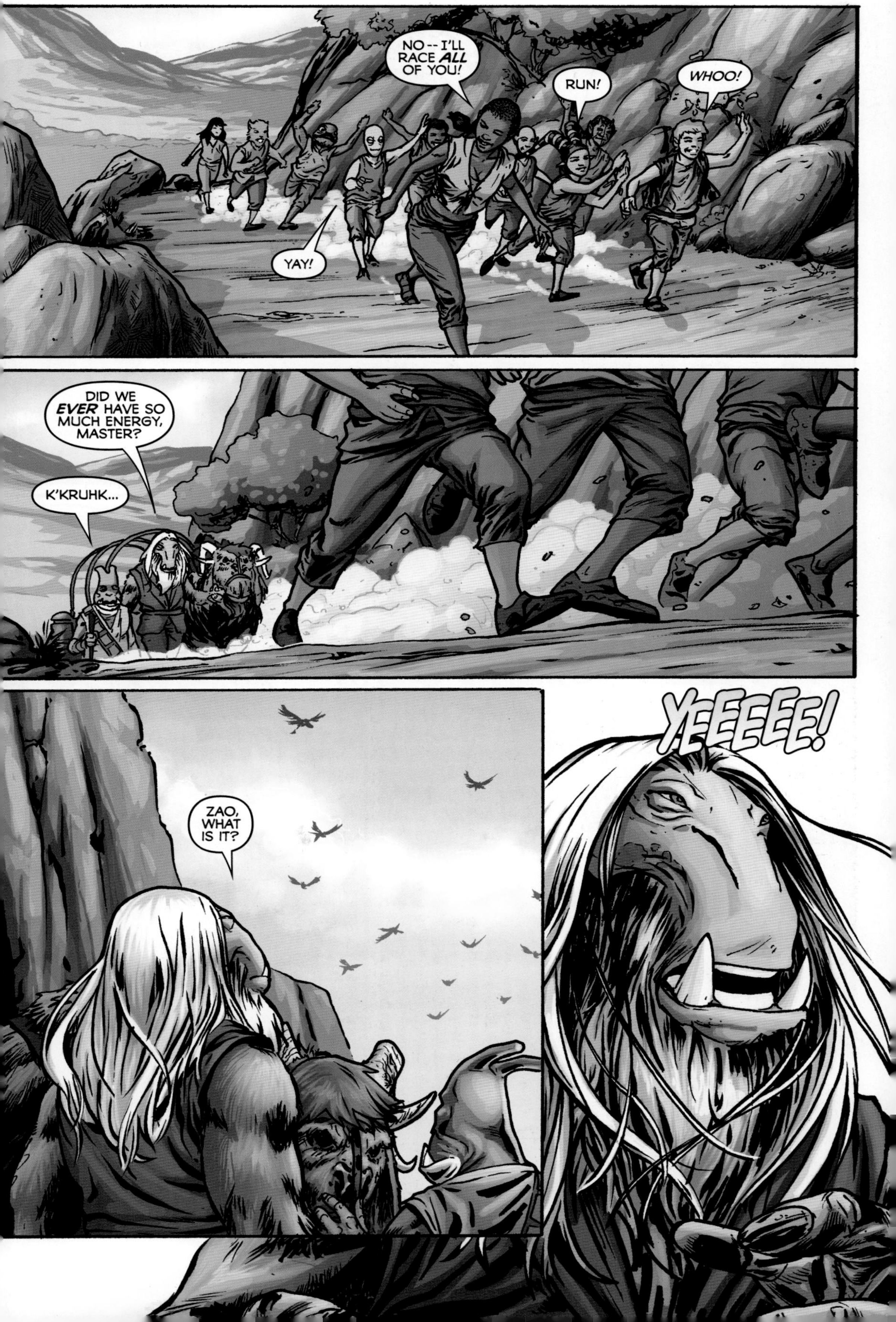
NO -- I'LL RACE ALL OF YOU!
RUN!
WHOO!
YAY!
DID WE EVER HAVE SO MUCH ENERGY, MASTER?
K'KRUHK...
ZAO, WHAT IS IT?
YEEEEEE!

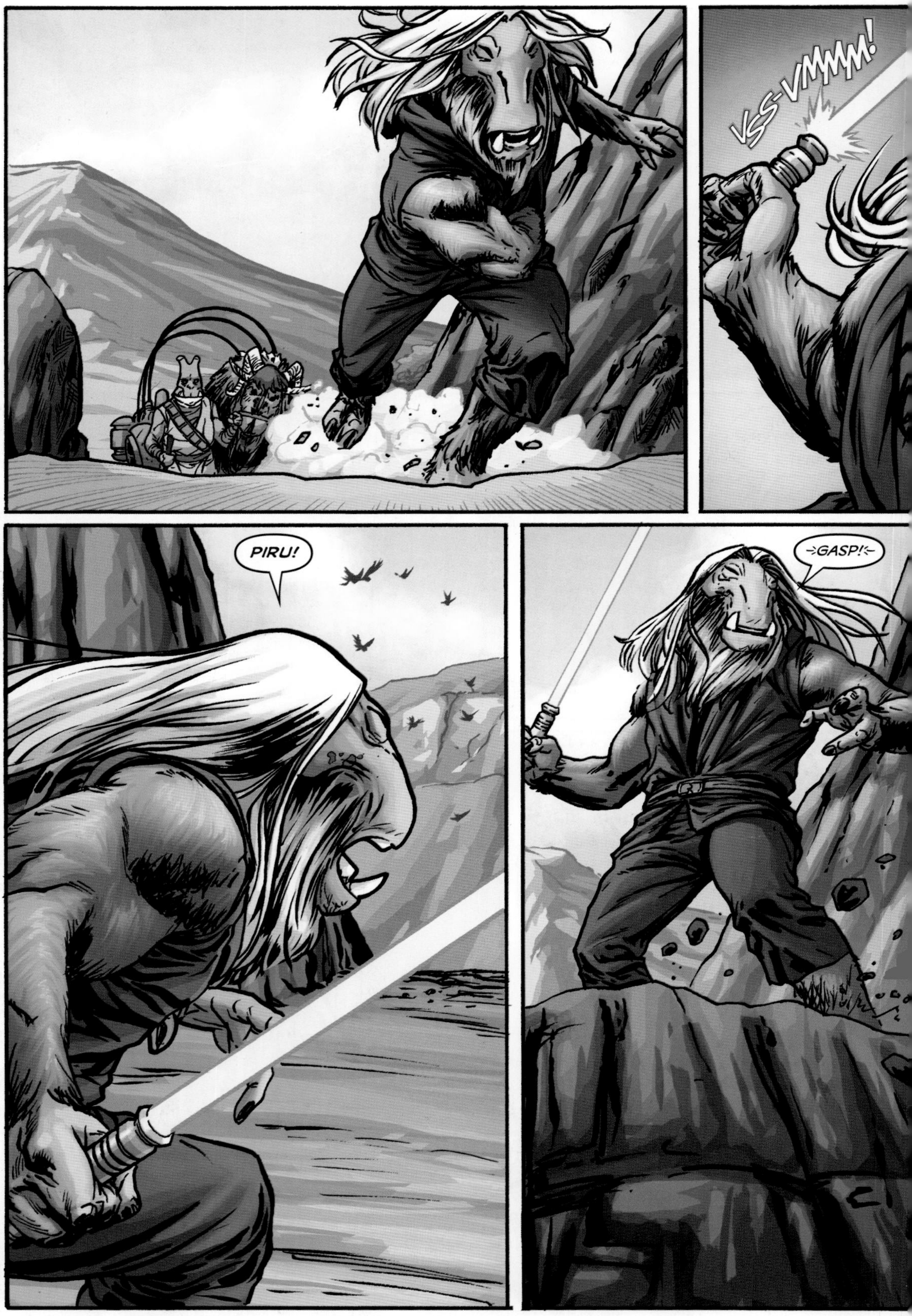
VSS-VMMM!
PIRU!
GASP!

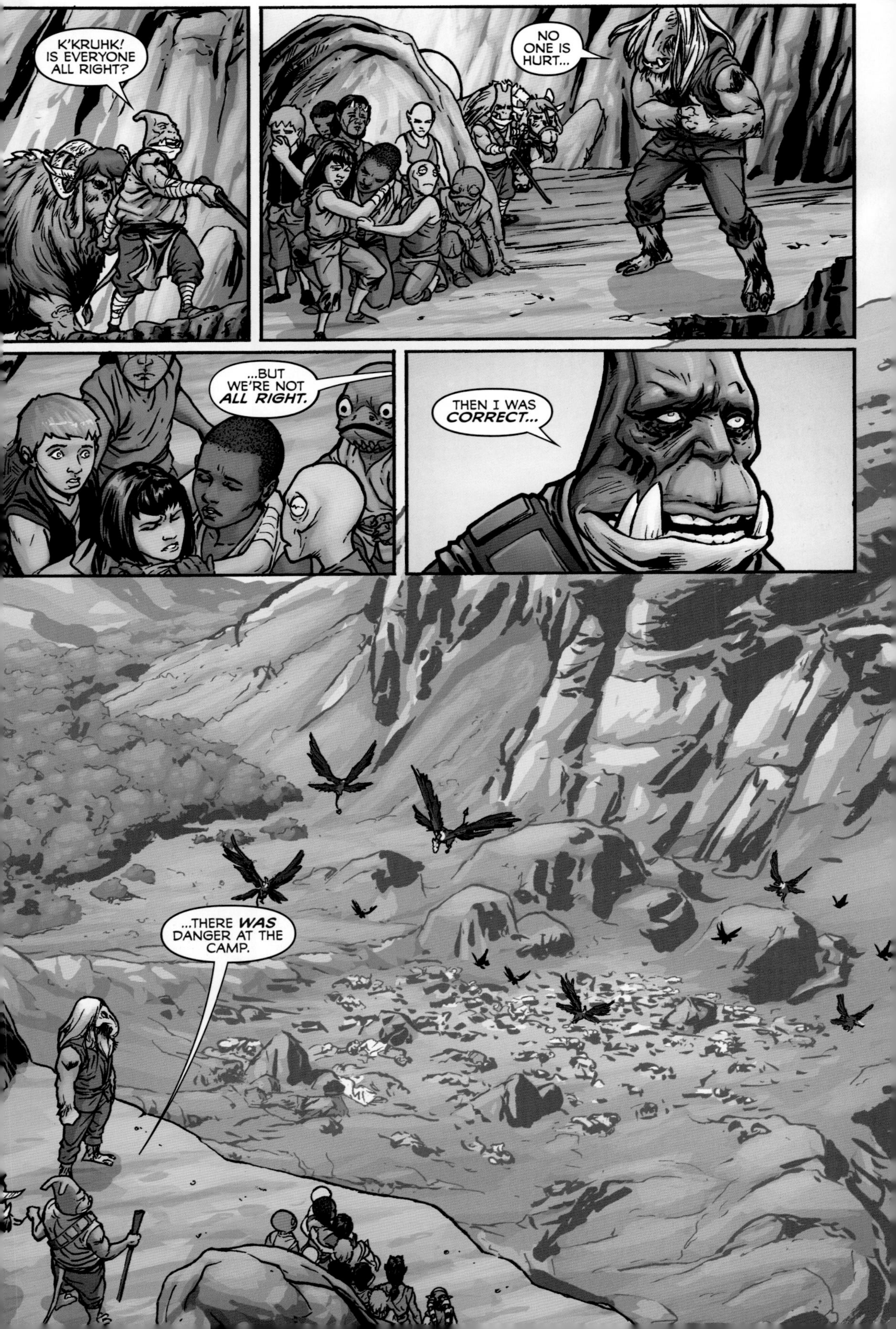
K'KRUHK! IS EVERYONE ALL RIGHT?
NO ONE IS HURT...
...BUT WE'RE NOT ALL RIGHT.
THEN I WAS CORRECT...
...THERE WAS DANGER AT THE CAMP.

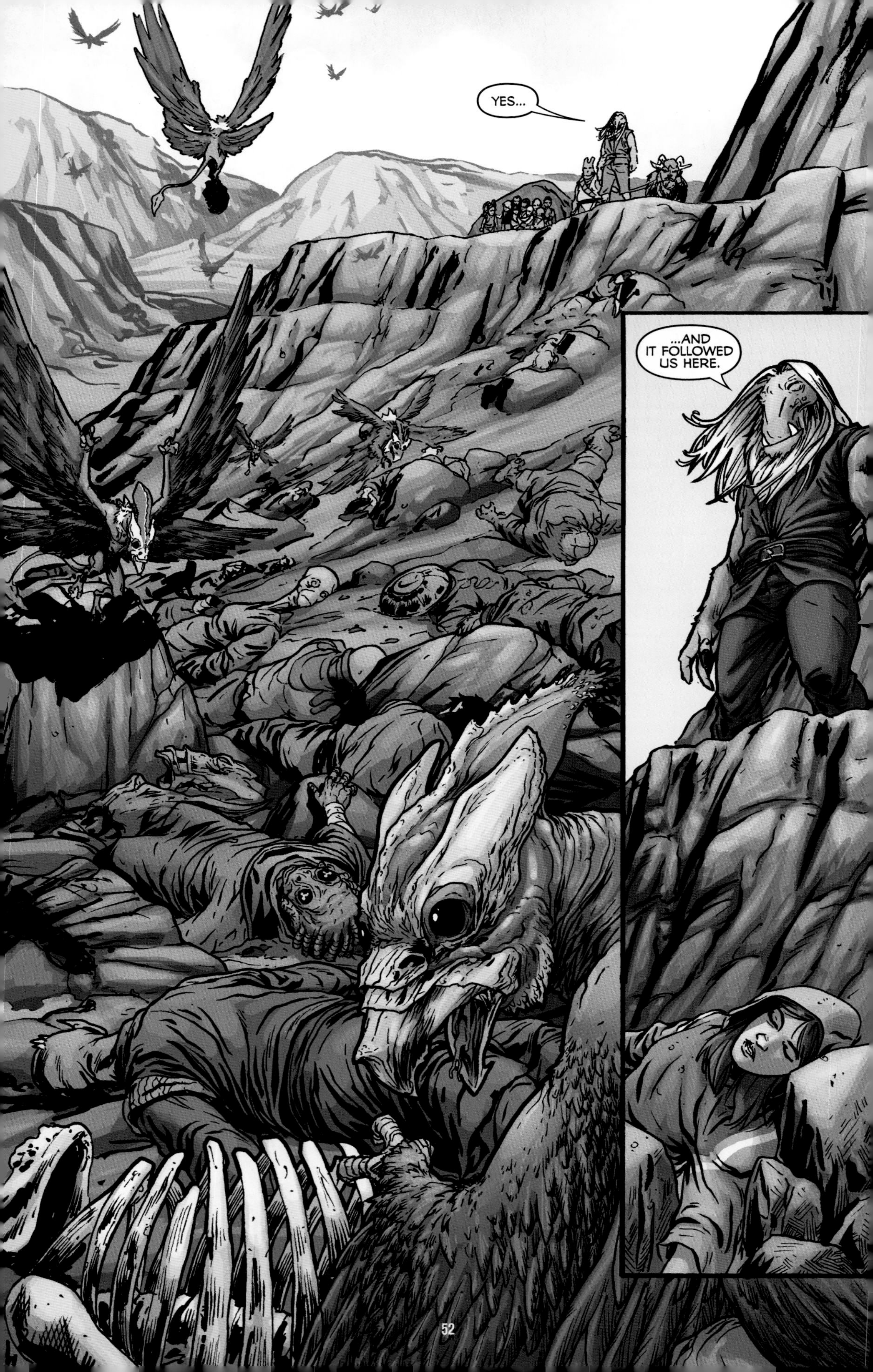
YES...
...AND IT FOLLOWED US HERE.

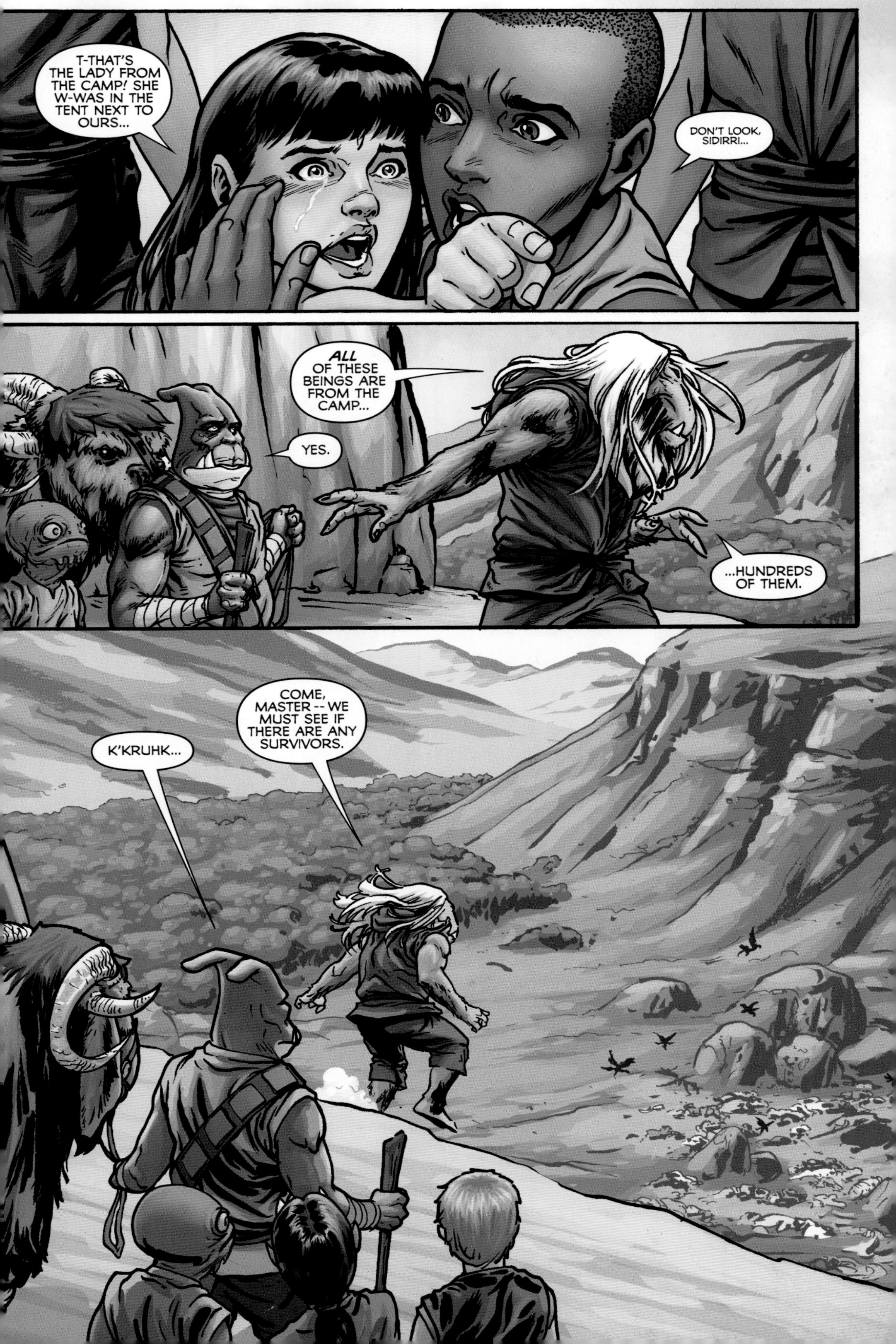
T-THAT'S THE LADY FROM THE CAMP! SHE W-WAS IN THE TENT NEXT TO OURS...
DON'T LOOK, SIDIRRI...
ALL OF THESE BEINGS ARE FROM THE CAMP...
YES.
...HUNDREDS OF THEM.
K'KRUHK...
COME, MASTER -- WE MUST SEE IF THERE ARE ANY SURVIVORS.

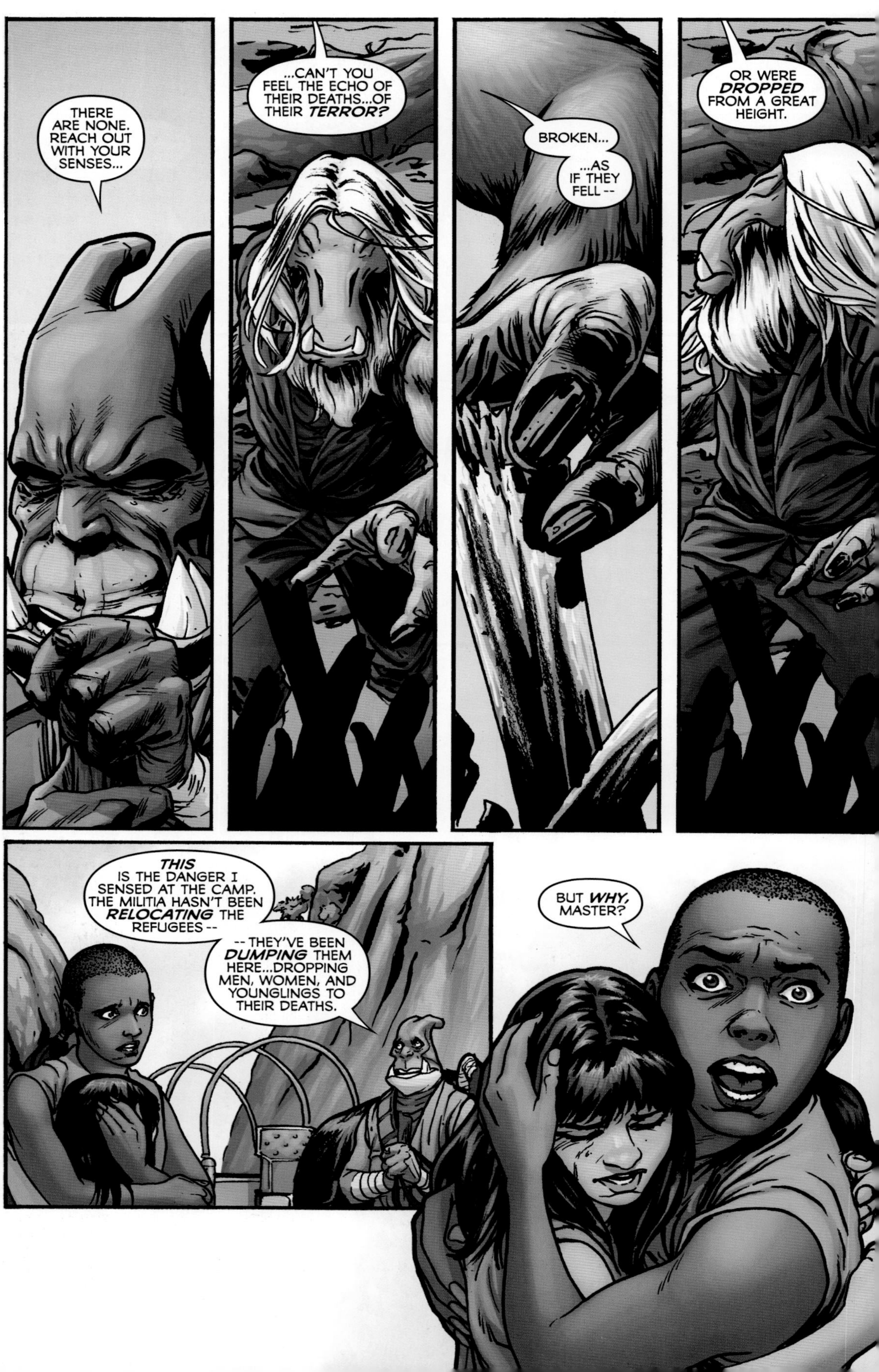
THERE ARE NONE. REACH OUT WITH YOUR SENSES...
...CAN'T YOU FEEL THE ECHO OF THEIR DEATHS...OF THEIR *TERROR?*
BROKEN...
...AS IF THEY FELL --
OR WERE *DROPPED* FROM A GREAT HEIGHT.
THIS IS THE DANGER I SENSED AT THE CAMP. THE MILITIA HASN'T BEEN *RELOCATING* THE REFUGEES --
-- THEY'VE BEEN *DUMPING* THEM HERE...DROPPING MEN, WOMEN, AND YOUNGLINGS TO THEIR DEATHS.
BUT *WHY,* MASTER?

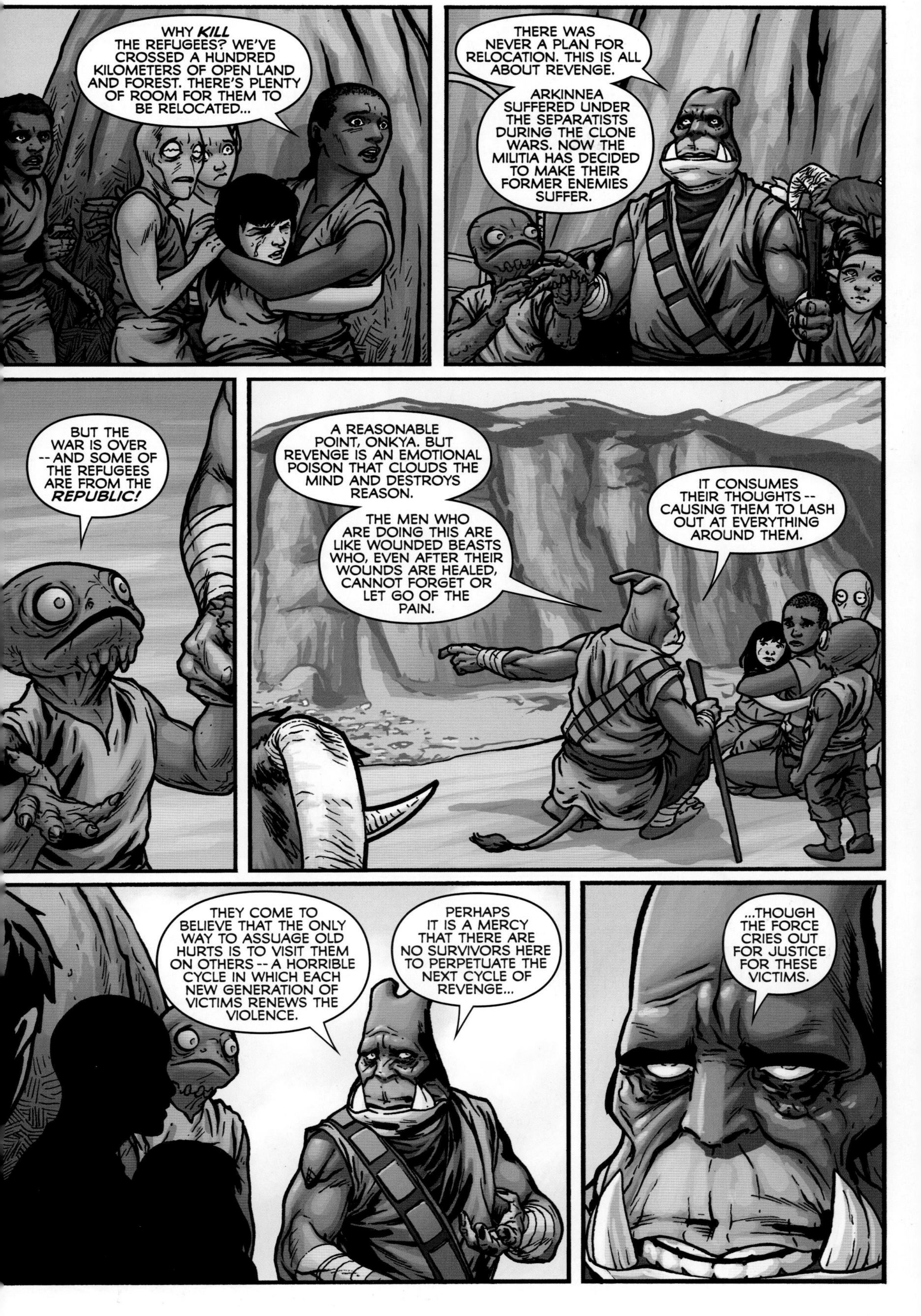
WHY KILL THE REFUGEES? WE'VE CROSSED A HUNDRED KILOMETERS OF OPEN LAND AND FOREST. THERE'S PLENTY OF ROOM FOR THEM TO BE RELOCATED...
THERE WAS NEVER A PLAN FOR RELOCATION. THIS IS ALL ABOUT REVENGE.
ARKINNEA SUFFERED UNDER THE SEPARATISTS DURING THE CLONE WARS. NOW THE MILITIA HAS DECIDED TO MAKE THEIR FORMER ENEMIES SUFFER.
BUT THE WAR IS OVER -- AND SOME OF THE REFUGEES ARE FROM THE REPUBLIC!
A REASONABLE POINT, ONKYA. BUT REVENGE IS AN EMOTIONAL POISON THAT CLOUDS THE MIND AND DESTROYS REASON.
THE MEN WHO ARE DOING THIS ARE LIKE WOUNDED BEASTS WHO, EVEN AFTER THEIR WOUNDS ARE HEALED, CANNOT FORGET OR LET GO OF THE PAIN.
IT CONSUMES THEIR THOUGHTS -- CAUSING THEM TO LASH OUT AT EVERYTHING AROUND THEM.
THEY COME TO BELIEVE THAT THE ONLY WAY TO ASSUAGE OLD HURTS IS TO VISIT THEM ON OTHERS -- A HORRIBLE CYCLE IN WHICH EACH NEW GENERATION OF VICTIMS RENEWS THE VIOLENCE.
PERHAPS IT IS A MERCY THAT THERE ARE NO SURVIVORS HERE TO PERPETUATE THE NEXT CYCLE OF REVENGE...
...THOUGH THE FORCE CRIES OUT FOR JUSTICE FOR THESE VICTIMS.

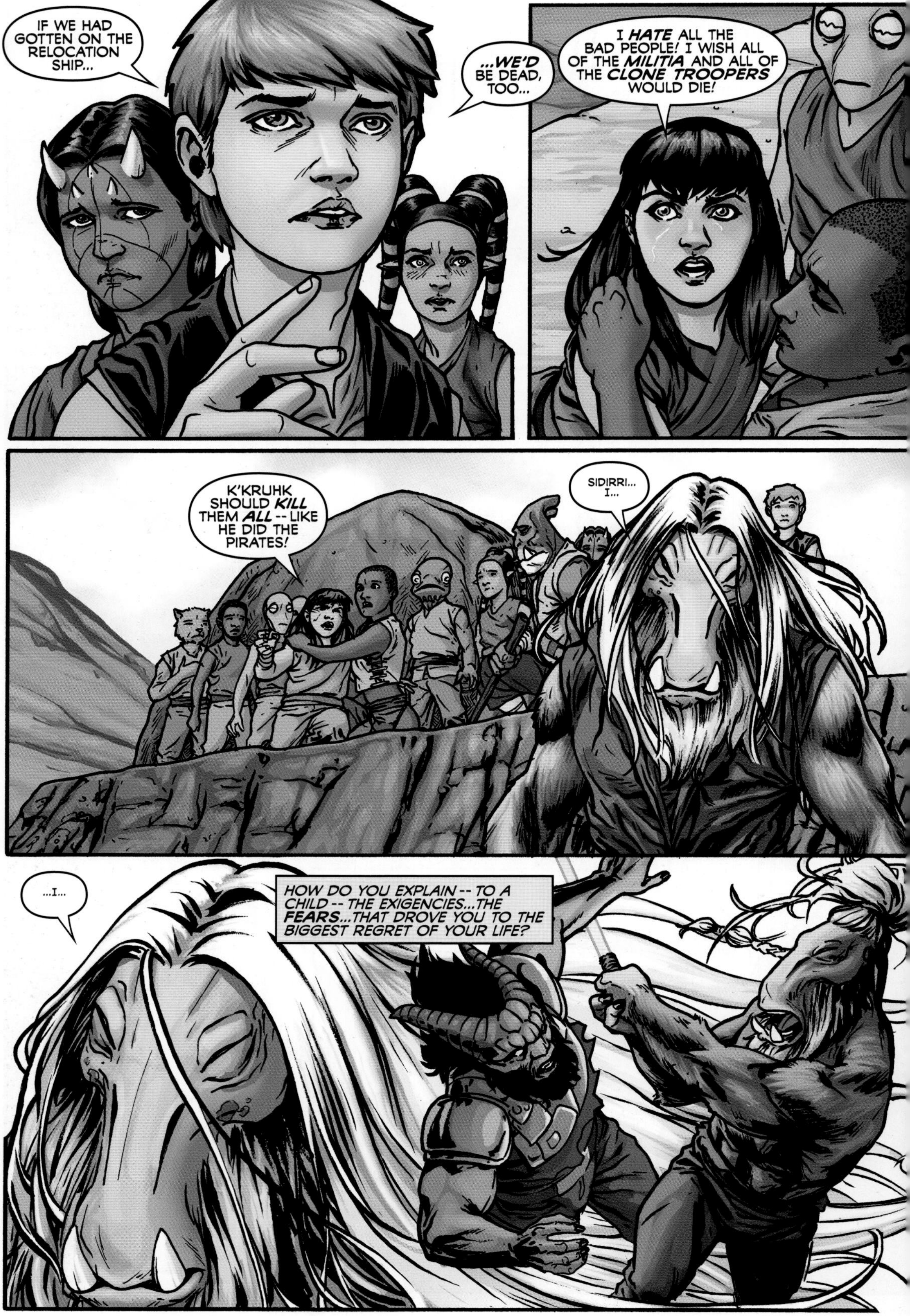
IF WE HAD GOTTEN ON THE RELOCATION SHIP...
...WE'D BE DEAD, TOO...
I HATE ALL THE BAD PEOPLE! I WISH ALL OF THE MILITIA AND ALL OF THE CLONE TROOPERS WOULD DIE!
K'KRUHK SHOULD KILL THEM ALL -- LIKE HE DID THE PIRATES!
SIDIRRI... I...
...I...
HOW DO YOU EXPLAIN -- TO A CHILD -- THE EXIGENCIES...THE FEARS...THAT DROVE YOU TO THE BIGGEST REGRET OF YOUR LIFE?

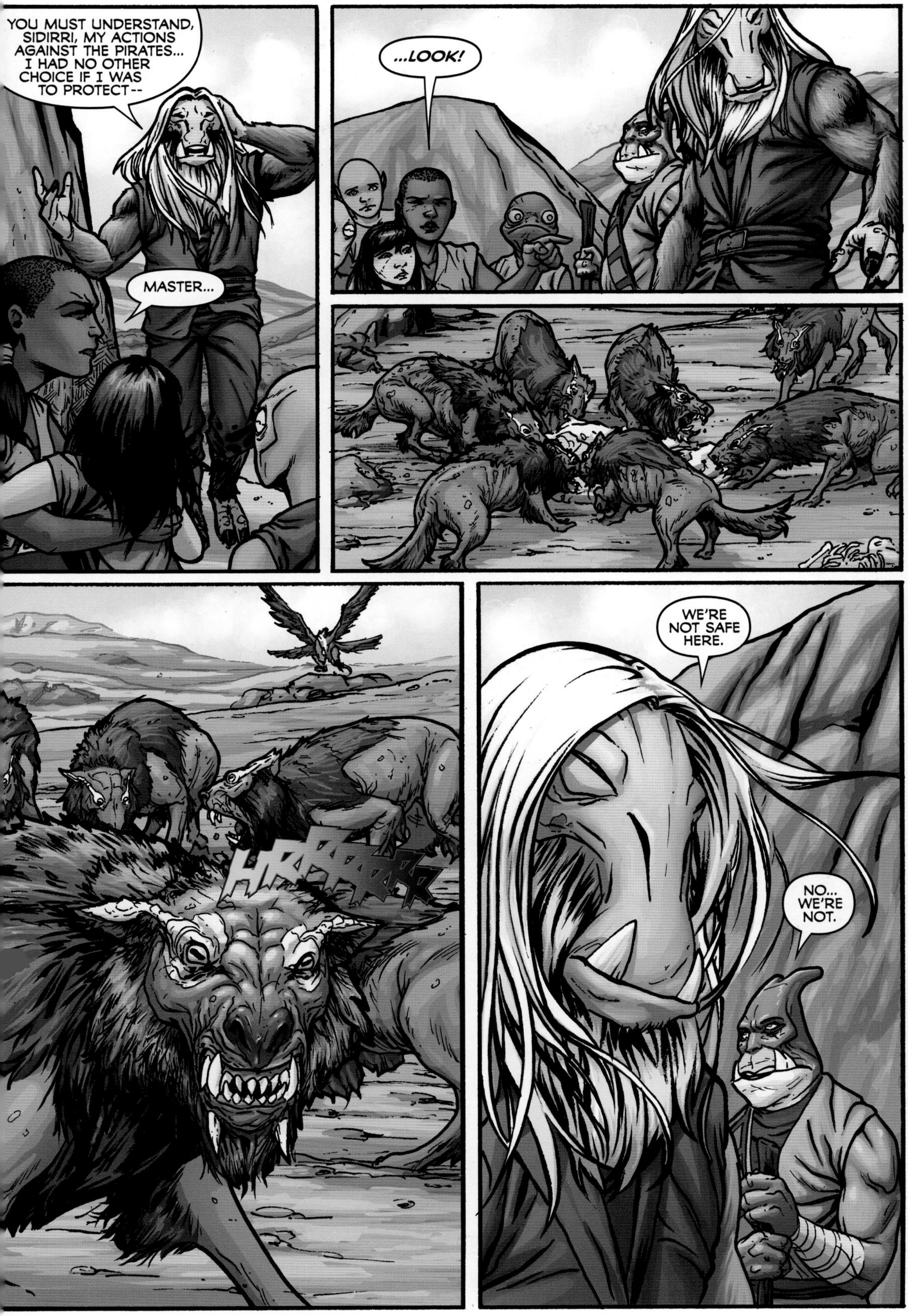
YOU MUST UNDERSTAND, SIDIRRI, MY ACTIONS AGAINST THE PIRATES... I HAD NO OTHER CHOICE IF I WAS TO PROTECT--
MASTER...
...LOOK!
WE'RE NOT SAFE HERE.
NO... WE'RE NOT.

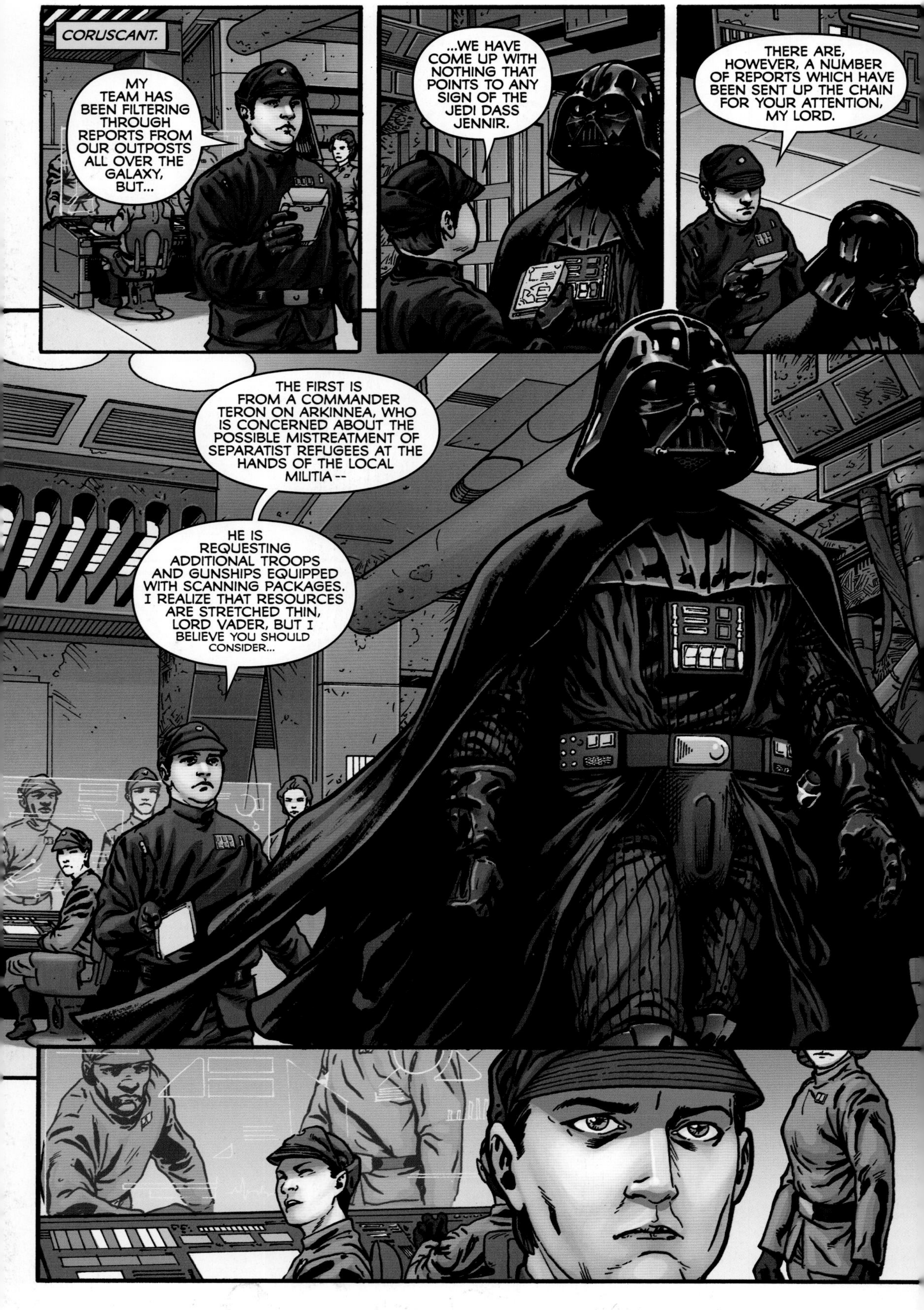
CORUSCANT.
MY TEAM HAS BEEN FILTERING THROUGH REPORTS FROM OUR OUTPOSTS ALL OVER THE GALAXY, BUT...
...WE HAVE COME UP WITH NOTHING THAT POINTS TO ANY SIGN OF THE JEDI DASS JENNIR.
THERE ARE, HOWEVER, A NUMBER OF REPORTS WHICH HAVE BEEN SENT UP THE CHAIN FOR YOUR ATTENTION, MY LORD.
THE FIRST IS FROM A COMMANDER TERON ON ARKINNEA, WHO IS CONCERNED ABOUT THE POSSIBLE MISTREATMENT OF SEPARATIST REFUGEES AT THE HANDS OF THE LOCAL MILITIA --
HE IS REQUESTING ADDITIONAL TROOPS AND GUNSHIPS EQUIPPED WITH SCANNING PACKAGES. I REALIZE THAT RESOURCES ARE STRETCHED THIN, LORD VADER, BUT I BELIEVE YOU SHOULD CONSIDER...

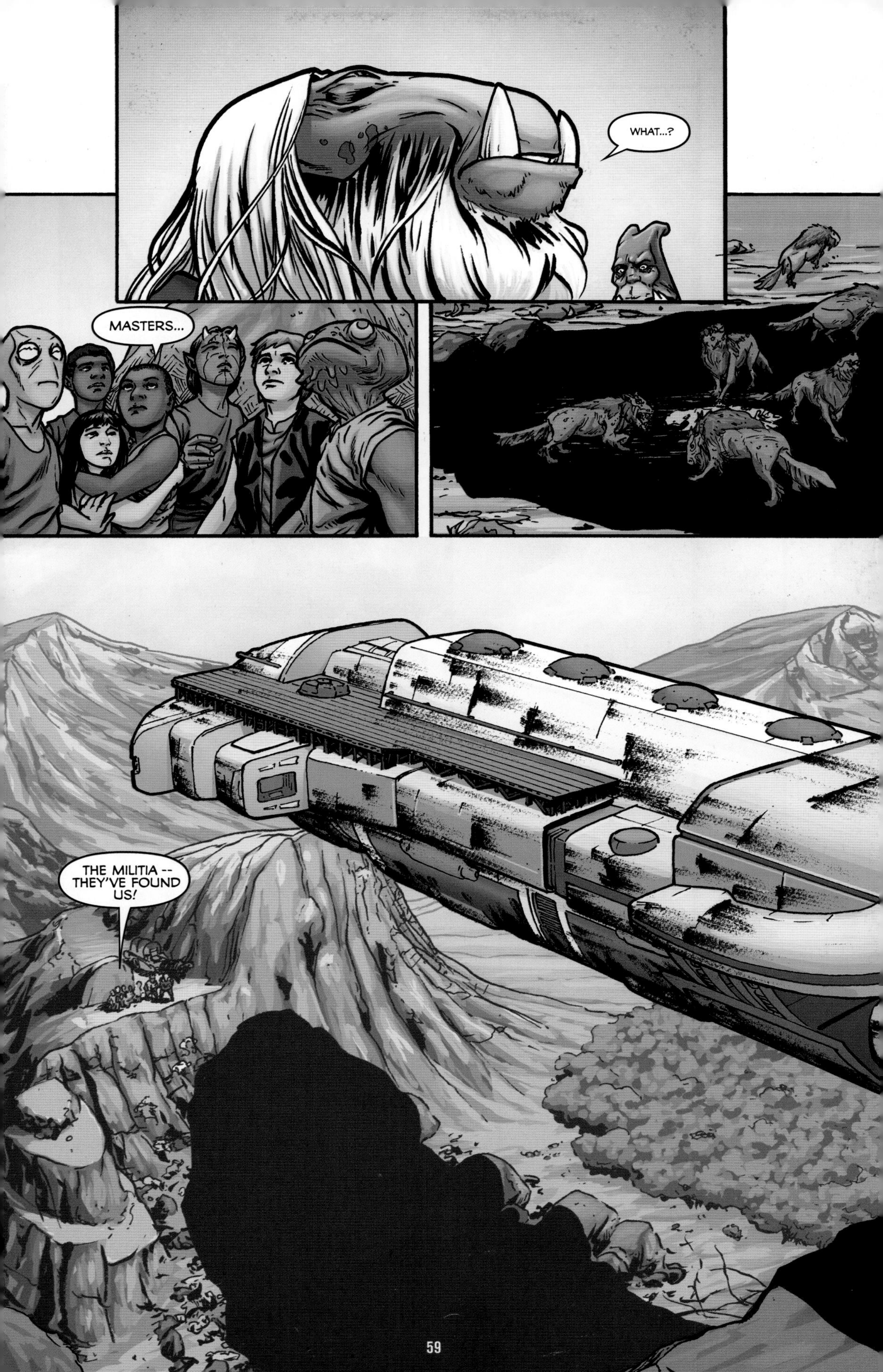
WHAT...?
MASTERS...
THE MILITIA -- THEY'VE FOUND US!

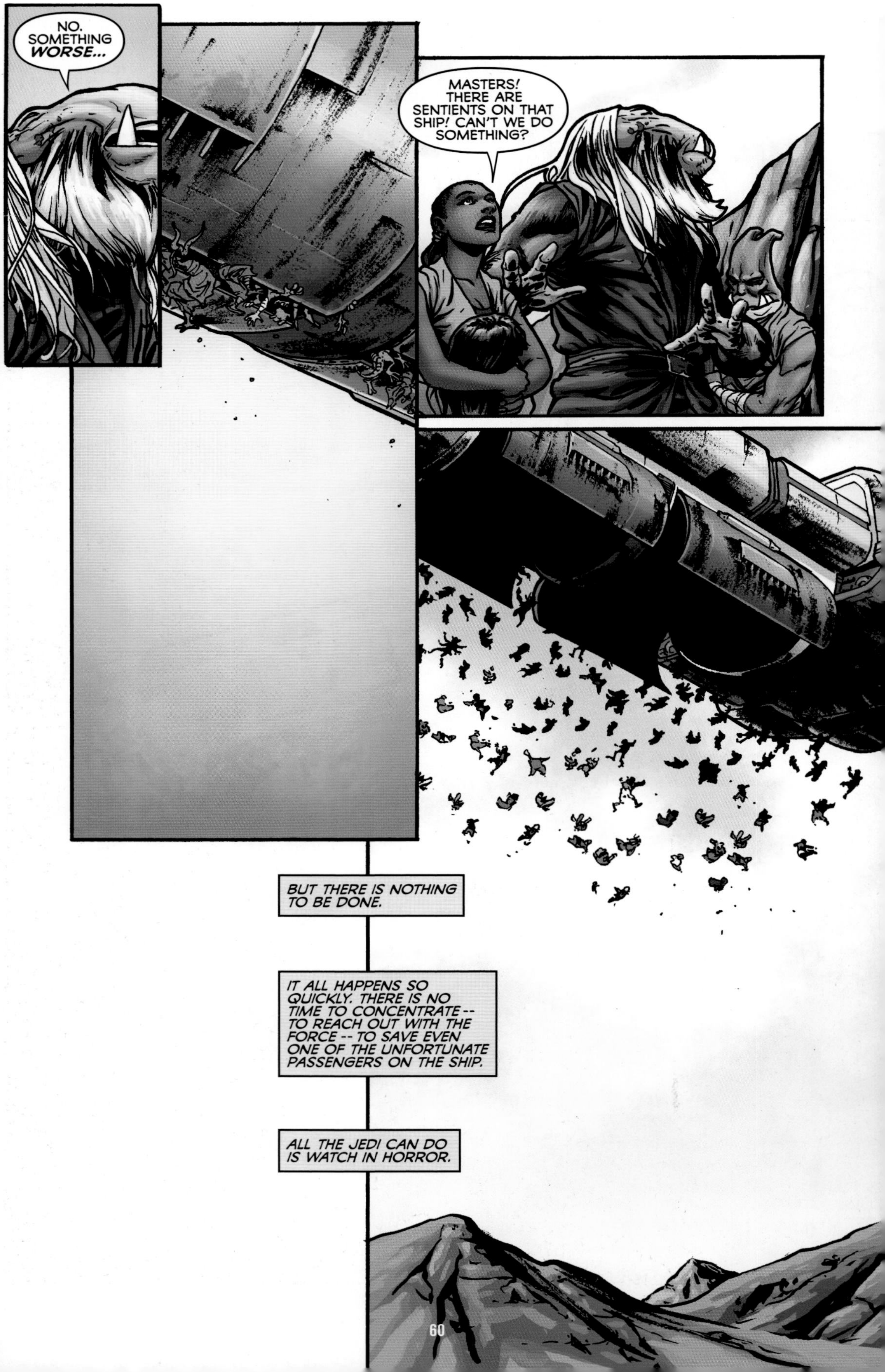
NO. SOMETHING WORSE...
MASTERS! THERE ARE SENTIENTS ON THAT SHIP! CAN'T WE DO SOMETHING?
BUT THERE IS NOTHING TO BE DONE.
IT ALL HAPPENS SO QUICKLY. THERE IS NO TIME TO CONCENTRATE -- TO REACH OUT WITH THE FORCE -- TO SAVE EVEN ONE OF THE UNFORTUNATE PASSENGERS ON THE SHIP.
ALL THE JEDI CAN DO IS WATCH IN HORROR.

IT IS OVER IN SECONDS, AS THE SCREAMS OF THE FALLING ARE ABRUPTLY CUT OFF BY CONTACT WITH THE GROUND.

BUT FOR THE WITNESSES, THOSE FEW SECONDS ARE AS HOURS, BURNED INTO THEIR MEMORIES FOREVER.

IS THE CARGO BAY CLEAR, MAKOS? ANY "CLINGERS"?

NO CLINGERS, LIEUTENANT -- SOMETHING WORSE ...WITNESSES! ON THE GROUND, ON THE TOP OF THAT RIDGE!

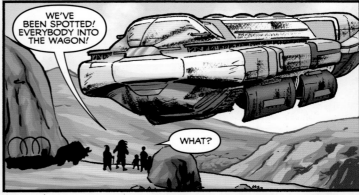

WE'VE BEEN SPOTTED! EVERYBODY INTO THE WAGON!

WHAT?

EVERYBODY. INTO. THE. WAGON!

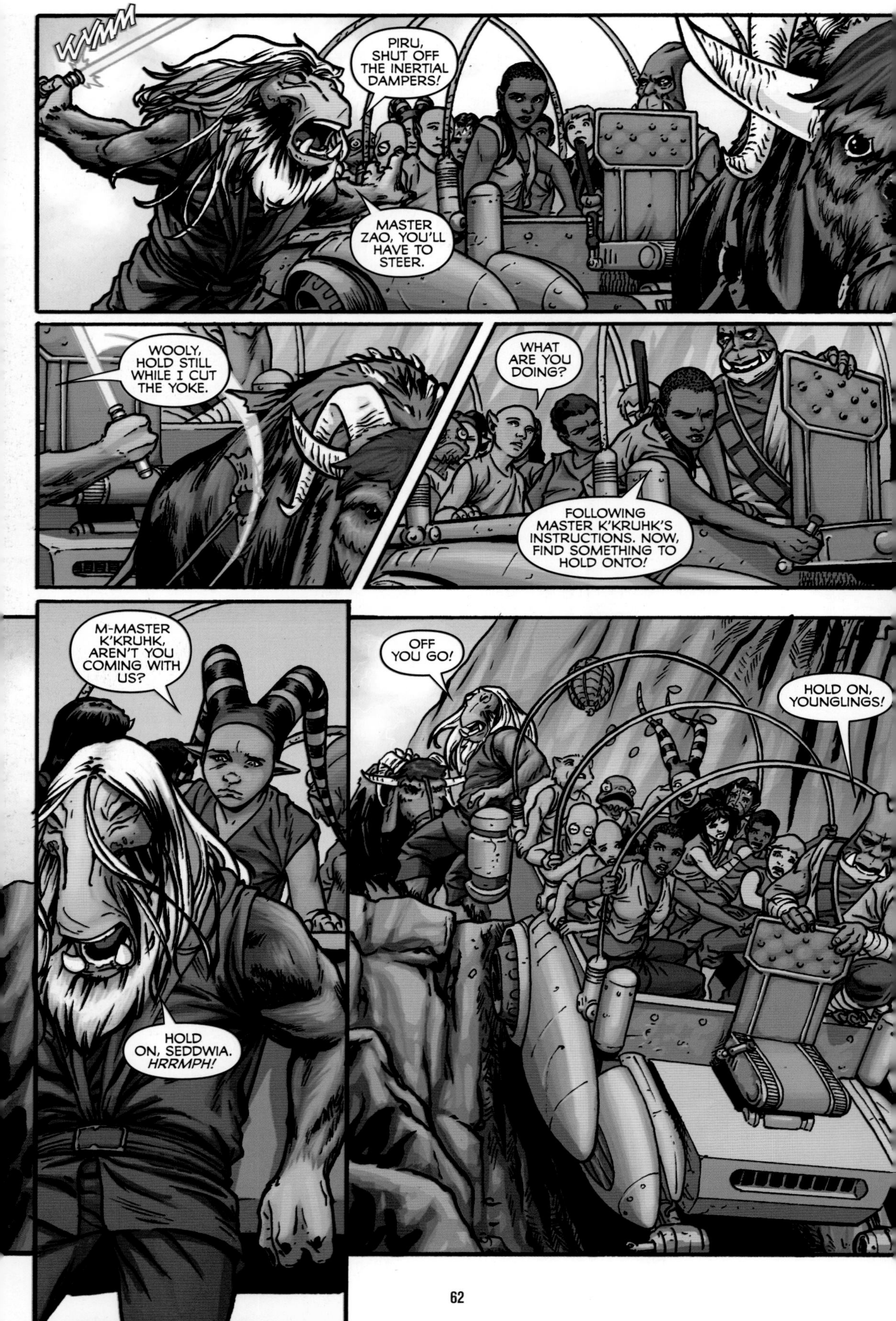

WVMM
PIRU, SHUT OFF THE INERTIAL DAMPERS!
MASTER ZAO, YOU'LL HAVE TO STEER.
WOOLY, HOLD STILL WHILE I CUT THE YOKE.
WHAT ARE YOU DOING?
FOLLOWING MASTER K'KRUHK'S INSTRUCTIONS. NOW, FIND SOMETHING TO HOLD ONTO!
M-MASTER K'KRUHK, AREN'T YOU COMING WITH US?
HOLD ON, SEDDWIA. *HRRMPH!*
OFF YOU GO!
HOLD ON, YOUNGLINGS!

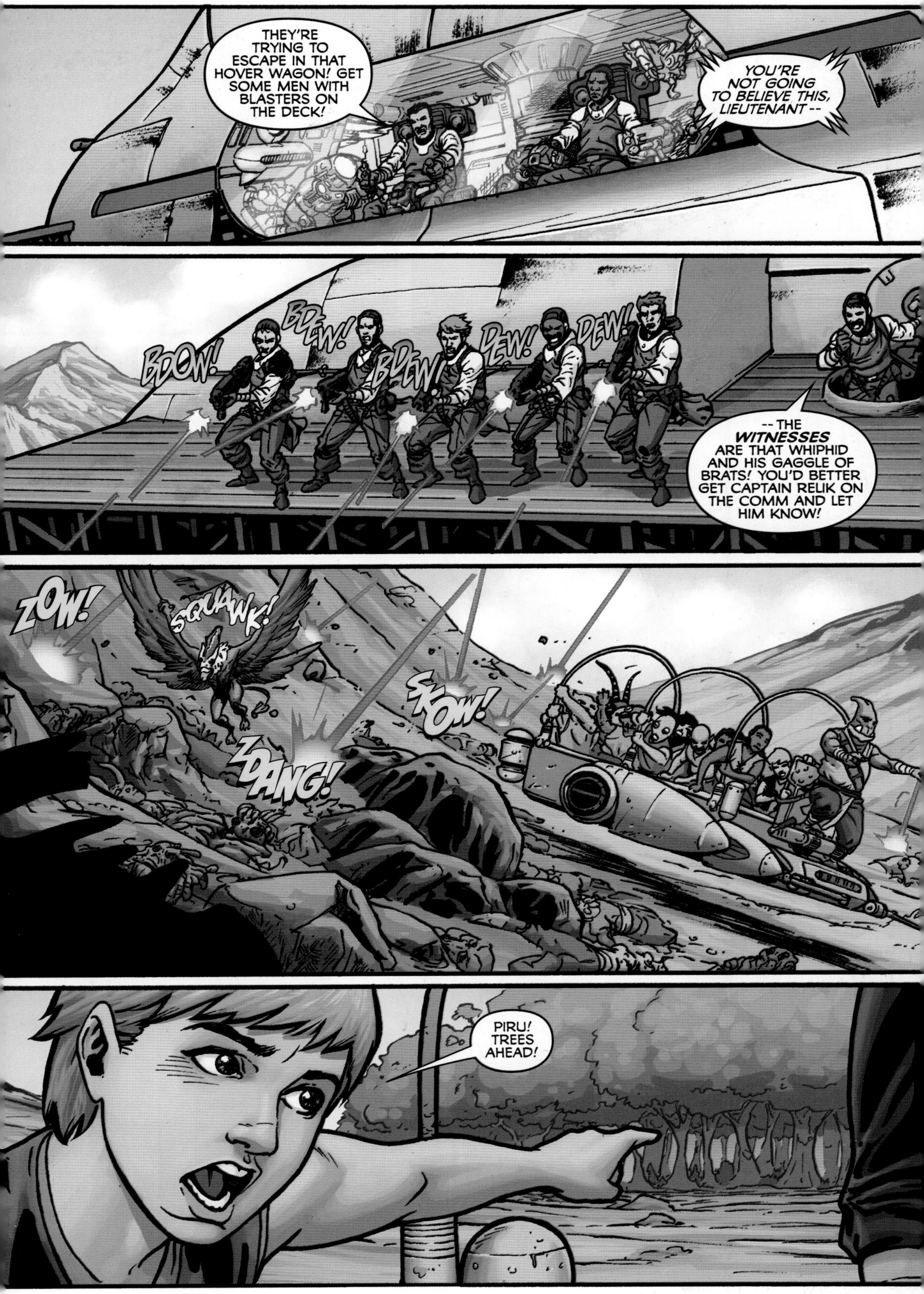
THEY'RE TRYING TO ESCAPE IN THAT HOVER WAGON! GET SOME MEN WITH BLASTERS ON THE DECK!
YOU'RE NOT GOING TO BELIEVE THIS, LIEUTENANT --
BDOW!
BDEW!
BDEW!
DEW!
DEW!
-- THE WITNESSES ARE THAT WHIPHID AND HIS GAGGLE OF BRATS! YOU'D BETTER GET CAPTAIN RELIK ON THE COMM AND LET HIM KNOW!
ZOW!
SQUAWK!
SKOW!
ZDANG!
PIRU! TREES AHEAD!

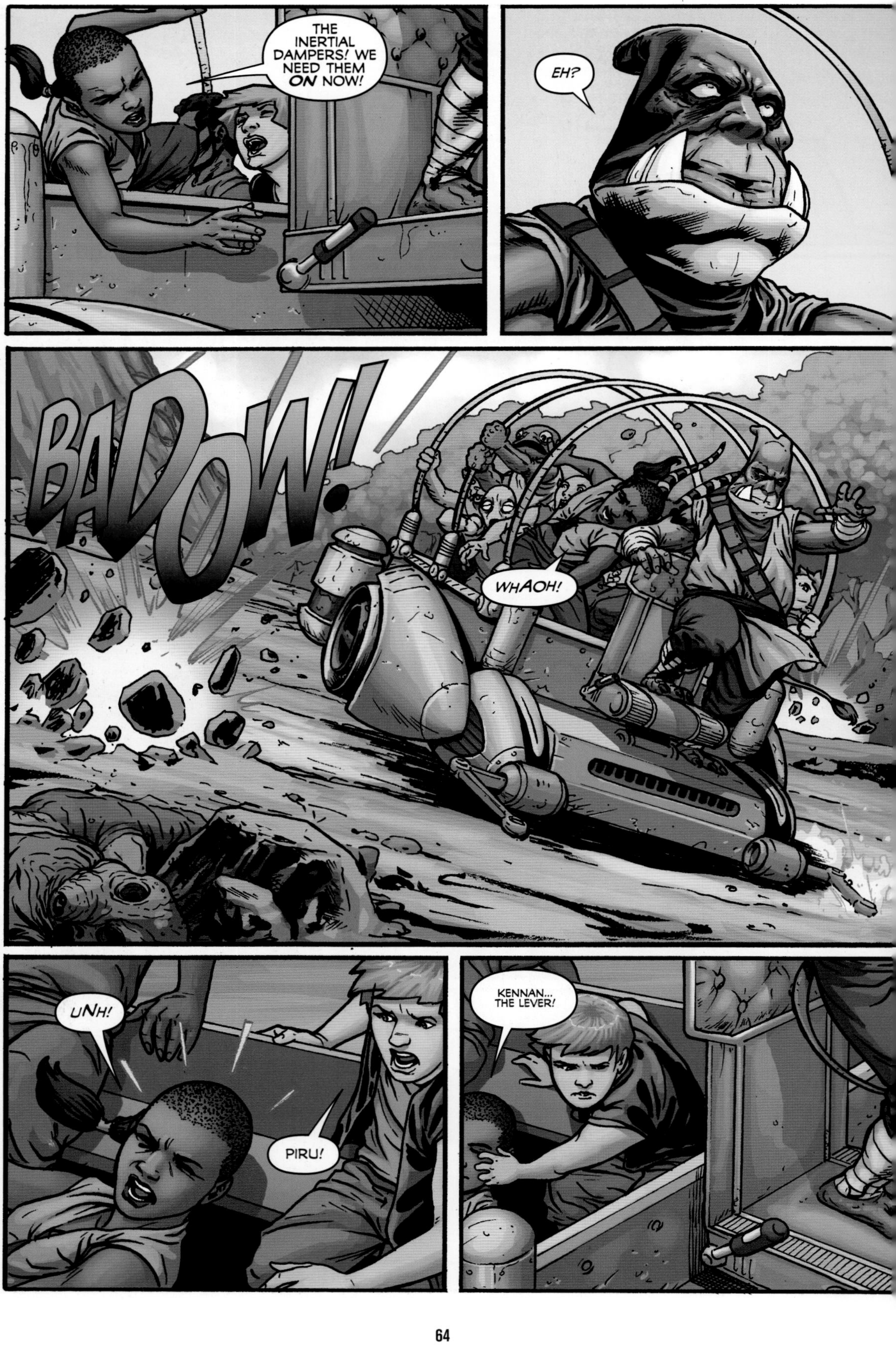
THE INERTIAL DAMPERS! WE NEED THEM ON NOW!
EH?
BADOW!!
WHAOH!
UNH!
PIRU!
KENNAN... THE LEVER!

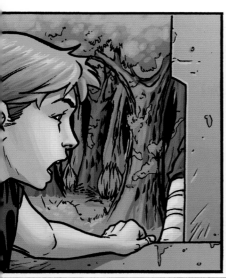

EVERYONE HANG --

WHAM!

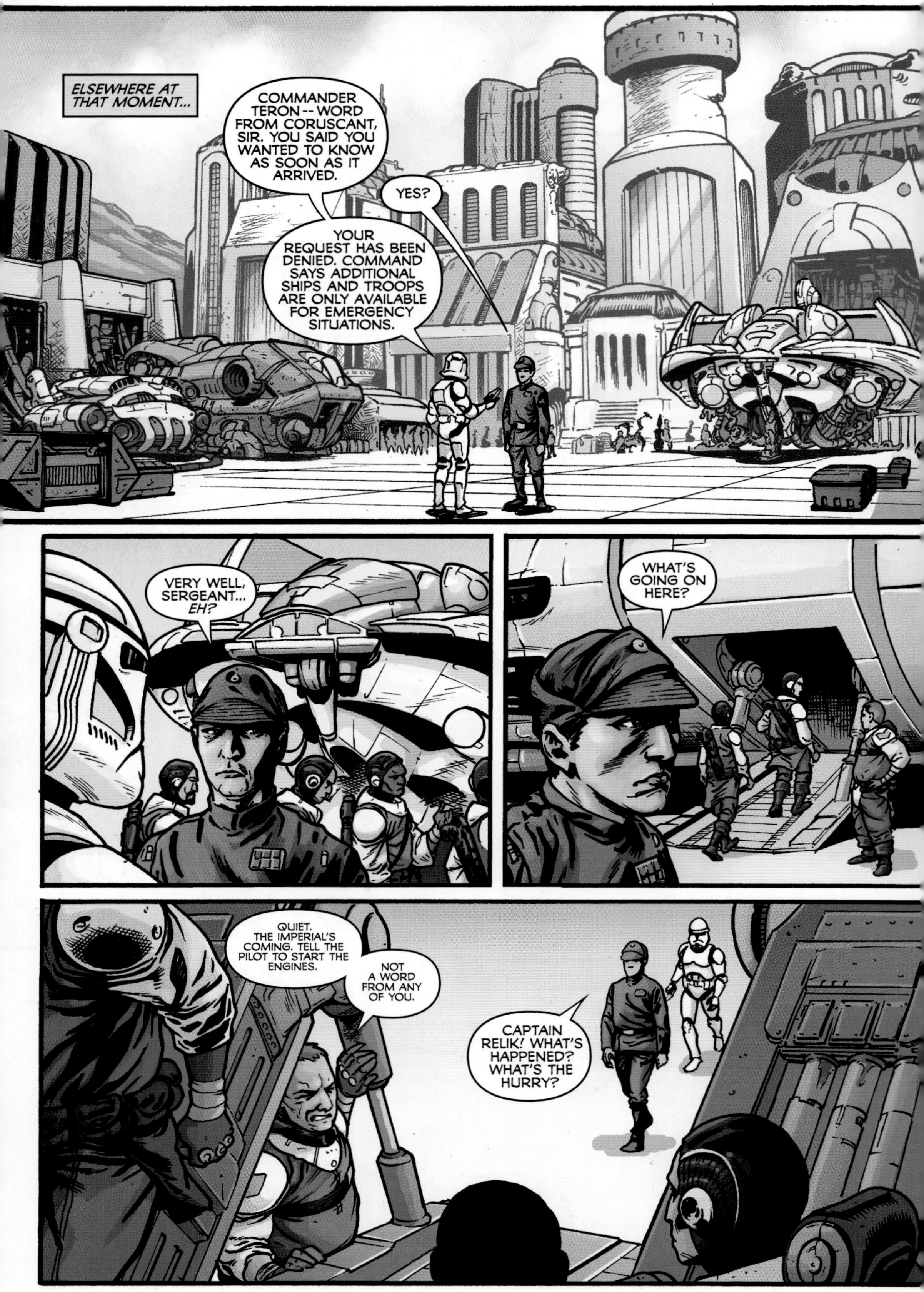
ELSEWHERE AT THAT MOMENT...
COMMANDER TERON--WORD FROM CORUSCANT, SIR. YOU SAID YOU WANTED TO KNOW AS SOON AS IT ARRIVED.
YES?
YOUR REQUEST HAS BEEN DENIED. COMMAND SAYS ADDITIONAL SHIPS AND TROOPS ARE ONLY AVAILABLE FOR EMERGENCY SITUATIONS.
VERY WELL, SERGEANT... EH?
WHAT'S GOING ON HERE?
QUIET. THE IMPERIAL'S COMING. TELL THE PILOT TO START THE ENGINES.
NOT A WORD FROM ANY OF YOU.
CAPTAIN RELIK! WHAT'S HAPPENED? WHAT'S THE HURRY?

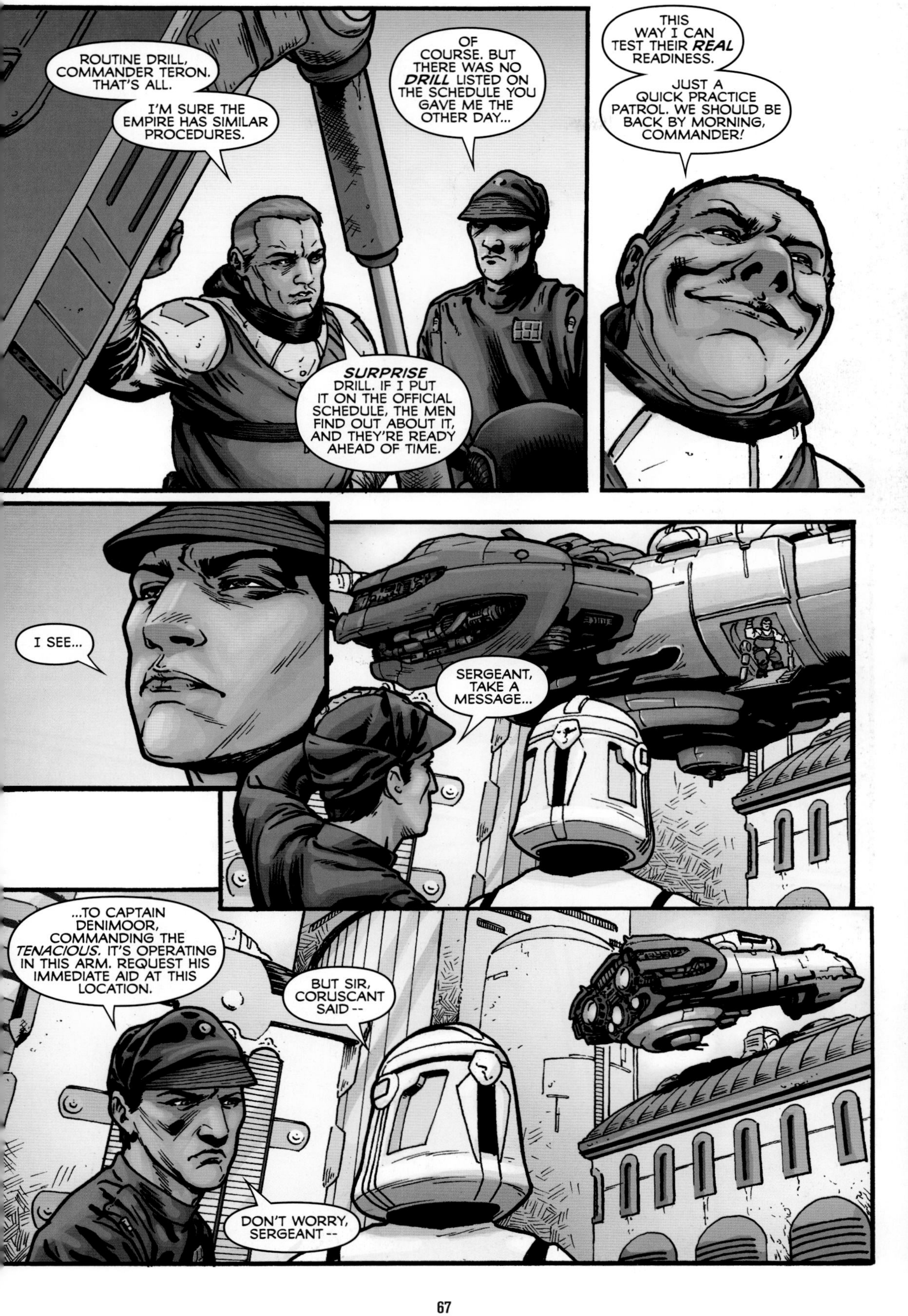
ROUTINE DRILL, COMMANDER TERON. THAT'S ALL.
I'M SURE THE EMPIRE HAS SIMILAR PROCEDURES.
OF COURSE. BUT THERE WAS NO DRILL LISTED ON THE SCHEDULE YOU GAVE ME THE OTHER DAY...
SURPRISE DRILL. IF I PUT IT ON THE OFFICIAL SCHEDULE, THE MEN FIND OUT ABOUT IT, AND THEY'RE READY AHEAD OF TIME.
THIS WAY I CAN TEST THEIR REAL READINESS.
JUST A QUICK PRACTICE PATROL. WE SHOULD BE BACK BY MORNING, COMMANDER!
I SEE...
SERGEANT, TAKE A MESSAGE...
...TO CAPTAIN DENIMOOR, COMMANDING THE TENACIOUS. IT'S OPERATING IN THIS ARM. REQUEST HIS IMMEDIATE AID AT THIS LOCATION.
BUT SIR, CORUSCANT SAID --
DON'T WORRY, SERGEANT --

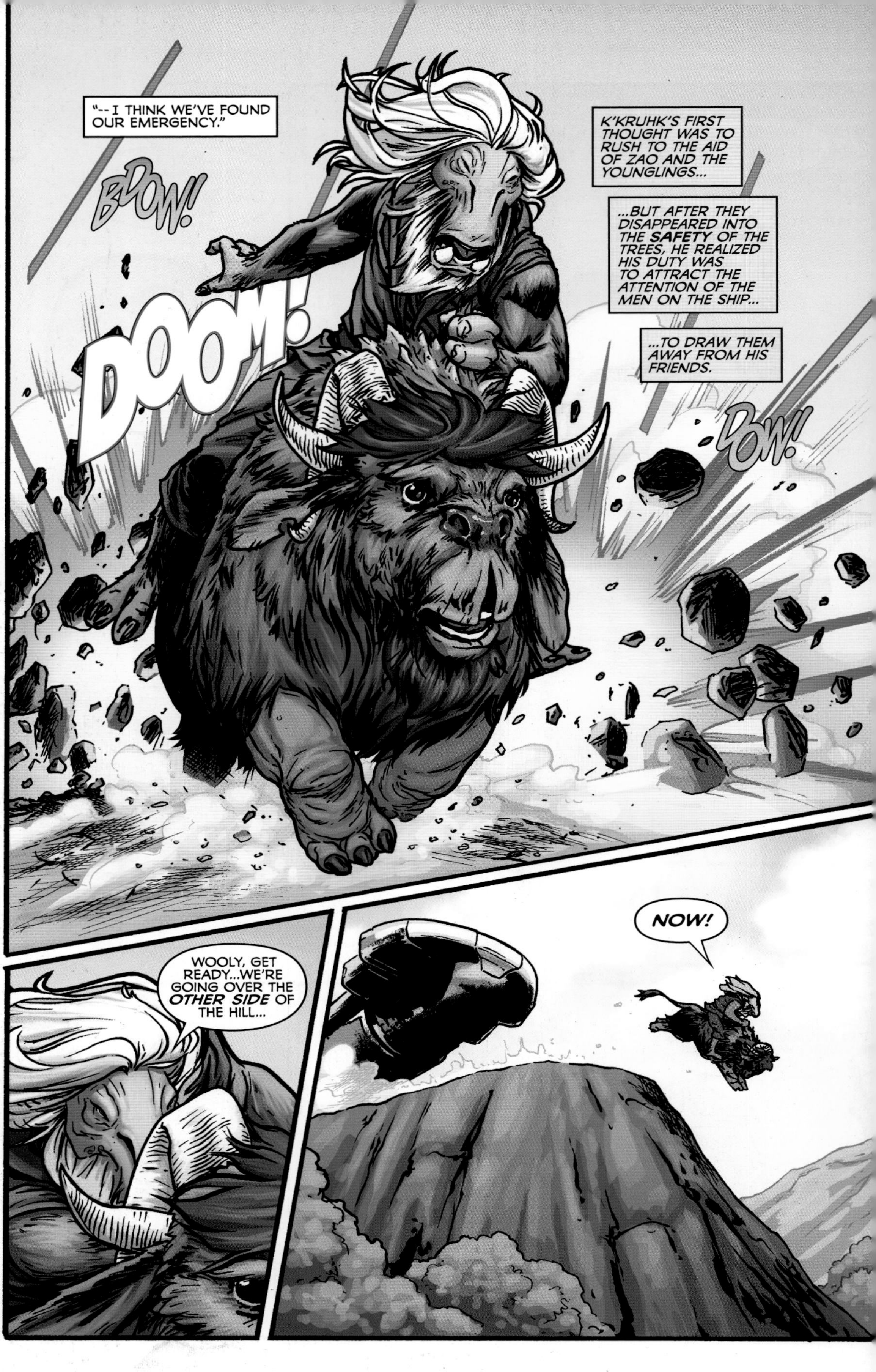
"-- I THINK WE'VE FOUND OUR EMERGENCY."
BDOW!
DOOM!
K'KRUHK'S FIRST THOUGHT WAS TO RUSH TO THE AID OF ZAO AND THE YOUNGLINGS...
...BUT AFTER THEY DISAPPEARED INTO THE SAFETY OF THE TREES, HE REALIZED HIS DUTY WAS TO ATTRACT THE ATTENTION OF THE MEN ON THE SHIP...
...TO DRAW THEM AWAY FROM HIS FRIENDS.
DOW!
WOOLY, GET READY...WE'RE GOING OVER THE OTHER SIDE OF THE HILL...
NOW!

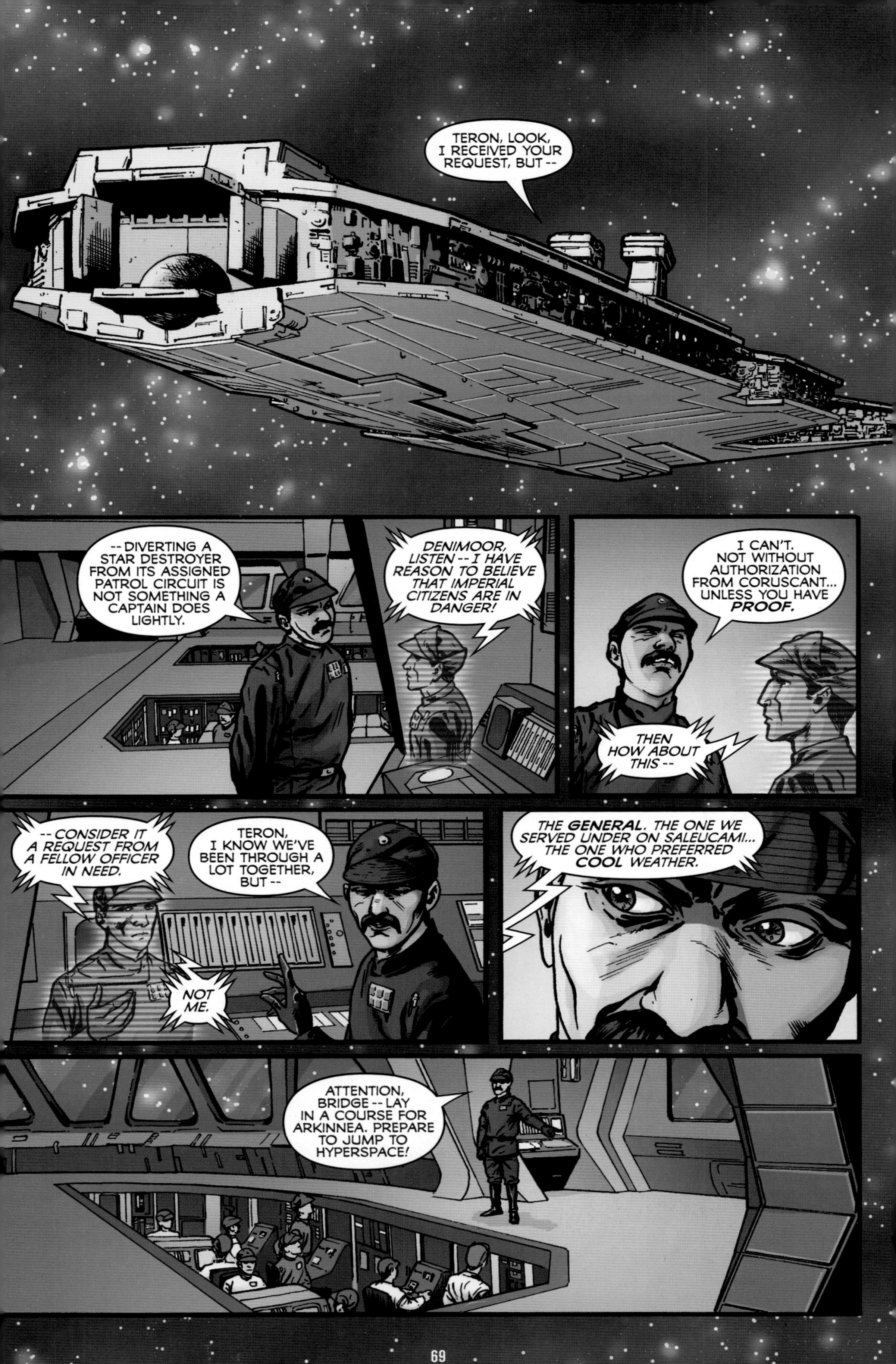
TERON, LOOK, I RECEIVED YOUR REQUEST, BUT --
-- DIVERTING A STAR DESTROYER FROM ITS ASSIGNED PATROL CIRCUIT IS NOT SOMETHING A CAPTAIN DOES LIGHTLY.
DENIMOOR, LISTEN -- I HAVE REASON TO BELIEVE THAT IMPERIAL CITIZENS ARE IN DANGER!
I CAN'T. NOT WITHOUT AUTHORIZATION FROM CORUSCANT... UNLESS YOU HAVE PROOF.
THEN HOW ABOUT THIS --
-- CONSIDER IT A REQUEST FROM A FELLOW OFFICER IN NEED.
TERON, I KNOW WE'VE BEEN THROUGH A LOT TOGETHER, BUT --
NOT ME.
THE GENERAL. THE ONE WE SERVED UNDER ON SALEUCAMI... THE ONE WHO PREFERRED COOL WEATHER.
ATTENTION, BRIDGE -- LAY IN A COURSE FOR ARKINNEA. PREPARE TO JUMP TO HYPERSPACE!

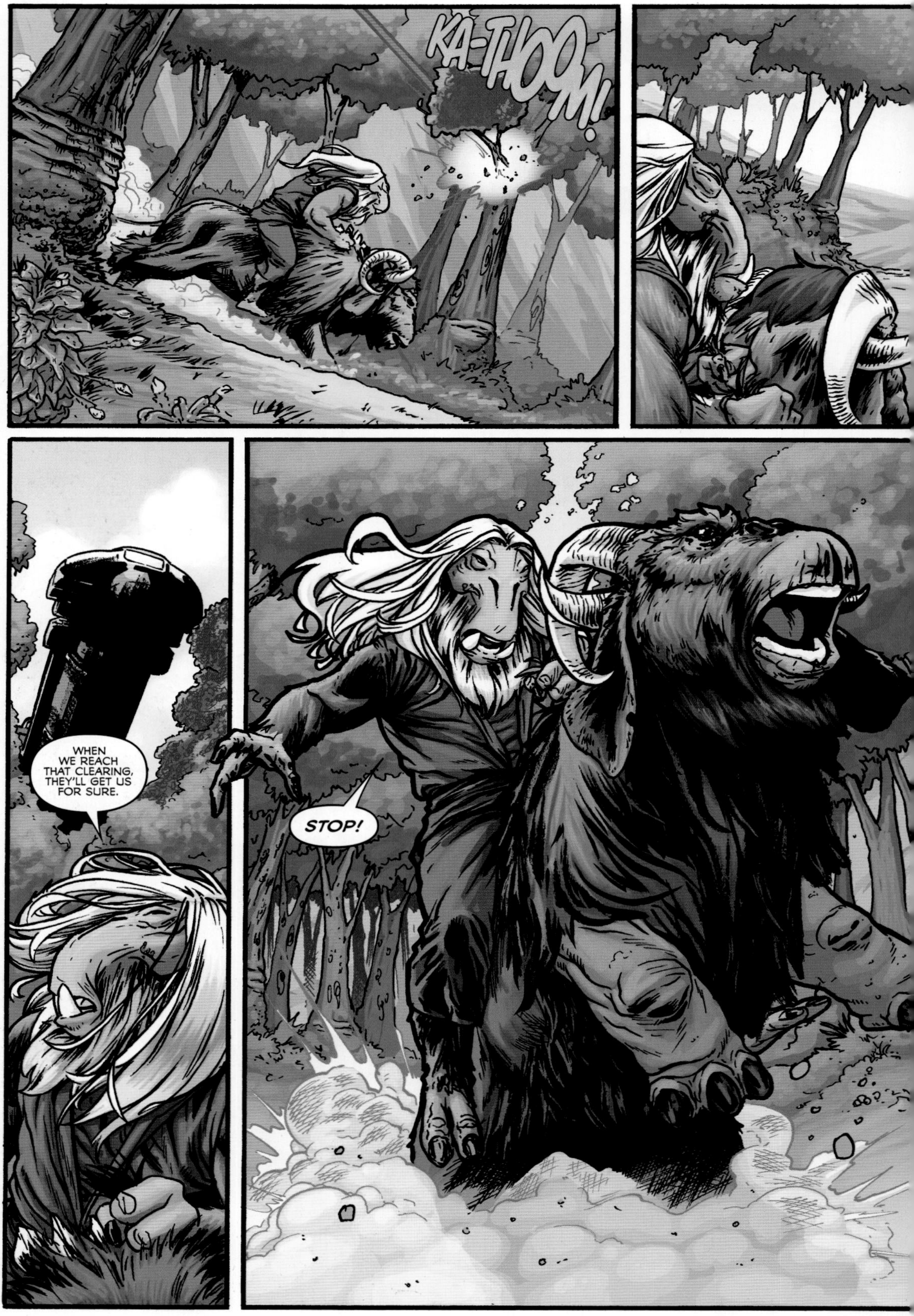
KA-THOOM!
WHEN WE REACH THAT CLEARING, THEY'LL GET US FOR SURE.
STOP!

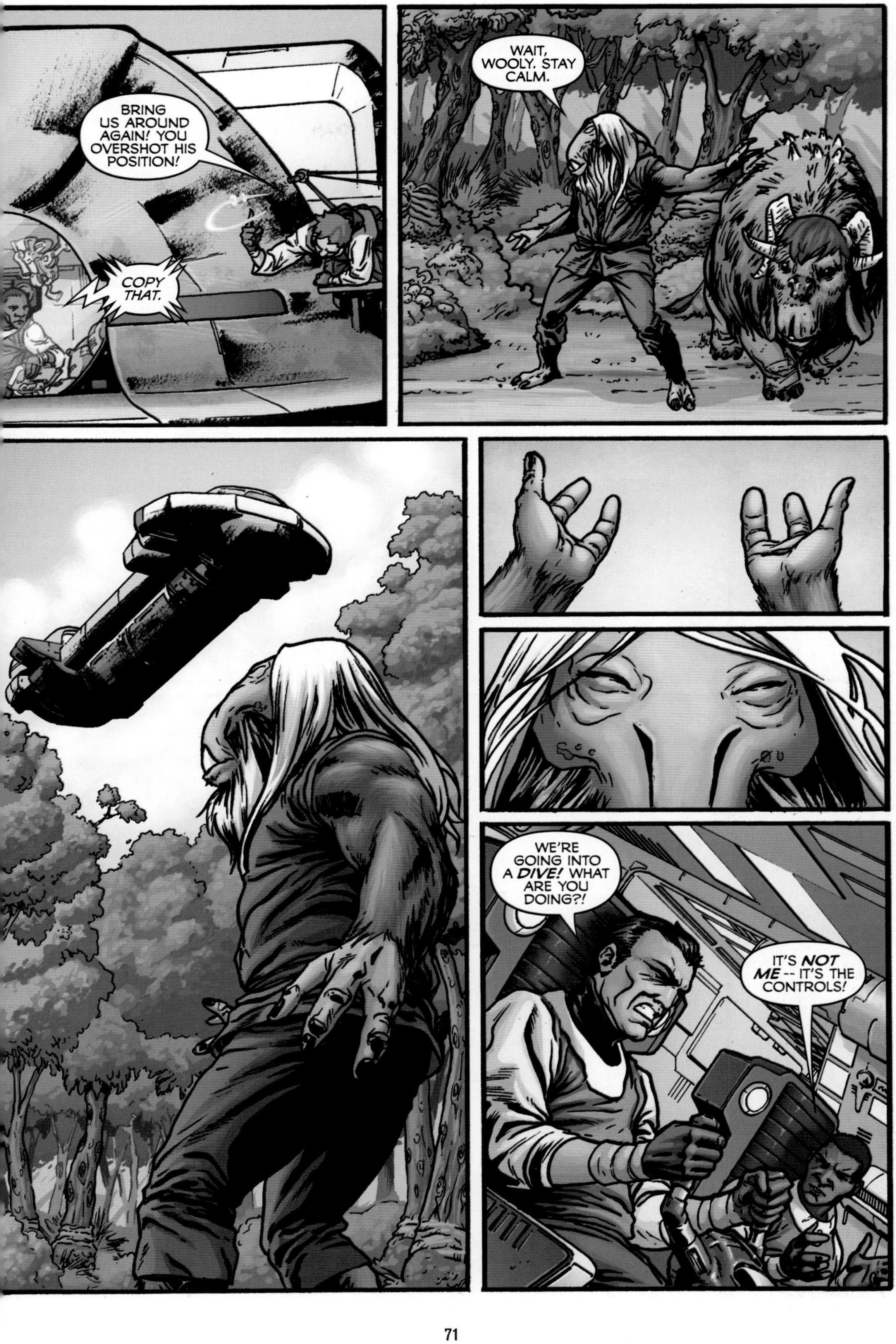
BRING US AROUND AGAIN! YOU OVERSHOT HIS POSITION!
COPY THAT.
WAIT, WOOLY. STAY CALM.
WE'RE GOING INTO A *DIVE!* WHAT ARE YOU DOING?!
IT'S ***NOT ME*** -- IT'S THE CONTROLS!

LIEUTENANT GREGG? I THOUGHT YOU'D WANT TO KNOW -- THE *TENACIOUS* HAS DEVIATED FROM ITS PATROL ROUTE AND IS EN ROUTE TO ARKINNEA.

AFTER LORD VADER HIMSELF TURNED DOWN ARKINNEA'S REQUEST FOR AID? INTERESTING...

THANK YOU, CORPORAL.

SO, THE EMPIRE'S GRIP ISN'T AS *TIGHT* AS EVERYONE THINKS. LOOKS LIKE I'M NOT THE *ONLY ONE* WHO DISOBEYS YOUR *"DARK LORD,"* EH, LIEUTENANT?

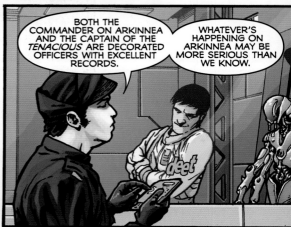

BOTH THE COMMANDER ON ARKINNEA AND THE CAPTAIN OF THE *TENACIOUS* ARE DECORATED OFFICERS WITH EXCELLENT RECORDS.

WHATEVER'S HAPPENING ON ARKINNEA MAY BE MORE SERIOUS THAN WE KNOW.

GET BACK TO YOUR TRAINING, SANG.

AGGH! BLAST YOU!

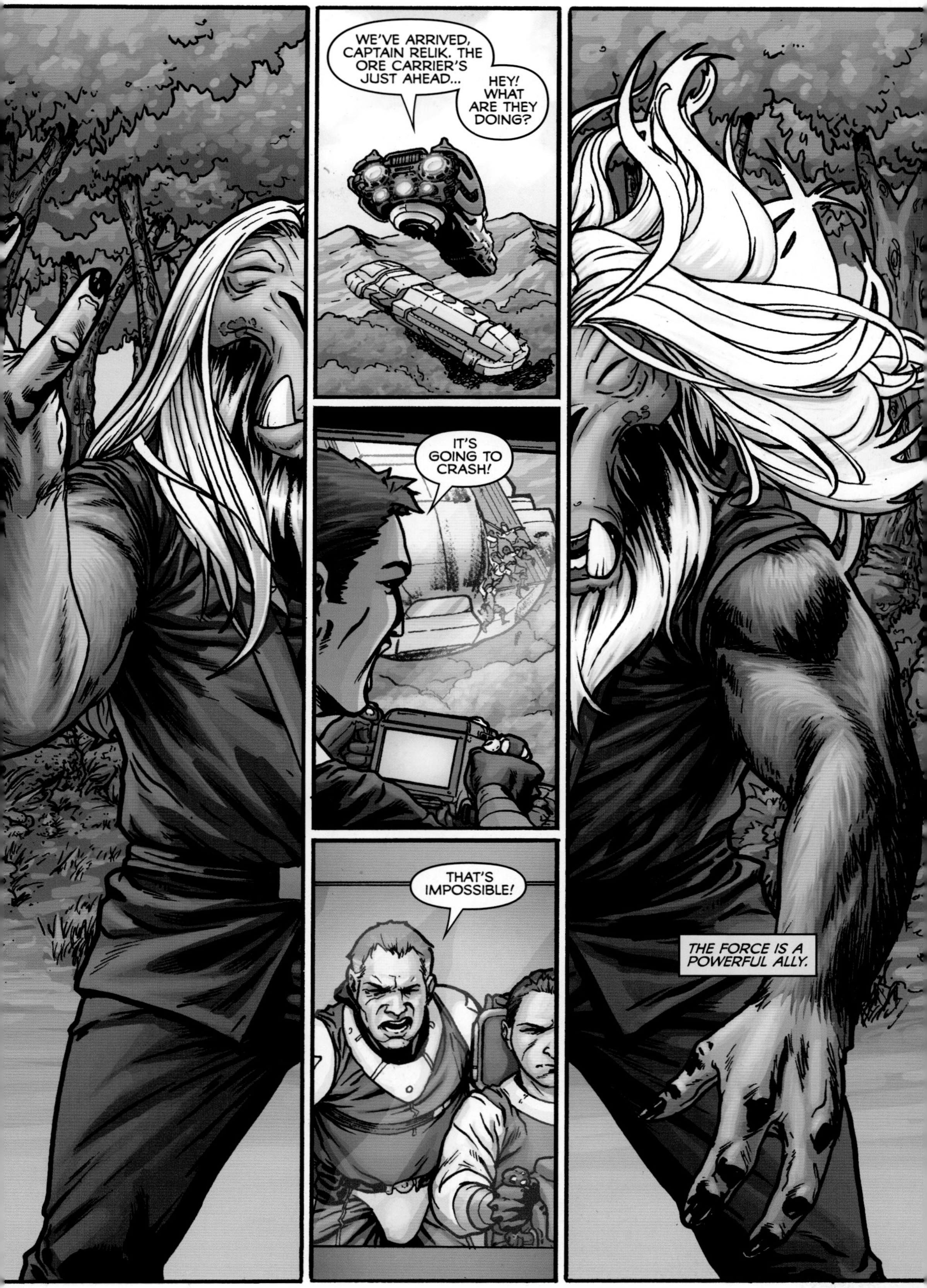
WE'VE ARRIVED, CAPTAIN RELIK. THE ORE CARRIER'S JUST AHEAD...
HEY! WHAT ARE THEY DOING?
IT'S GOING TO CRASH!
THAT'S IMPOSSIBLE!
THE FORCE IS A POWERFUL ALLY.

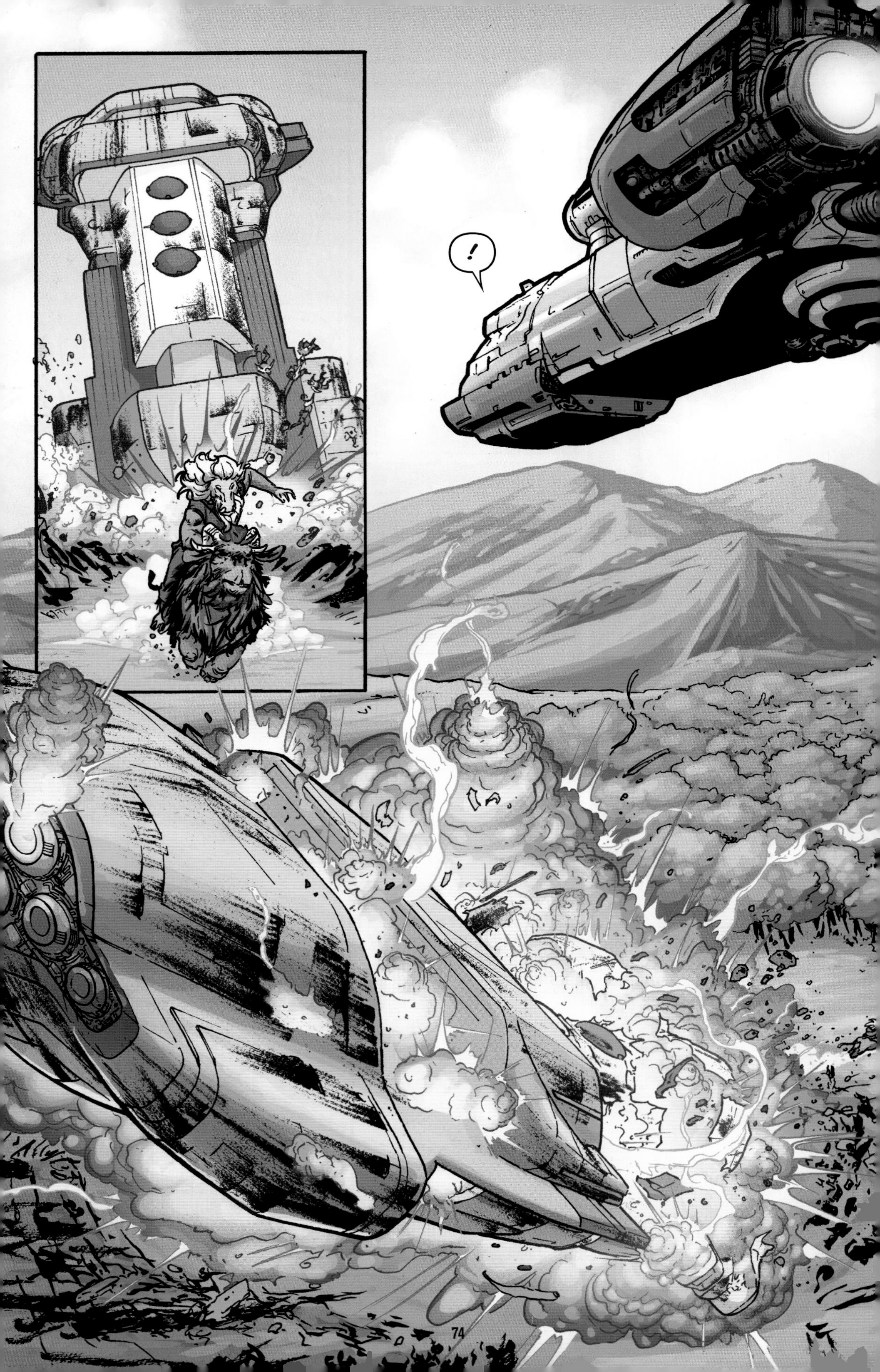
!

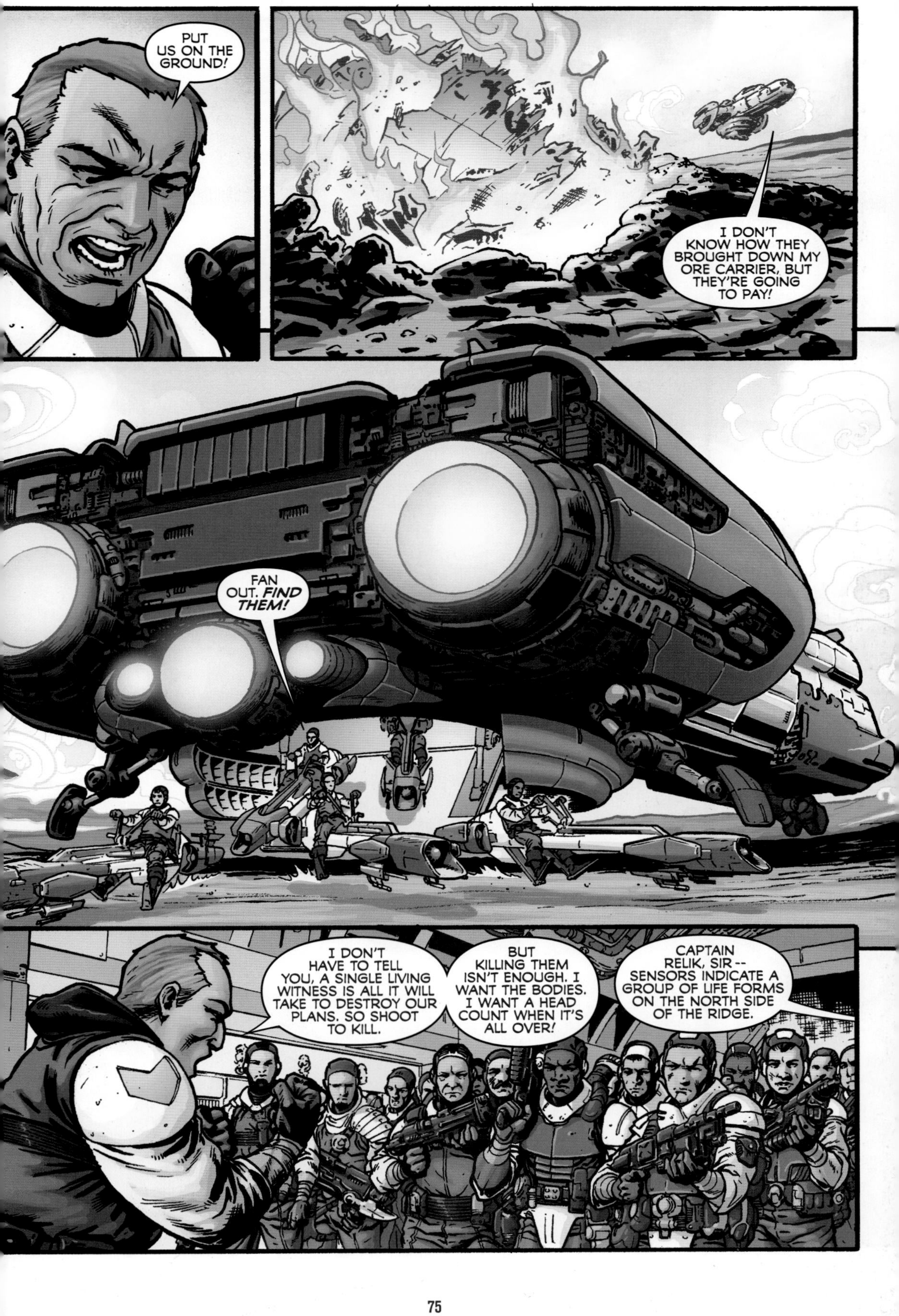
PUT US ON THE GROUND!
I DON'T KNOW HOW THEY BROUGHT DOWN MY ORE CARRIER, BUT THEY'RE GOING TO PAY!
FAN OUT. FIND THEM!
I DON'T HAVE TO TELL YOU, A SINGLE LIVING WITNESS IS ALL IT WILL TAKE TO DESTROY OUR PLANS. SO SHOOT TO KILL.
BUT KILLING THEM ISN'T ENOUGH. I WANT THE BODIES. I WANT A HEAD COUNT WHEN IT'S ALL OVER!
CAPTAIN RELIK, SIR-- SENSORS INDICATE A GROUP OF LIFE FORMS ON THE NORTH SIDE OF THE RIDGE.

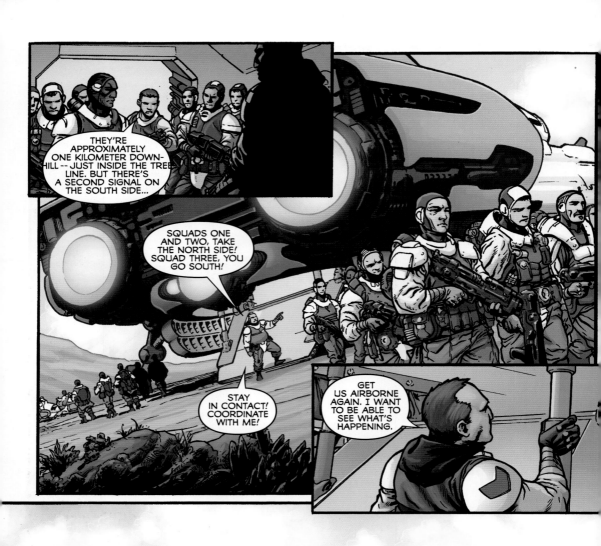

THEY'RE APPROXIMATELY ONE KILOMETER DOWNHILL -- JUST INSIDE THE TREE LINE. BUT THERE'S A SECOND SIGNAL ON THE SOUTH SIDE...

SQUADS ONE AND TWO, TAKE THE NORTH SIDE! SQUAD THREE, YOU GO SOUTH!

STAY IN CONTACT! COORDINATE WITH ME!

GET US AIRBORNE AGAIN. I WANT TO BE ABLE TO SEE WHAT'S HAPPENING.

THEY'RE SOMEWHERE IN THAT FOREST, SIR.

MASTER ZAO STRUGGLES TO CLEAR HIS HEAD. HE RECALLS THE SECONDS LEADING UP TO THE CRASH, BUT NOT THE IMPACT. HIS LAST MEMORY WAS...

...FEELING PIRU SWEEP THEM ALL UP IN THE FORCE--

-- AND HURL THEM CLEAR OF THE WAGON.

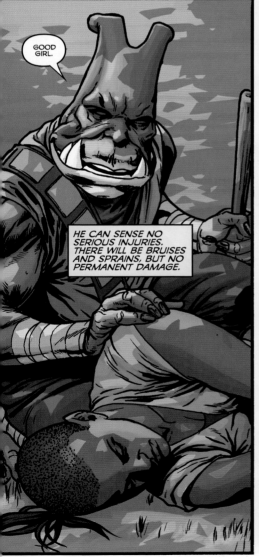

GOOD GIRL.

HE CAN SENSE NO SERIOUS INJURIES. THERE WILL BE BRUISES AND SPRAINS, BUT NO PERMANENT DAMAGE.

EH?

SIDIRRI?

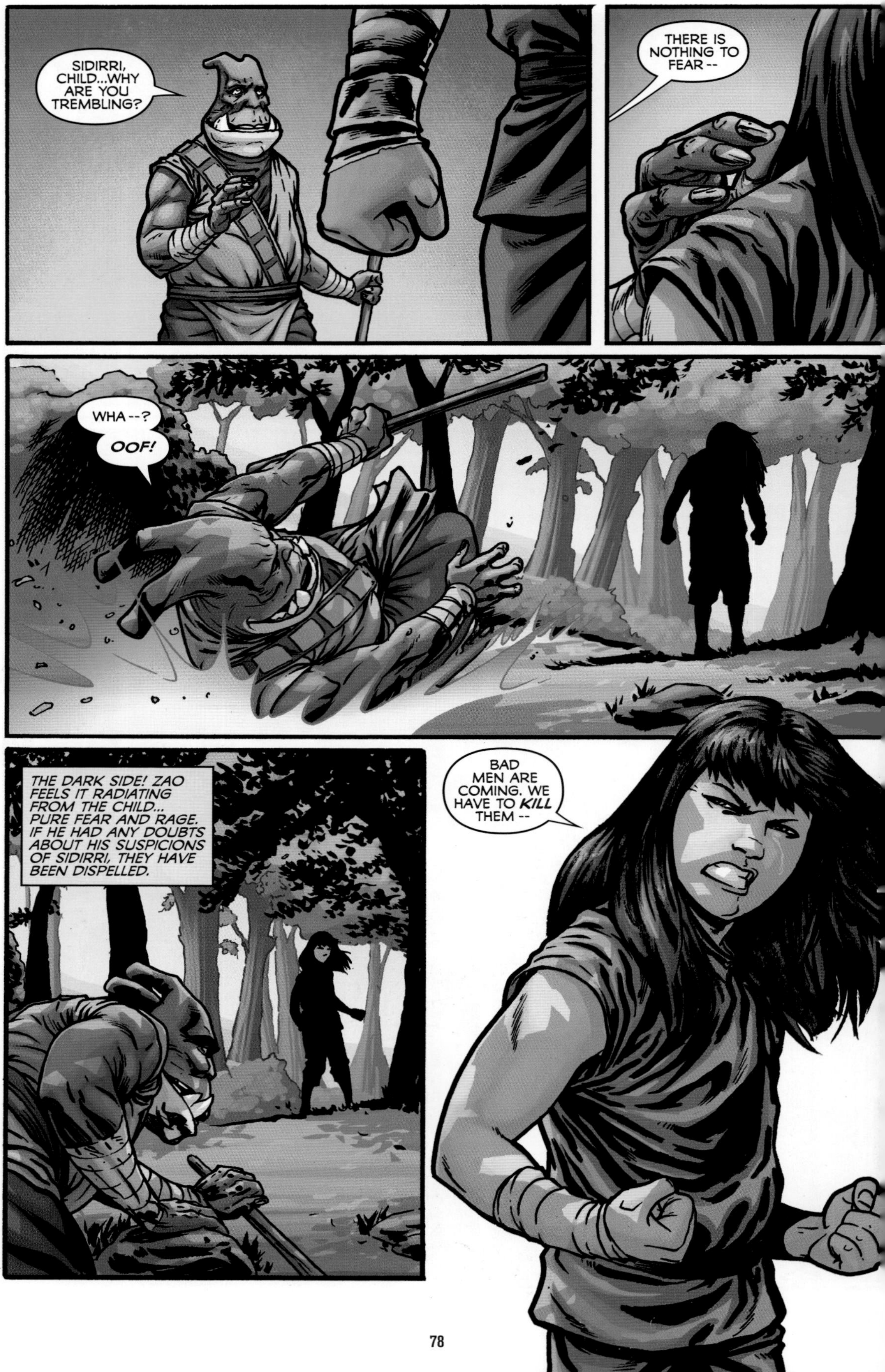
SIDIRRI, CHILD...WHY ARE YOU TREMBLING?
THERE IS NOTHING TO FEAR --
WHA --?
OOF!
THE DARK SIDE! ZAO FEELS IT RADIATING FROM THE CHILD... PURE FEAR AND RAGE. IF HE HAD ANY DOUBTS ABOUT HIS SUSPICIONS OF SIDIRRI, THEY HAVE BEEN DISPELLED.
BAD MEN ARE COMING. WE HAVE TO KILL THEM --

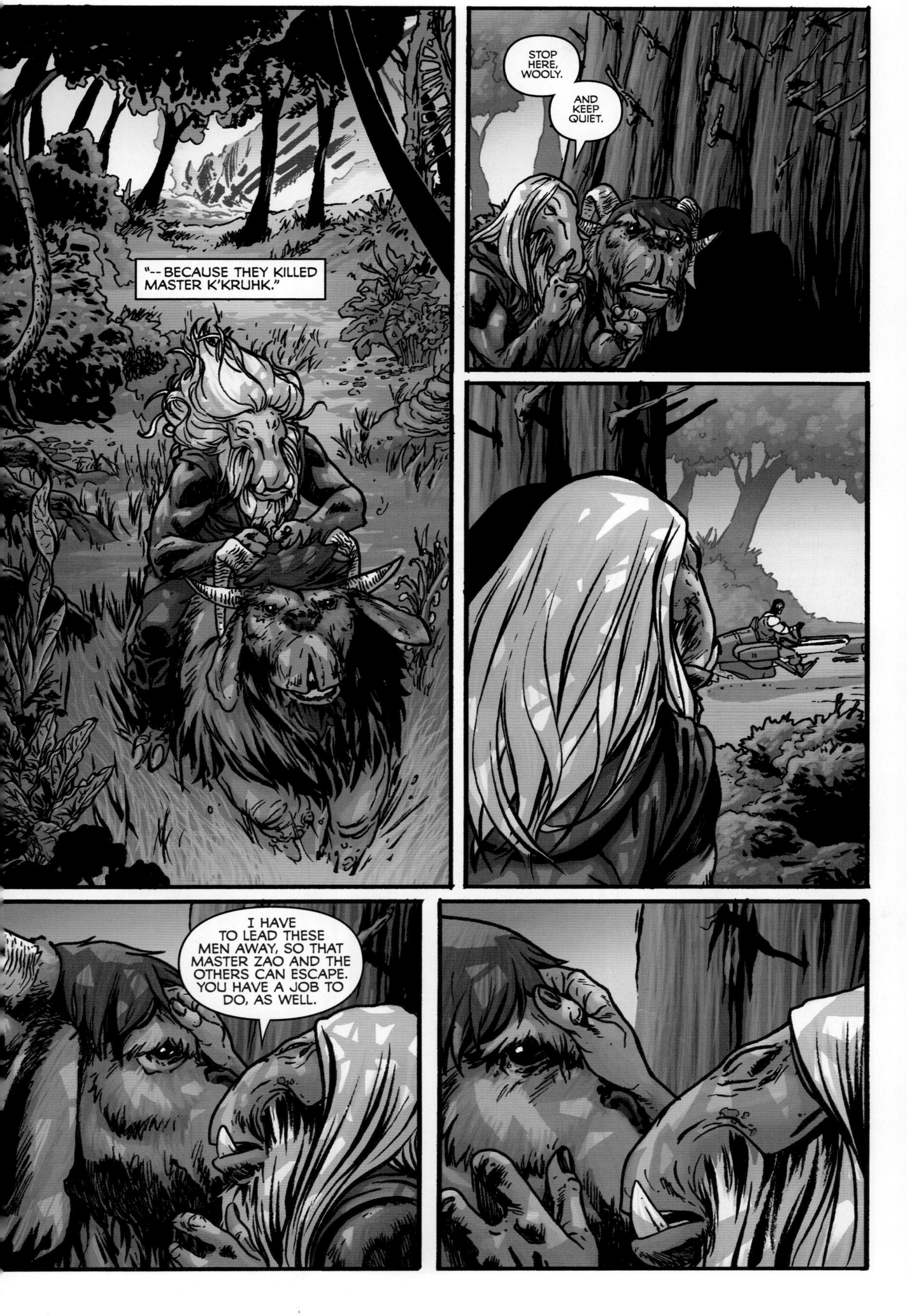
"--BECAUSE THEY KILLED MASTER K'KRUHK."
STOP HERE, WOOLY.
AND KEEP QUIET.
I HAVE TO LEAD THESE MEN AWAY, SO THAT MASTER ZAO AND THE OTHERS CAN ESCAPE. YOU HAVE A JOB TO DO, AS WELL.

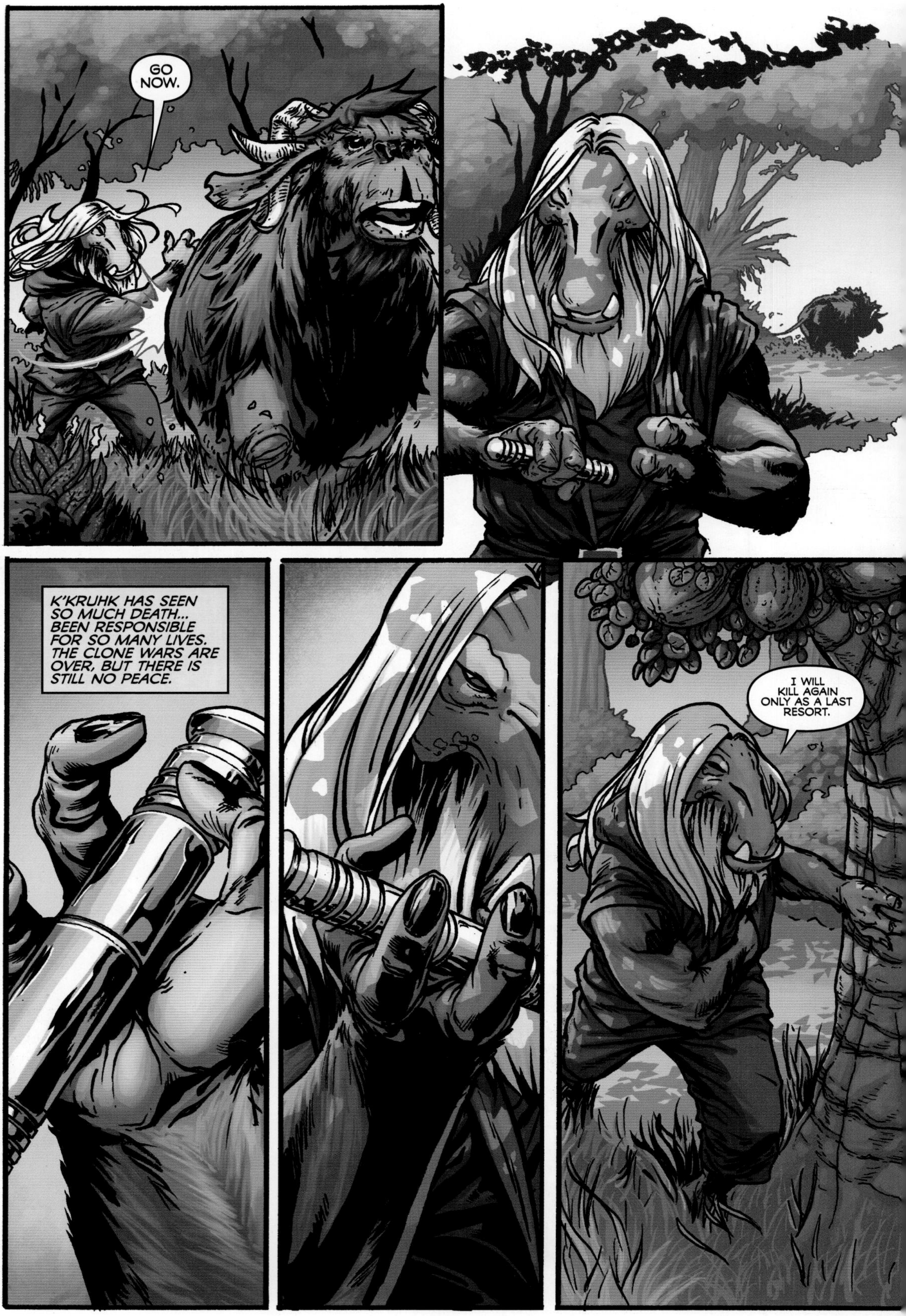
GO NOW.
K'KRUHK HAS SEEN SO MUCH DEATH... BEEN RESPONSIBLE FOR SO MANY LIVES. THE CLONE WARS ARE OVER, BUT THERE IS STILL NO PEACE.
I WILL KILL AGAIN ONLY AS A LAST RESORT.

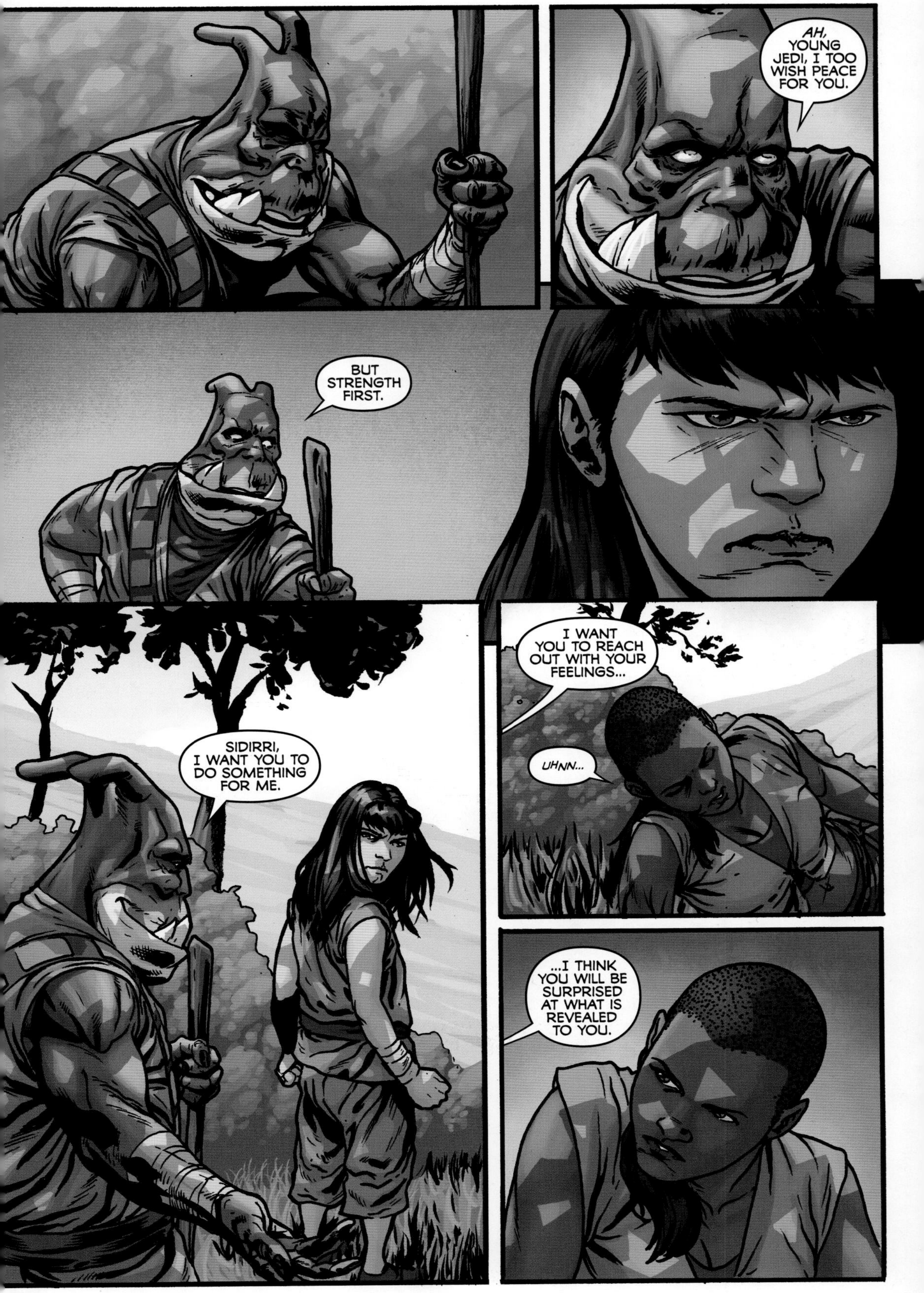

AH, YOUNG JEDI, I TOO WISH PEACE FOR YOU.
BUT STRENGTH FIRST.
SIDIRRI, I WANT YOU TO DO SOMETHING FOR ME.
I WANT YOU TO REACH OUT WITH YOUR FEELINGS...
UHNN...
...I THINK YOU WILL BE SURPRISED AT WHAT IS REVEALED TO YOU.

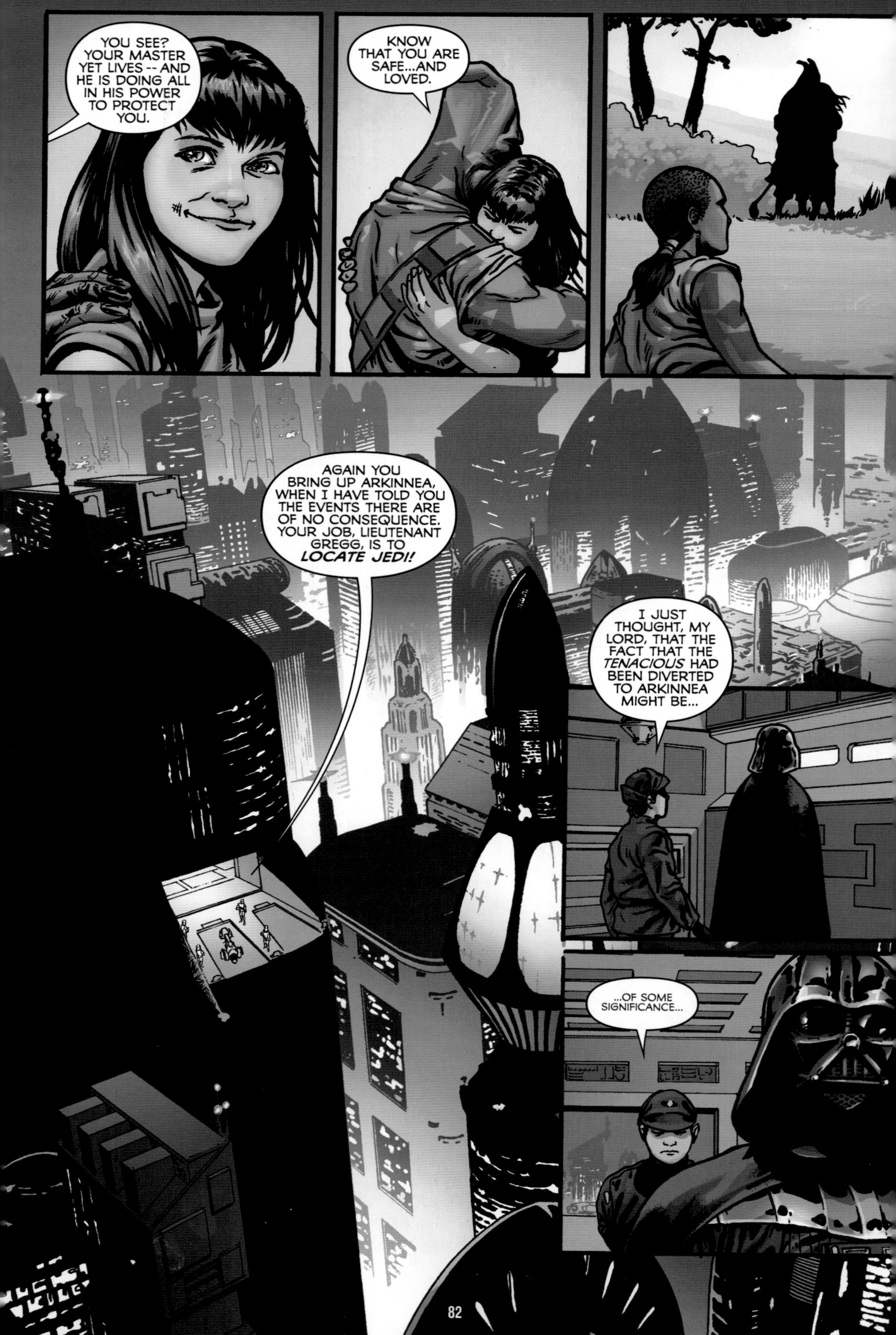
YOU SEE? YOUR MASTER YET LIVES -- AND HE IS DOING ALL IN HIS POWER TO PROTECT YOU.
KNOW THAT YOU ARE SAFE...AND LOVED.
AGAIN YOU BRING UP ARKINNEA, WHEN I HAVE TOLD YOU THE EVENTS THERE ARE OF NO CONSEQUENCE. YOUR JOB, LIEUTENANT GREGG, IS TO ***LOCATE JEDI!***
I JUST THOUGHT, MY LORD, THAT THE FACT THAT THE *TENACIOUS* HAD BEEN DIVERTED TO ARKINNEA MIGHT BE...
...OF SOME SIGNIFICANCE...

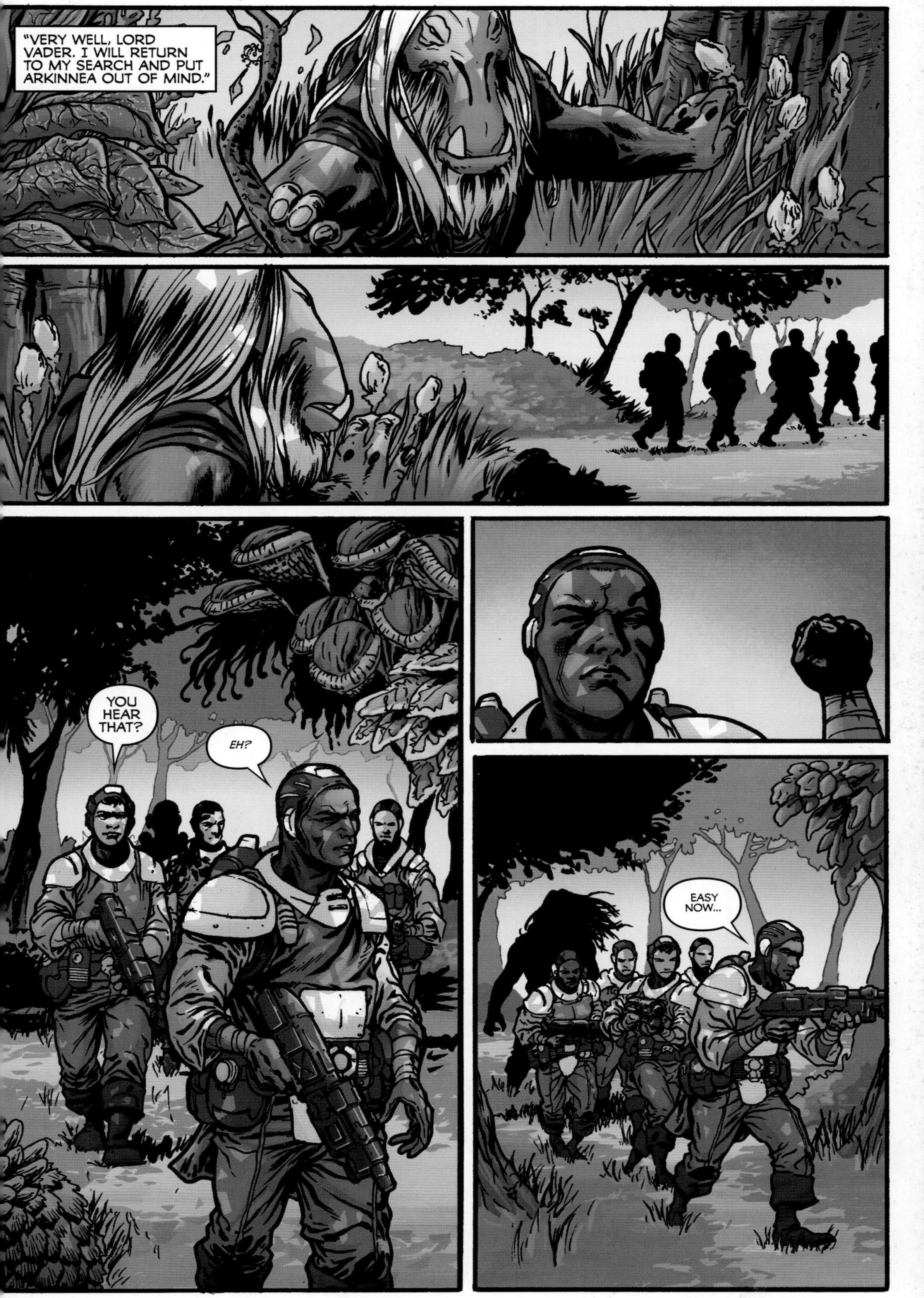
"VERY WELL, LORD VADER. I WILL RETURN TO MY SEARCH AND PUT ARKINNEA OUT OF MIND."
YOU HEAR THAT?
EH?
EASY NOW...

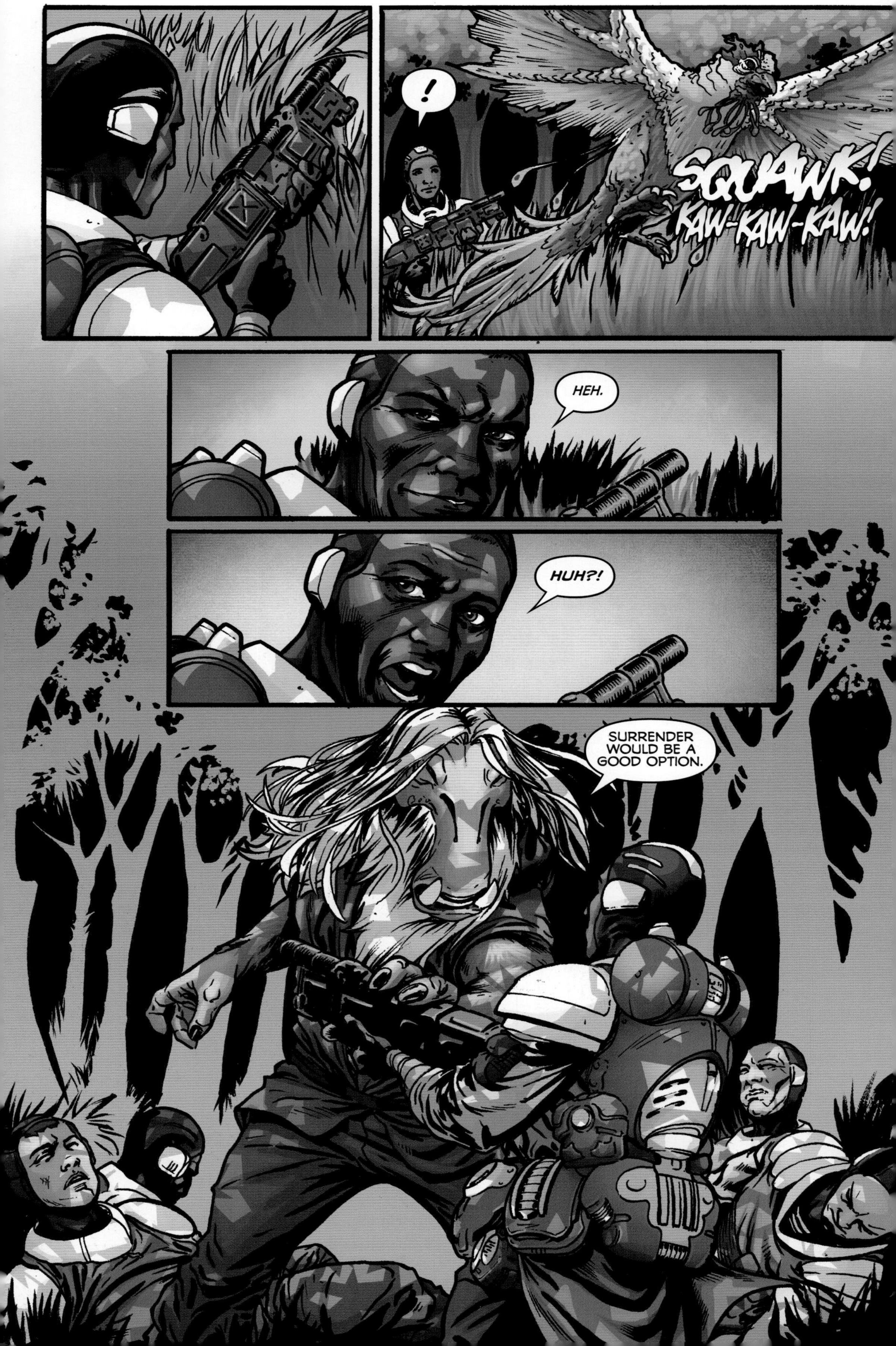
!
SQUAWK!
KAW-KAW-KAW!
HEH.
HUH?!
SURRENDER WOULD BE A GOOD OPTION.

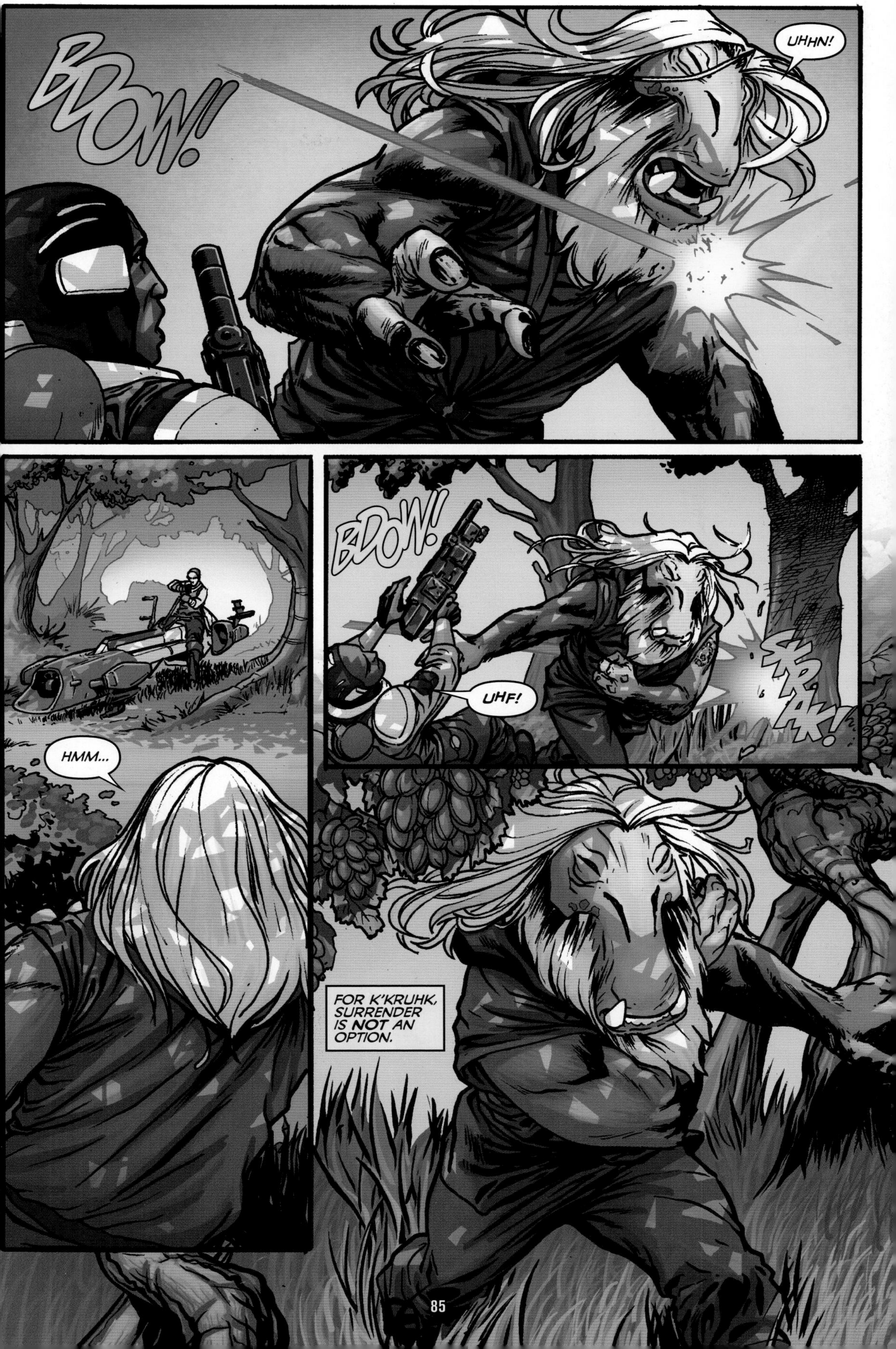
BDOW!!
UHHN!
HMM...
BDOW!!
UHF!
SKRAK!
FOR K'KRUHK, SURRENDER IS **NOT** AN OPTION.

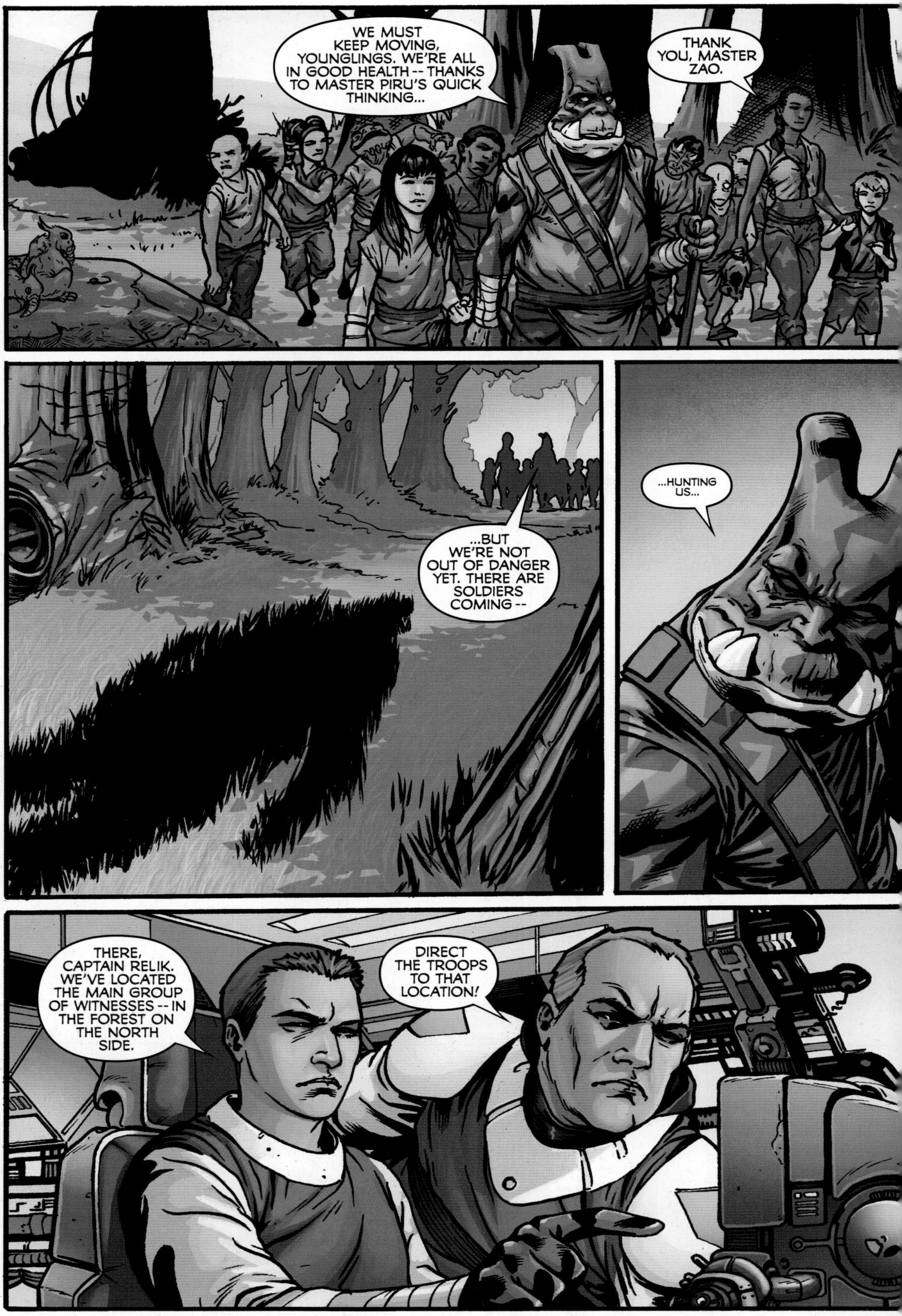

WE MUST KEEP MOVING, YOUNGLINGS. WE'RE ALL IN GOOD HEALTH -- THANKS TO MASTER PIRU'S QUICK THINKING...
THANK YOU, MASTER ZAO.
...BUT WE'RE NOT OUT OF DANGER YET. THERE ARE SOLDIERS COMING --
...HUNTING US...
THERE, CAPTAIN RELIK. WE'VE LOCATED THE MAIN GROUP OF WITNESSES -- IN THE FOREST ON THE NORTH SIDE.
DIRECT THE TROOPS TO THAT LOCATION!

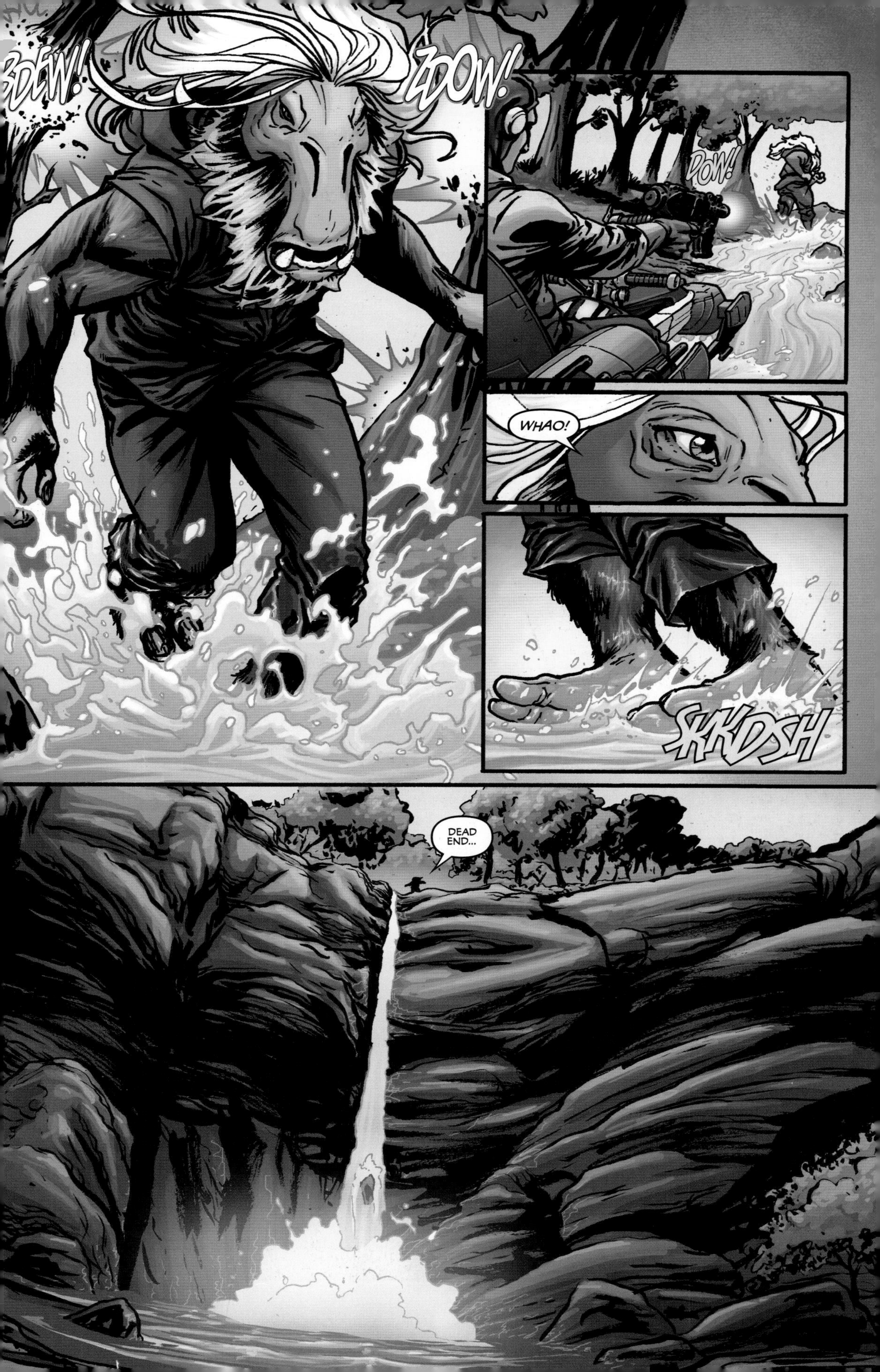
BDEW!
ZDOW!
DOW!
WHAO!
SKKDSH
DEAD END...

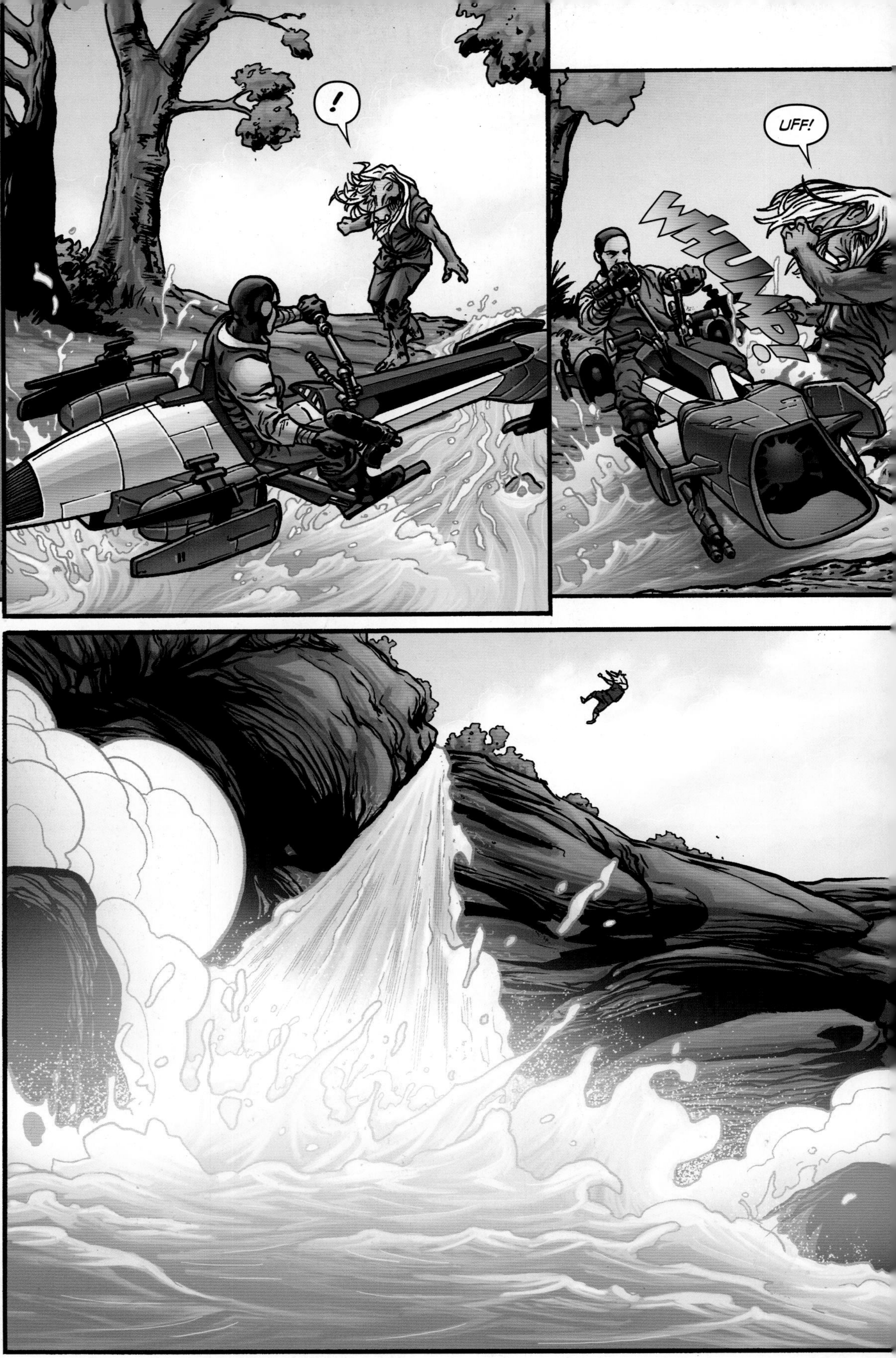
!
UFF!
WHUMP!

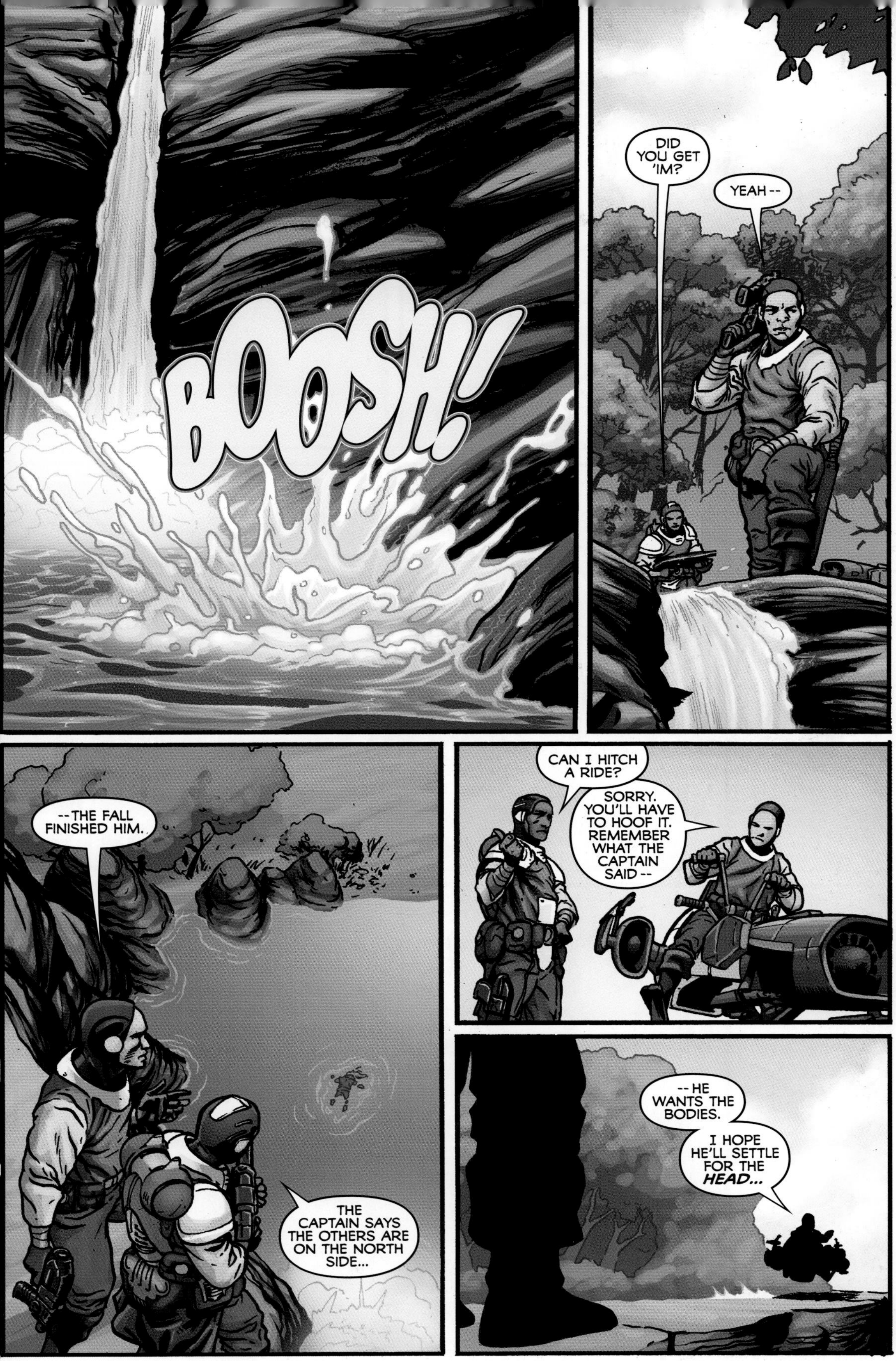
BOOSH!
DID YOU GET 'IM?
YEAH --
--THE FALL FINISHED HIM.
THE CAPTAIN SAYS THE OTHERS ARE ON THE NORTH SIDE...
CAN I HITCH A RIDE?
SORRY. YOU'LL HAVE TO HOOF IT. REMEMBER WHAT THE CAPTAIN SAID --
-- HE WANTS THE BODIES.
I HOPE HE'LL SETTLE FOR THE *HEAD...*

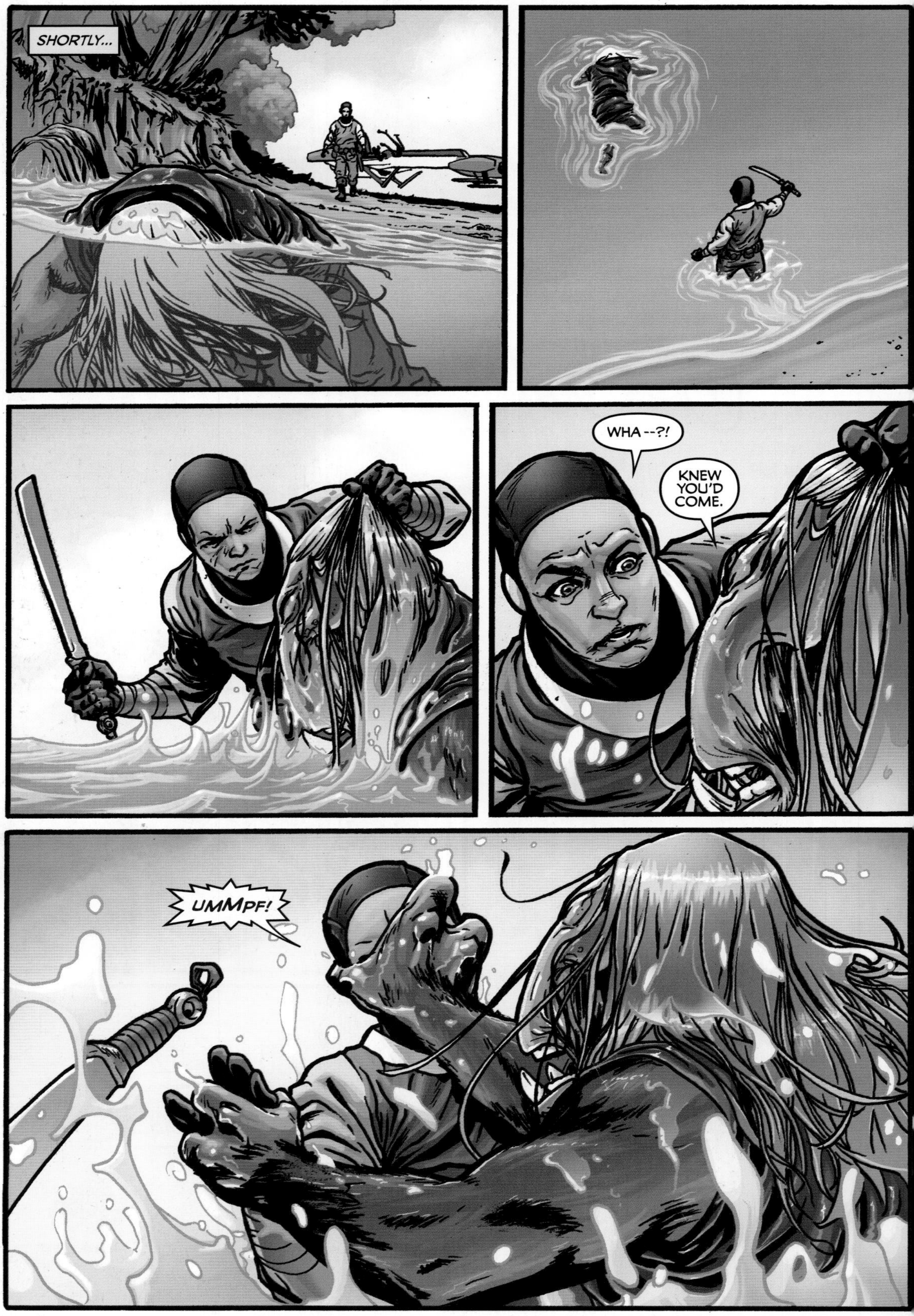
SHORTLY...
WHA--?!
KNEW YOU'D COME.
UMMPF!

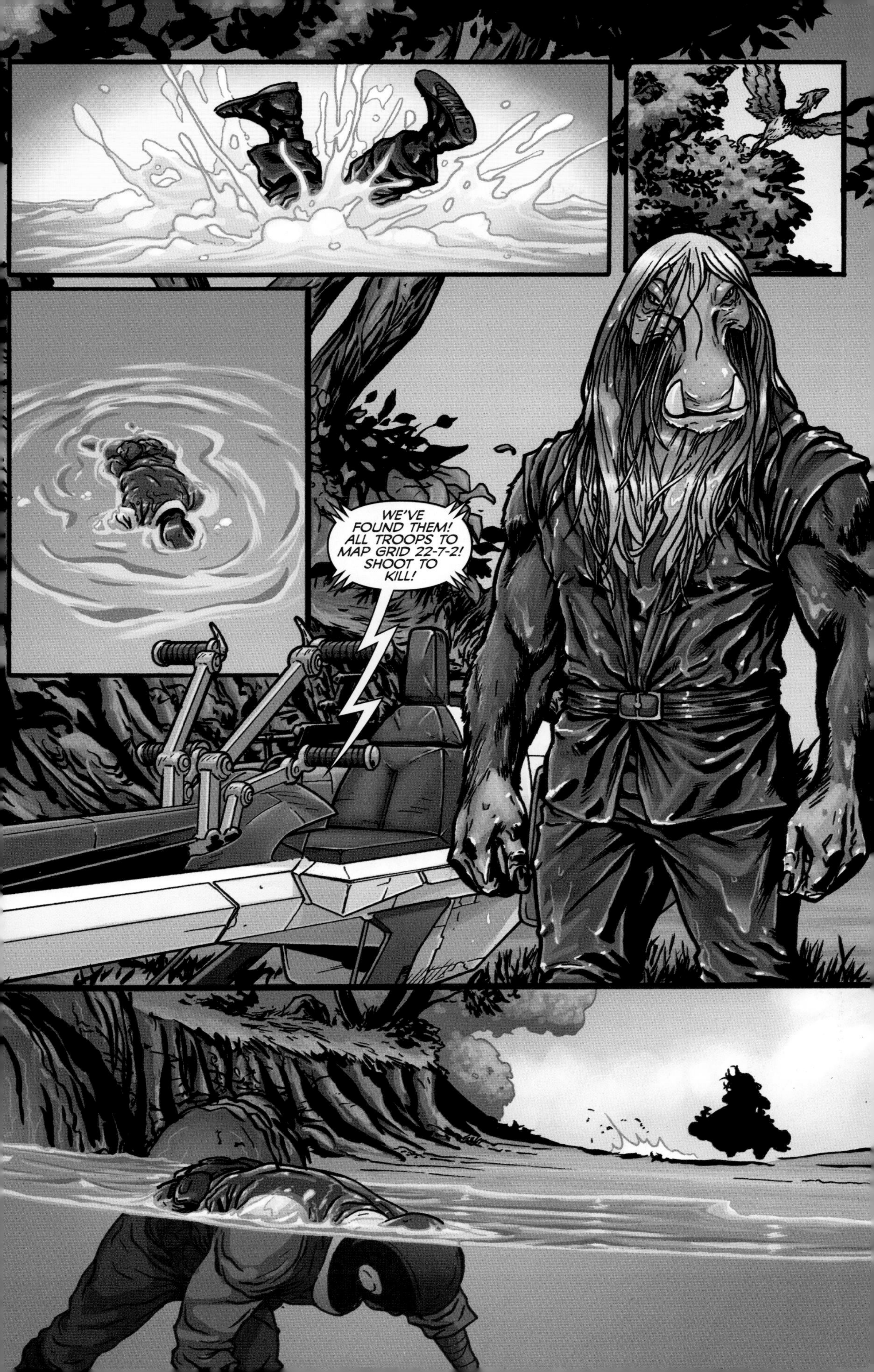
WE'VE FOUND THEM! ALL TROOPS TO MAP GRID 22-7-2! SHOOT TO KILL!

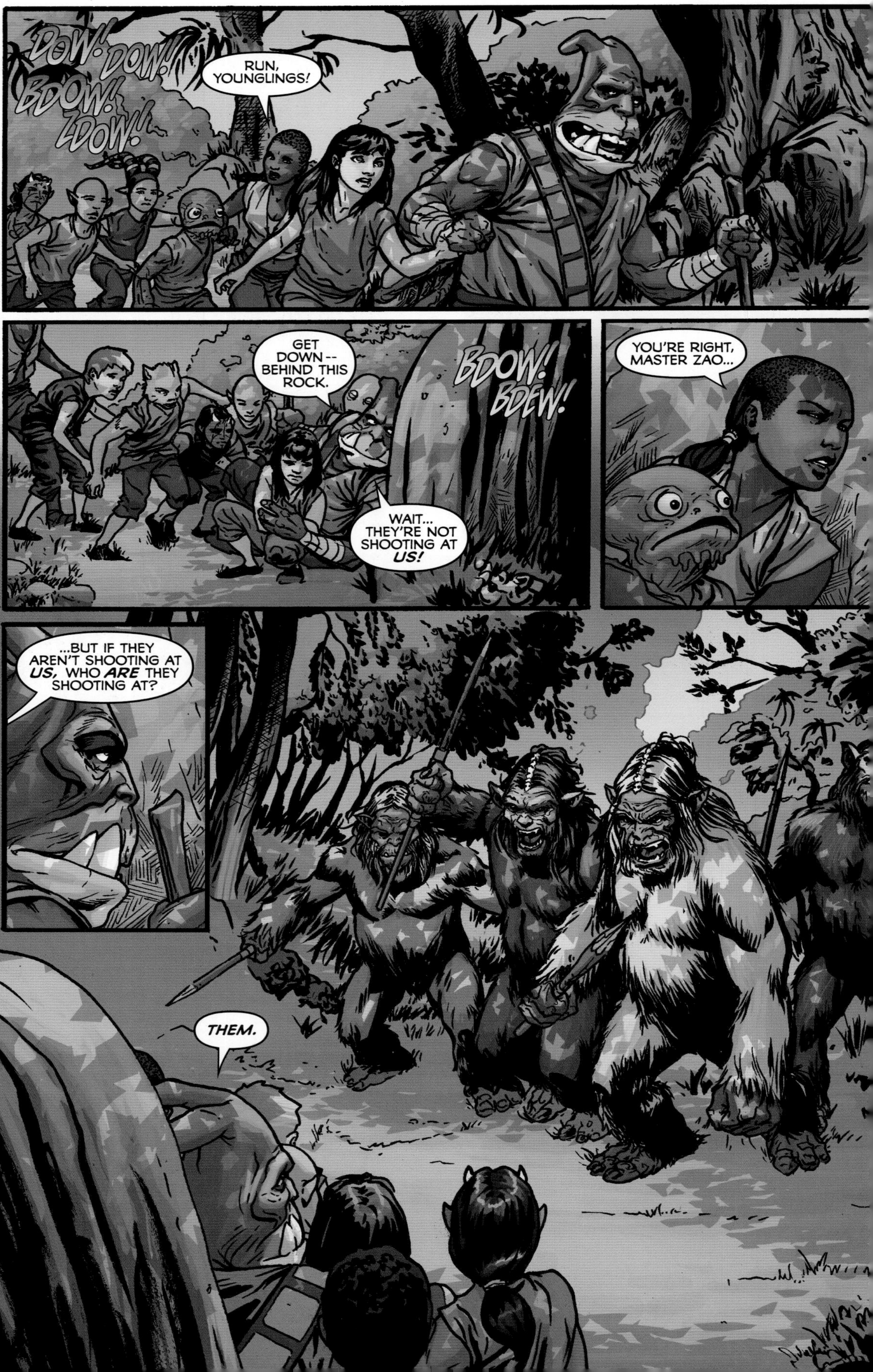
DOW! DOW!
BDOW!
ZDOW!
RUN, YOUNGLINGS!
GET DOWN -- BEHIND THIS ROCK.
BDOW! BDEW!
WAIT... THEY'RE NOT SHOOTING AT US!
YOU'RE RIGHT, MASTER ZAO...
...BUT IF THEY AREN'T SHOOTING AT US, WHO ARE THEY SHOOTING AT?
THEM.

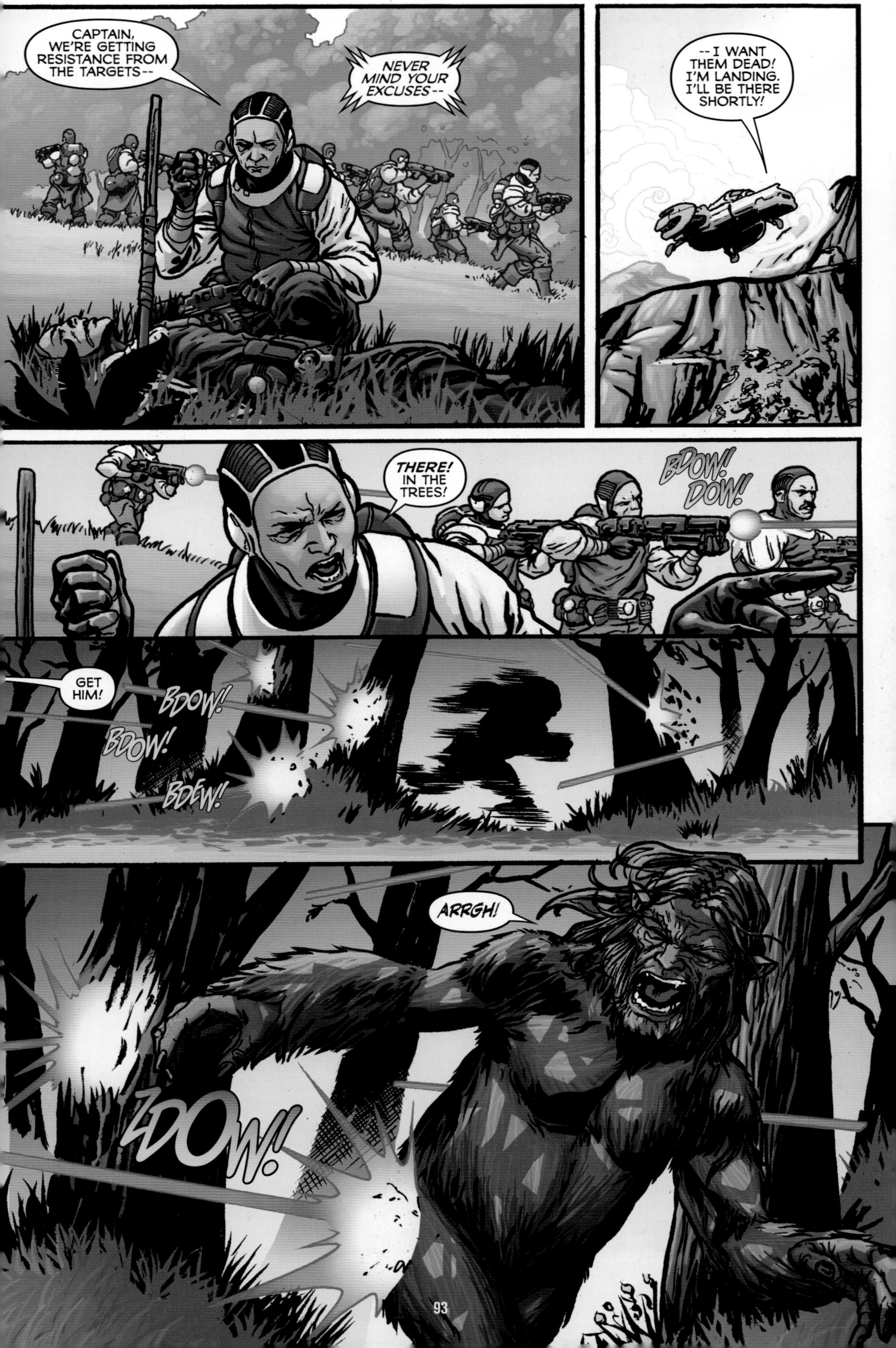
CAPTAIN, WE'RE GETTING RESISTANCE FROM THE TARGETS--
NEVER MIND YOUR EXCUSES--
--I WANT THEM DEAD! I'M LANDING. I'LL BE THERE SHORTLY!
THERE! IN THE TREES!
BDOW! DOW!
GET HIM!
BDOW!
BDOW!
BDEW!
ARRGH!
ZDOW!

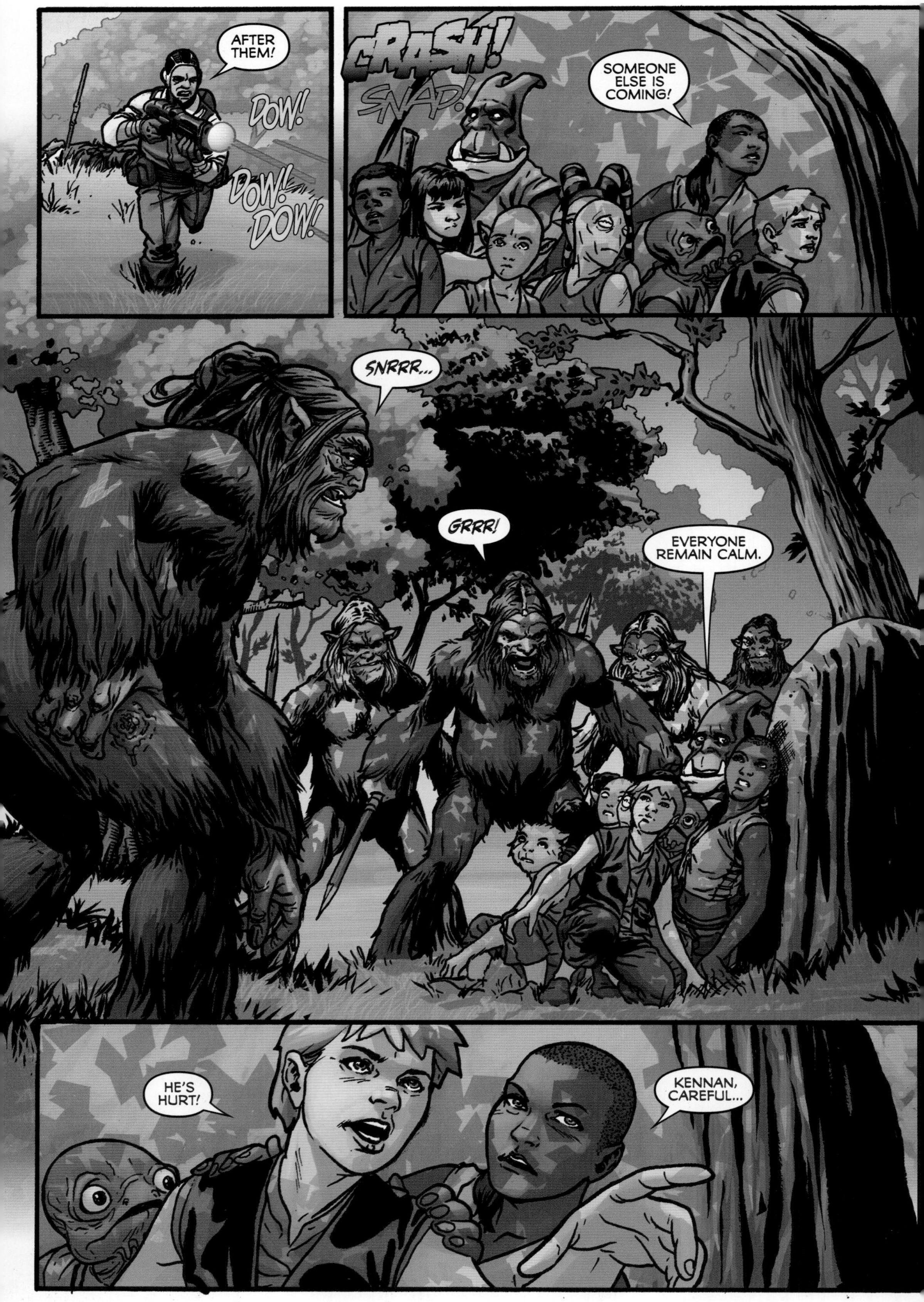
AFTER THEM!
DOW!
DOW! DOW!
CRASH!
SNAP!
SOMEONE ELSE IS COMING!
SNRRR...
GRRR!
EVERYONE REMAIN CALM.
HE'S HURT!
KENNAN, CAREFUL...

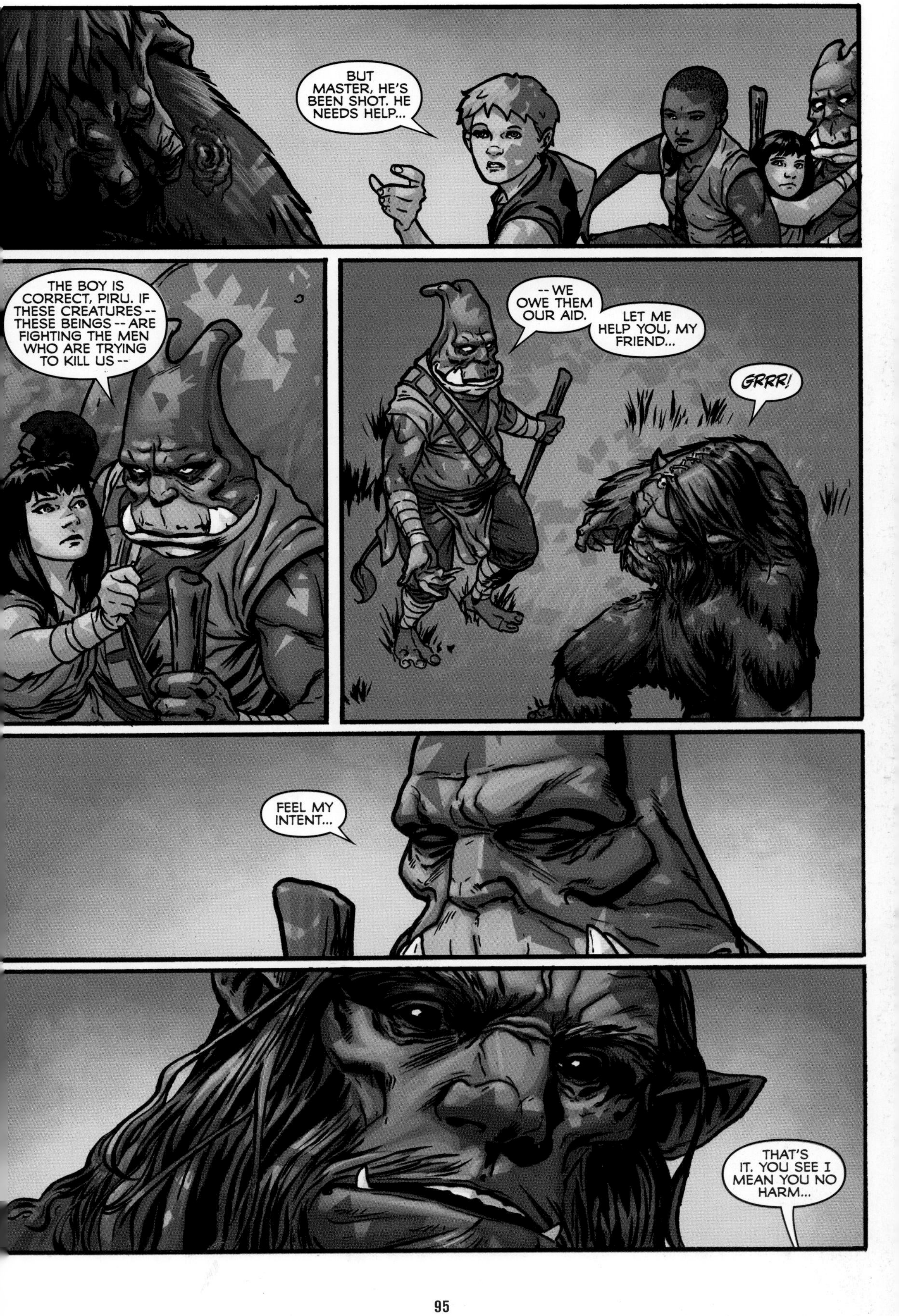
BUT MASTER, HE'S BEEN SHOT. HE NEEDS HELP...
THE BOY IS CORRECT, PIRU. IF THESE CREATURES -- THESE BEINGS -- ARE FIGHTING THE MEN WHO ARE TRYING TO KILL US --
-- WE OWE THEM OUR AID.
LET ME HELP YOU, MY FRIEND...
GRRR!
FEEL MY INTENT...
THAT'S IT. YOU SEE I MEAN YOU NO HARM...

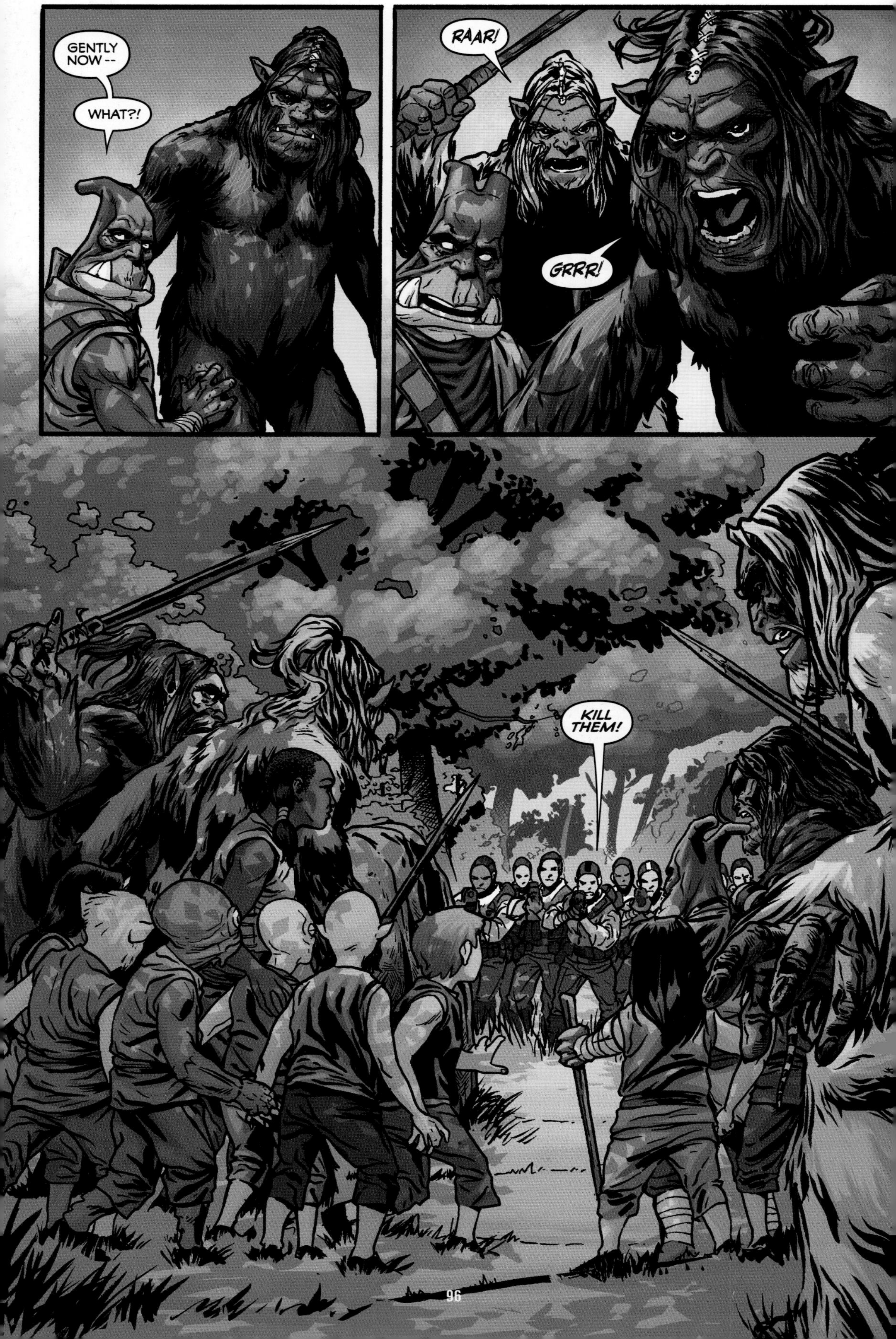
GENTLY NOW --
WHAT?!
RAAR!
GRRR!
KILL THEM!

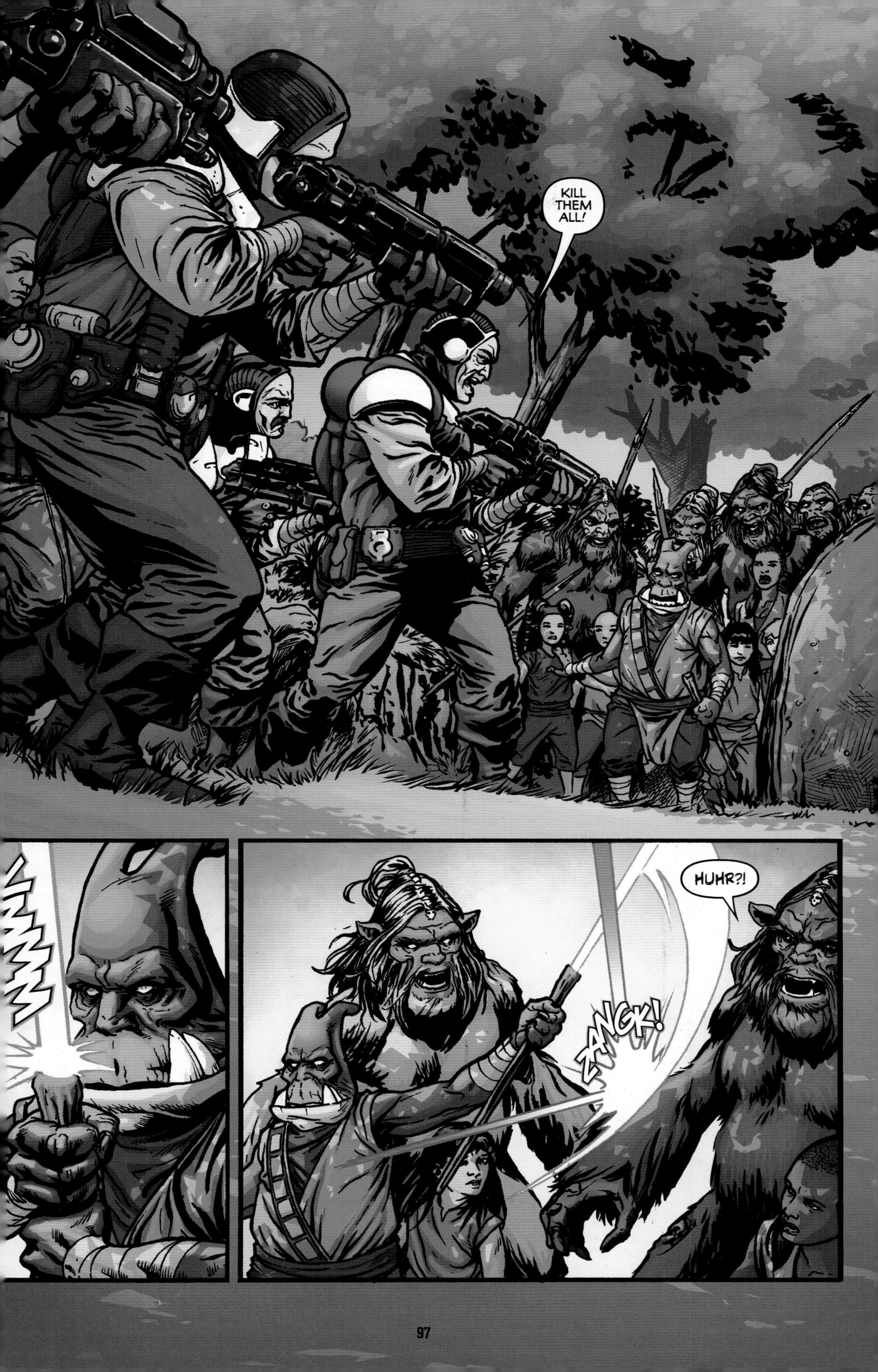
KILL THEM ALL!
HUHR?!
ZANGK!

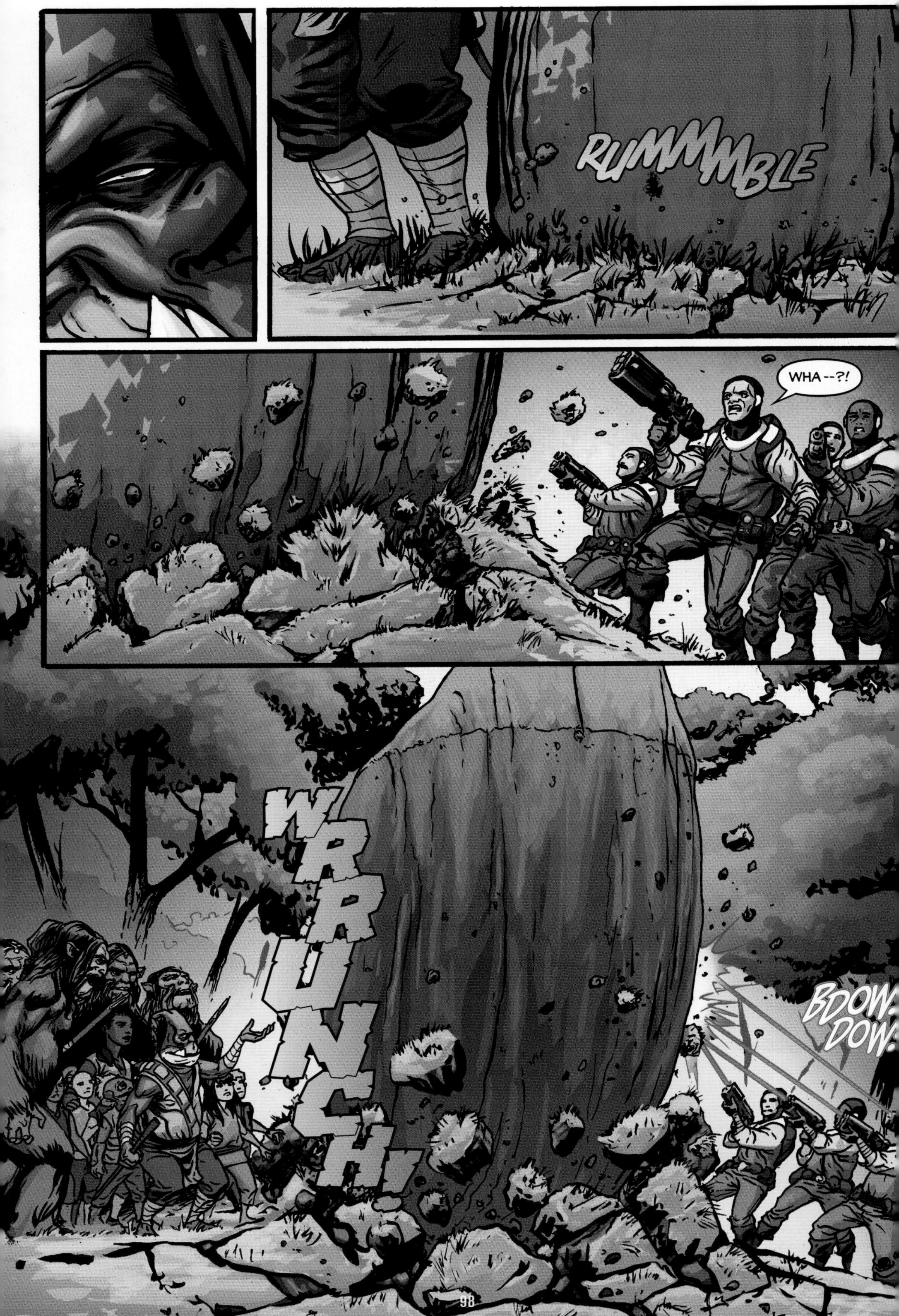
RUMMMMBLE
WHA--?!
WRRUNCH!
BDOW! DOW!

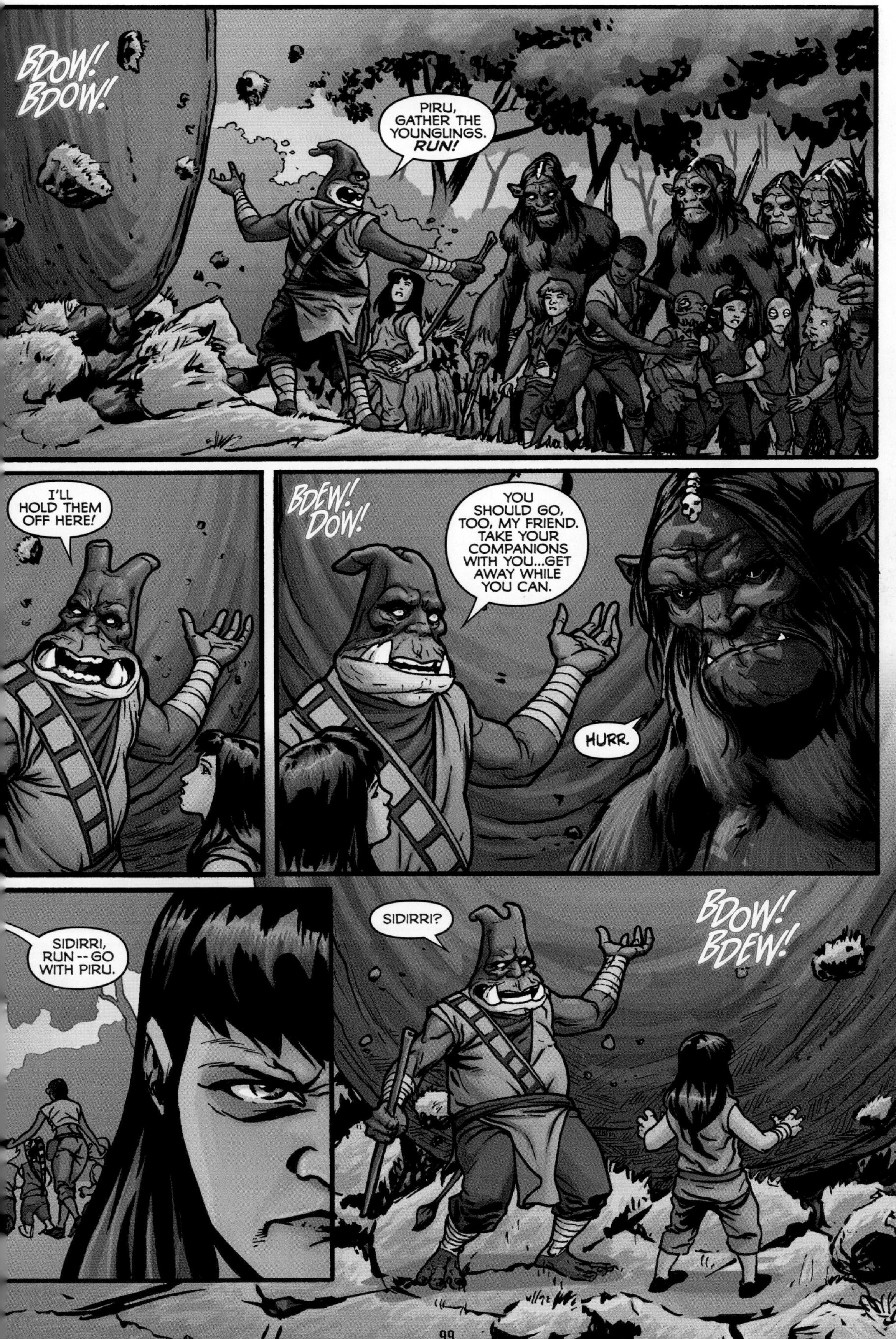
BDOW! BDOW!
PIRU, GATHER THE YOUNGLINGS. RUN!
I'LL HOLD THEM OFF HERE!
BDEW! DOW!
YOU SHOULD GO, TOO, MY FRIEND. TAKE YOUR COMPANIONS WITH YOU...GET AWAY WHILE YOU CAN.
HURR.
SIDIRRI, RUN -- GO WITH PIRU.
SIDIRRI?
BDOW! BDEW!

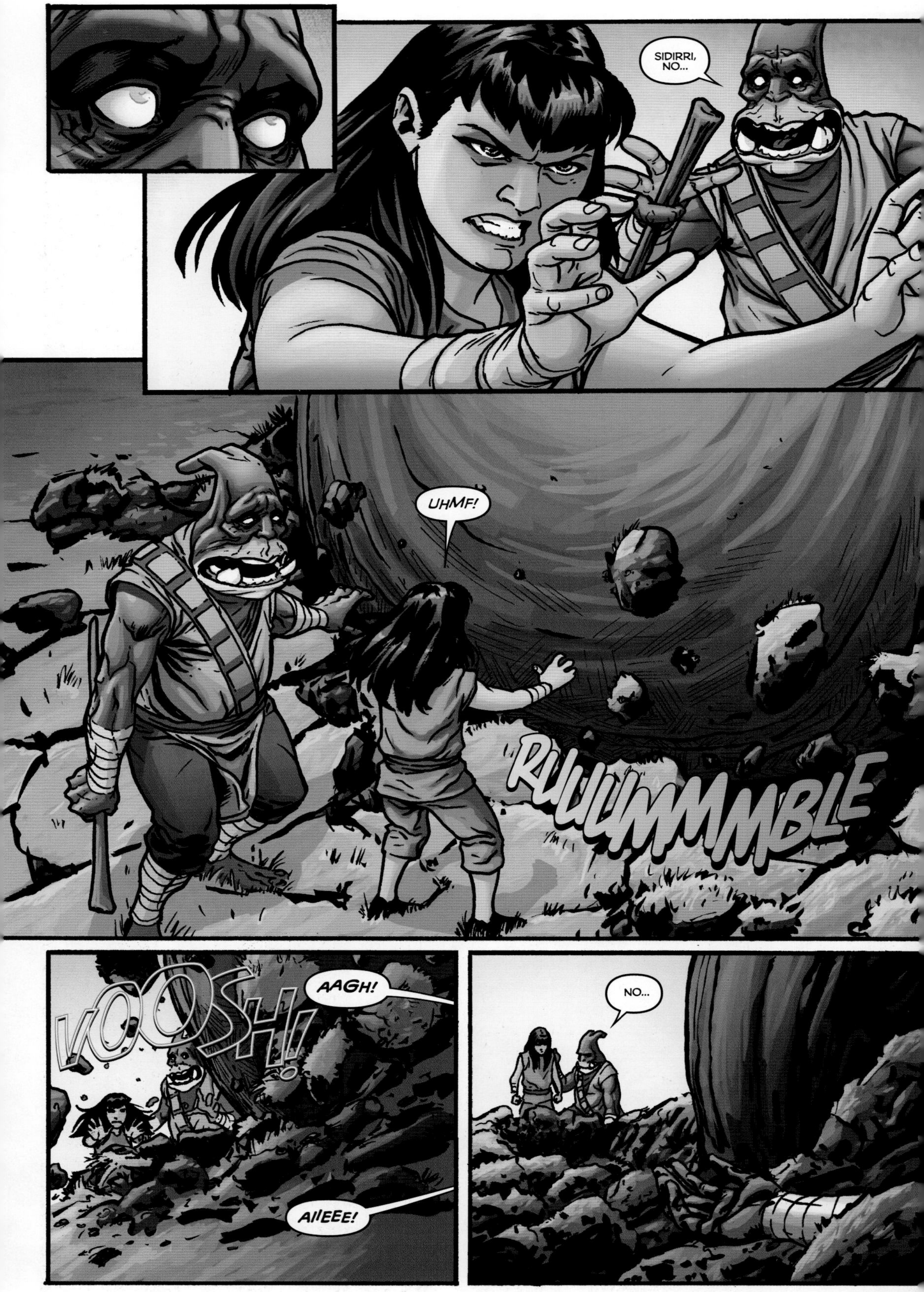
SIDIRRI, NO...
UHMF!
RUUUMMMBLE
VOOSH!
AAGH!
AIIEEE!
NO...

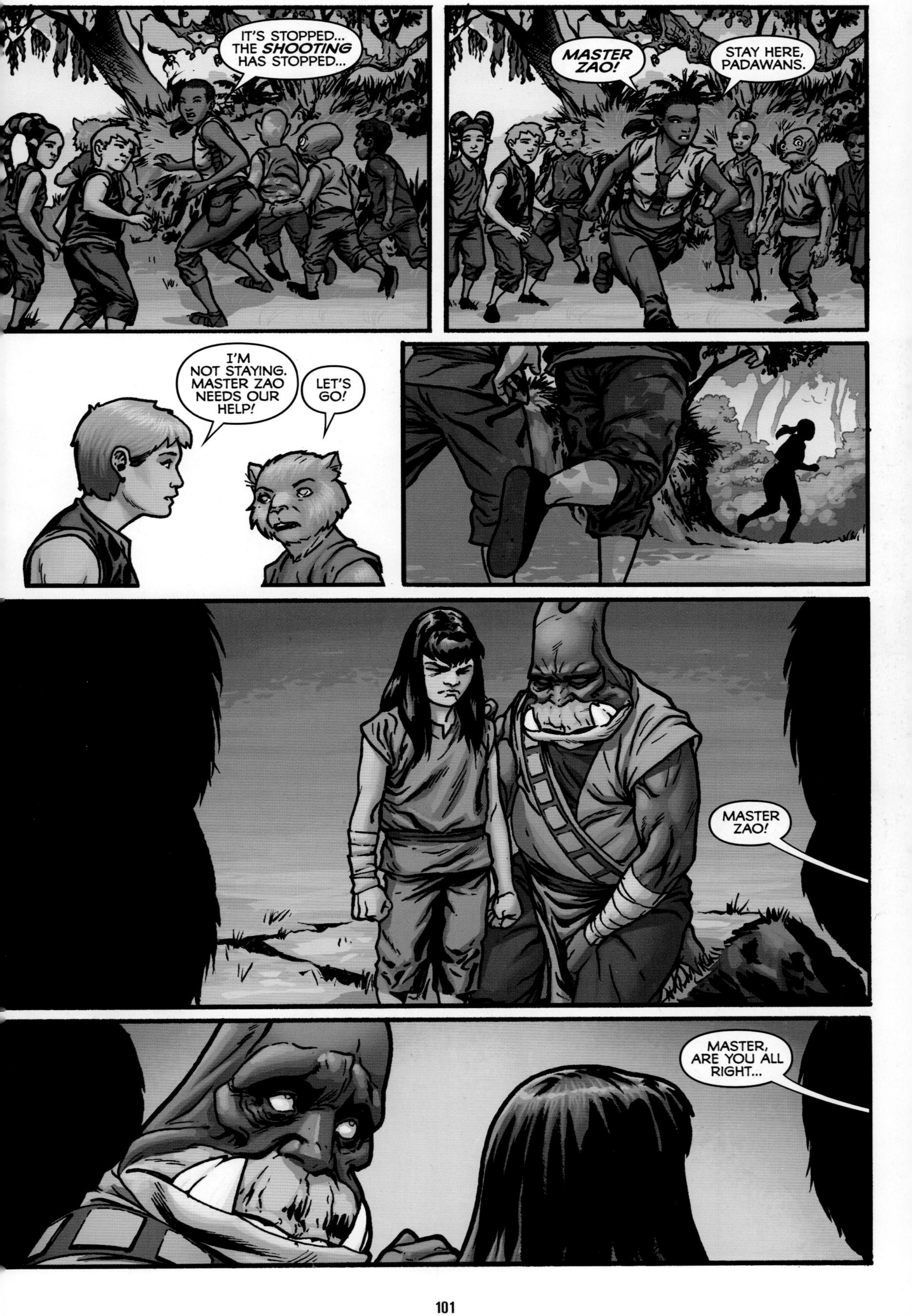
IT'S STOPPED... THE SHOOTING HAS STOPPED...
MASTER ZAO!
STAY HERE, PADAWANS.
I'M NOT STAYING. MASTER ZAO NEEDS OUR HELP!
LET'S GO!
MASTER ZAO!
MASTER, ARE YOU ALL RIGHT...

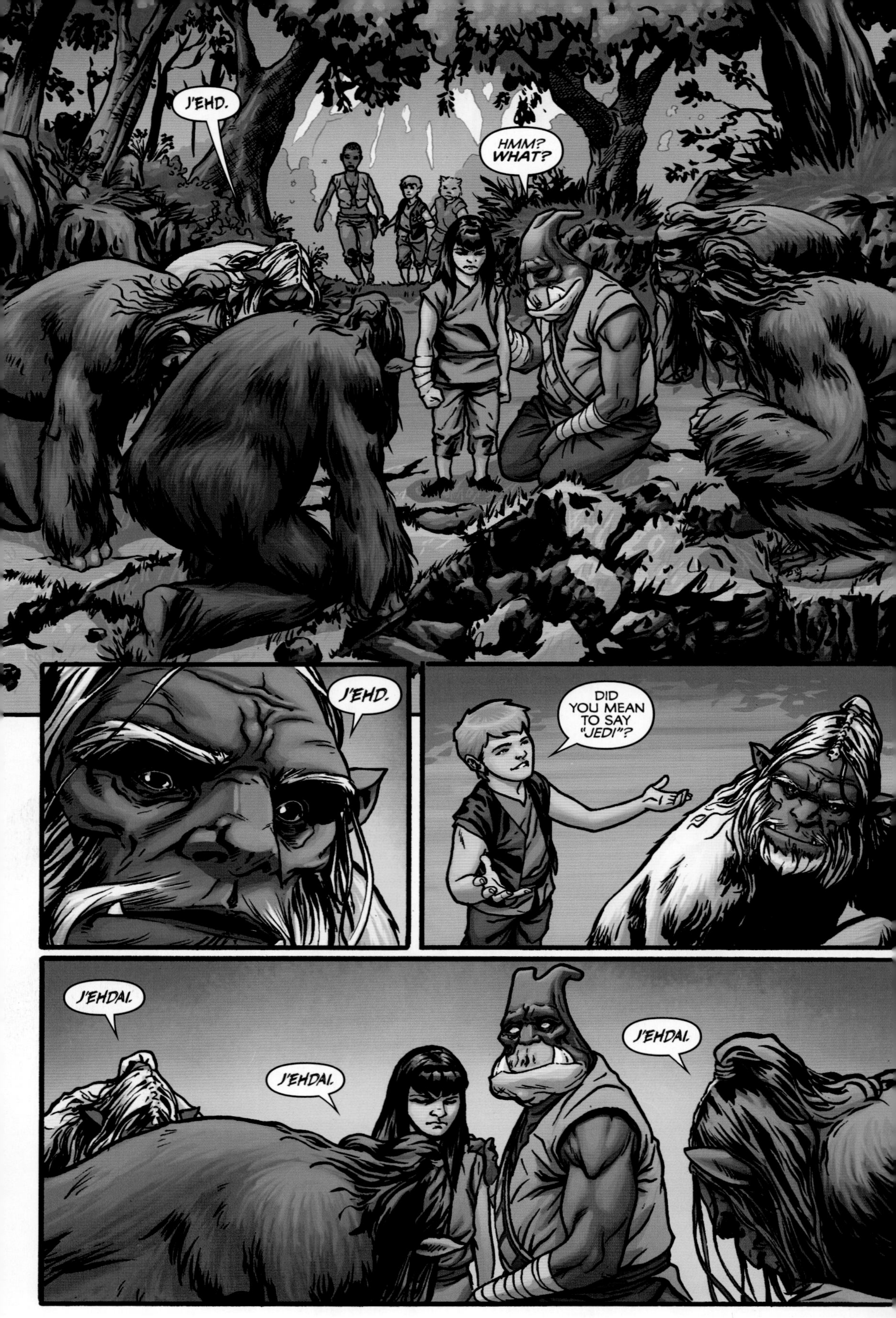
J'EHD.
HMM? WHAT?
J'EHD.
DID YOU MEAN TO SAY "JEDI"?
J'EHDAI.
J'EHDAI.
J'EHDAI.

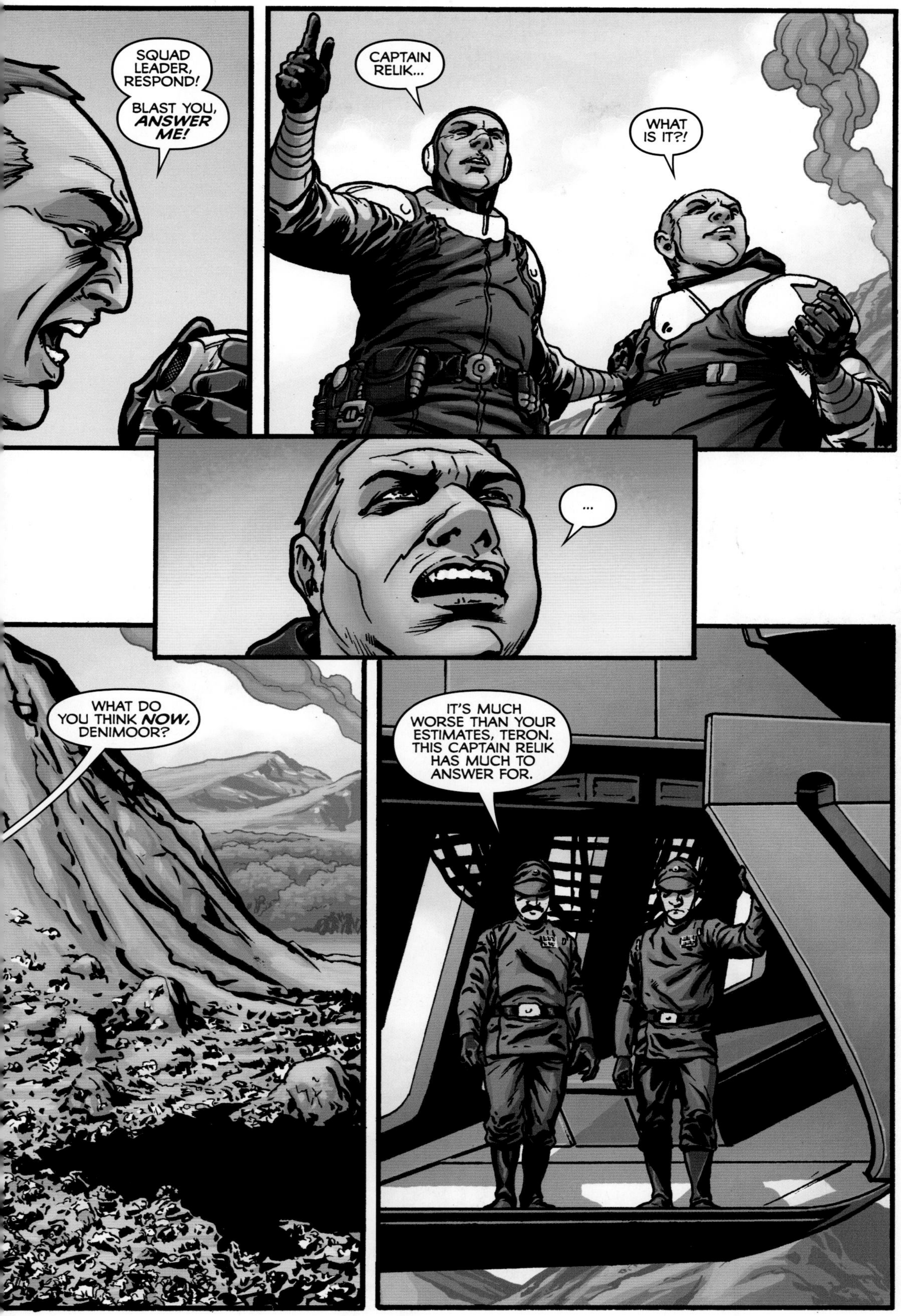
SQUAD LEADER, RESPOND!
BLAST YOU, *ANSWER ME!*
CAPTAIN RELIK...
WHAT IS IT?!
...
WHAT DO YOU THINK *NOW,* DENIMOOR?
IT'S MUCH WORSE THAN YOUR ESTIMATES, TERON. THIS CAPTAIN RELIK HAS MUCH TO ANSWER FOR.

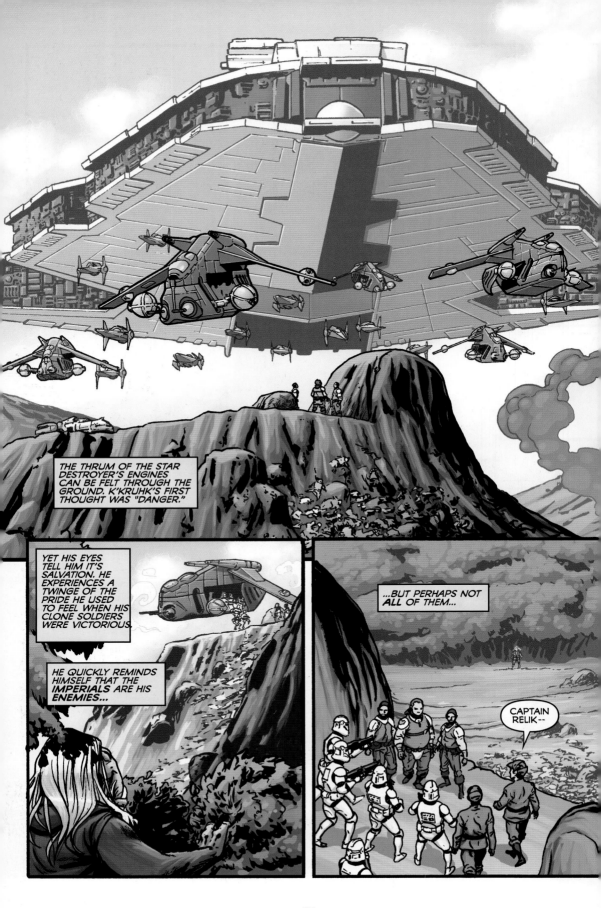

THE THRUM OF THE STAR DESTROYER'S ENGINES CAN BE FELT THROUGH THE GROUND. K'KRUHK'S FIRST THOUGHT WAS "DANGER."

YET HIS EYES TELL HIM IT'S SALVATION. HE EXPERIENCES A TWINGE OF THE PRIDE HE USED TO FEEL WHEN HIS CLONE SOLDIERS WERE VICTORIOUS.

HE QUICKLY REMINDS HIMSELF THAT THE IMPERIALS ARE HIS ENEMIES...

...BUT PERHAPS NOT ALL OF THEM...

CAPTAIN RELIK--

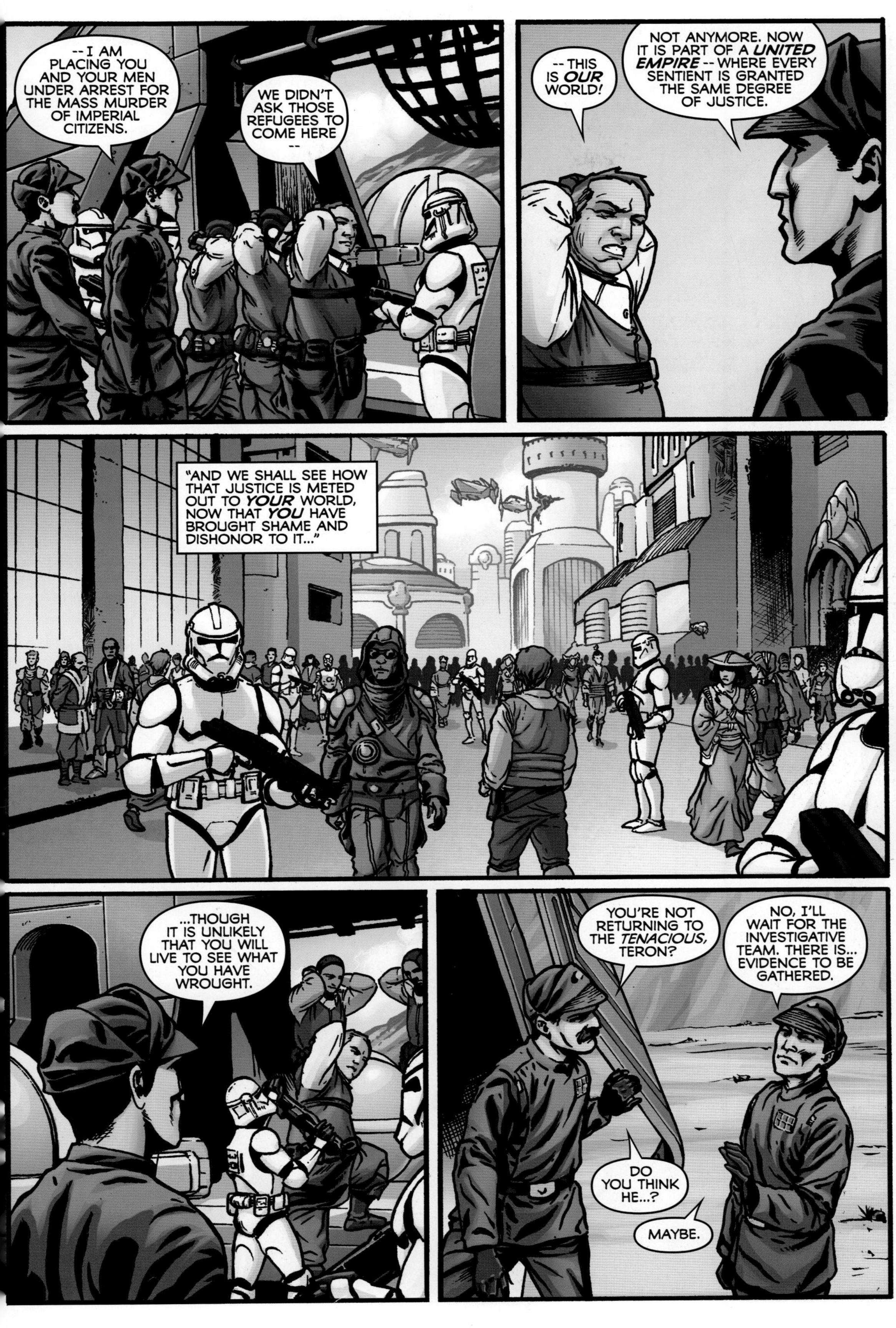
--I AM PLACING YOU AND YOUR MEN UNDER ARREST FOR THE MASS MURDER OF IMPERIAL CITIZENS.
WE DIDN'T ASK THOSE REFUGEES TO COME HERE --
-- THIS IS *OUR* WORLD!
NOT ANYMORE. NOW IT IS PART OF A *UNITED EMPIRE* -- WHERE EVERY SENTIENT IS GRANTED THE SAME DEGREE OF JUSTICE.
"AND WE SHALL SEE HOW THAT JUSTICE IS METED OUT TO *YOUR* WORLD, NOW THAT *YOU* HAVE BROUGHT SHAME AND DISHONOR TO IT..."
...THOUGH IT IS UNLIKELY THAT YOU WILL LIVE TO SEE WHAT YOU HAVE WROUGHT.
YOU'RE NOT RETURNING TO THE *TENACIOUS,* TERON?
NO, I'LL WAIT FOR THE INVESTIGATIVE TEAM. THERE IS... EVIDENCE TO BE GATHERED.
DO YOU THINK HE...?
MAYBE.

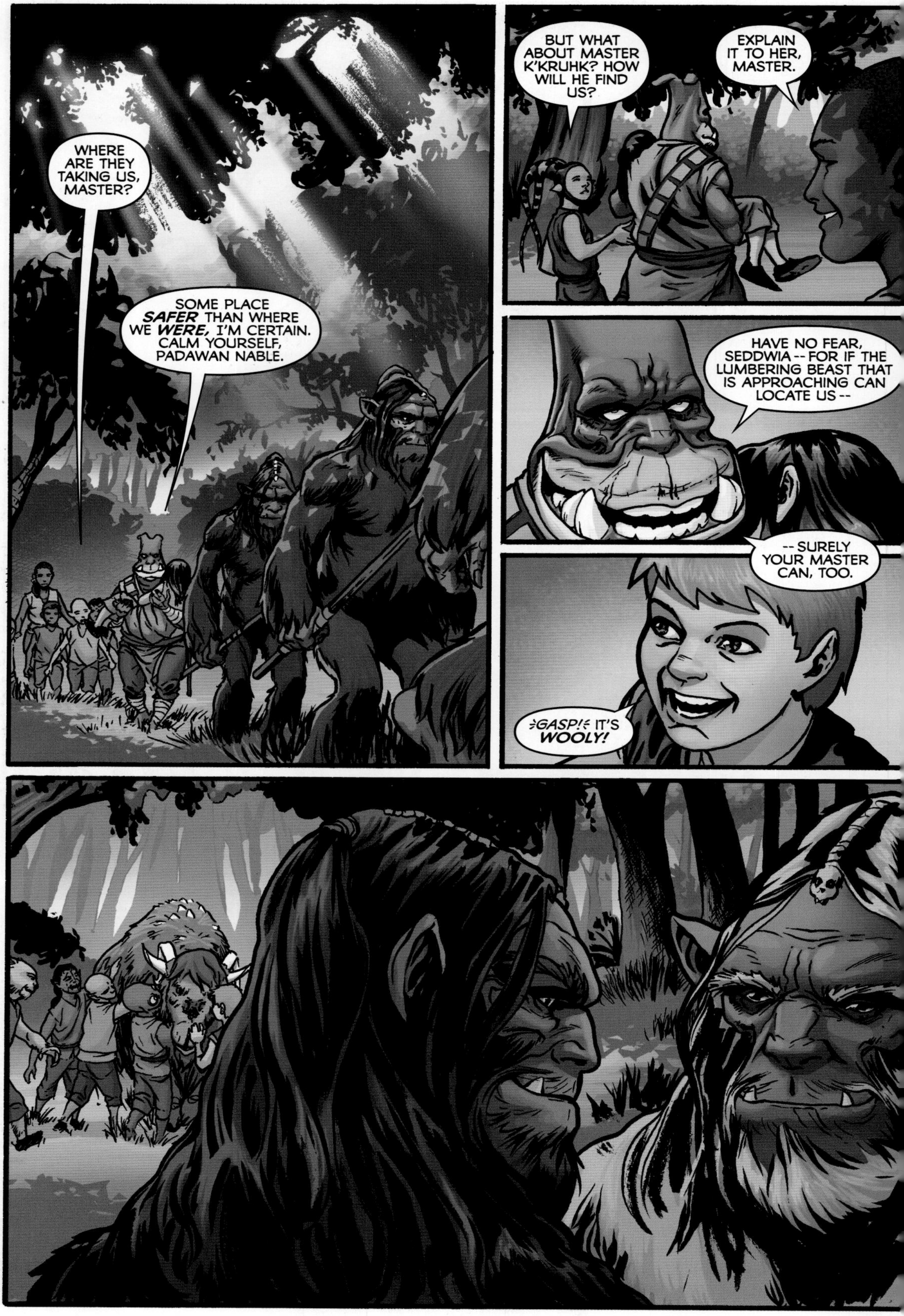
WHERE ARE THEY TAKING US, MASTER?
SOME PLACE *SAFER* THAN WHERE WE *WERE,* I'M CERTAIN. CALM YOURSELF, PADAWAN NABLE.
BUT WHAT ABOUT MASTER K'KRUHK? HOW WILL HE FIND US?
EXPLAIN IT TO HER, MASTER.
HAVE NO FEAR, SEDDWIA -- FOR IF THE LUMBERING BEAST THAT IS APPROACHING CAN LOCATE US --
-- SURELY YOUR MASTER CAN, TOO.
GASP! IT'S *WOOLY!*

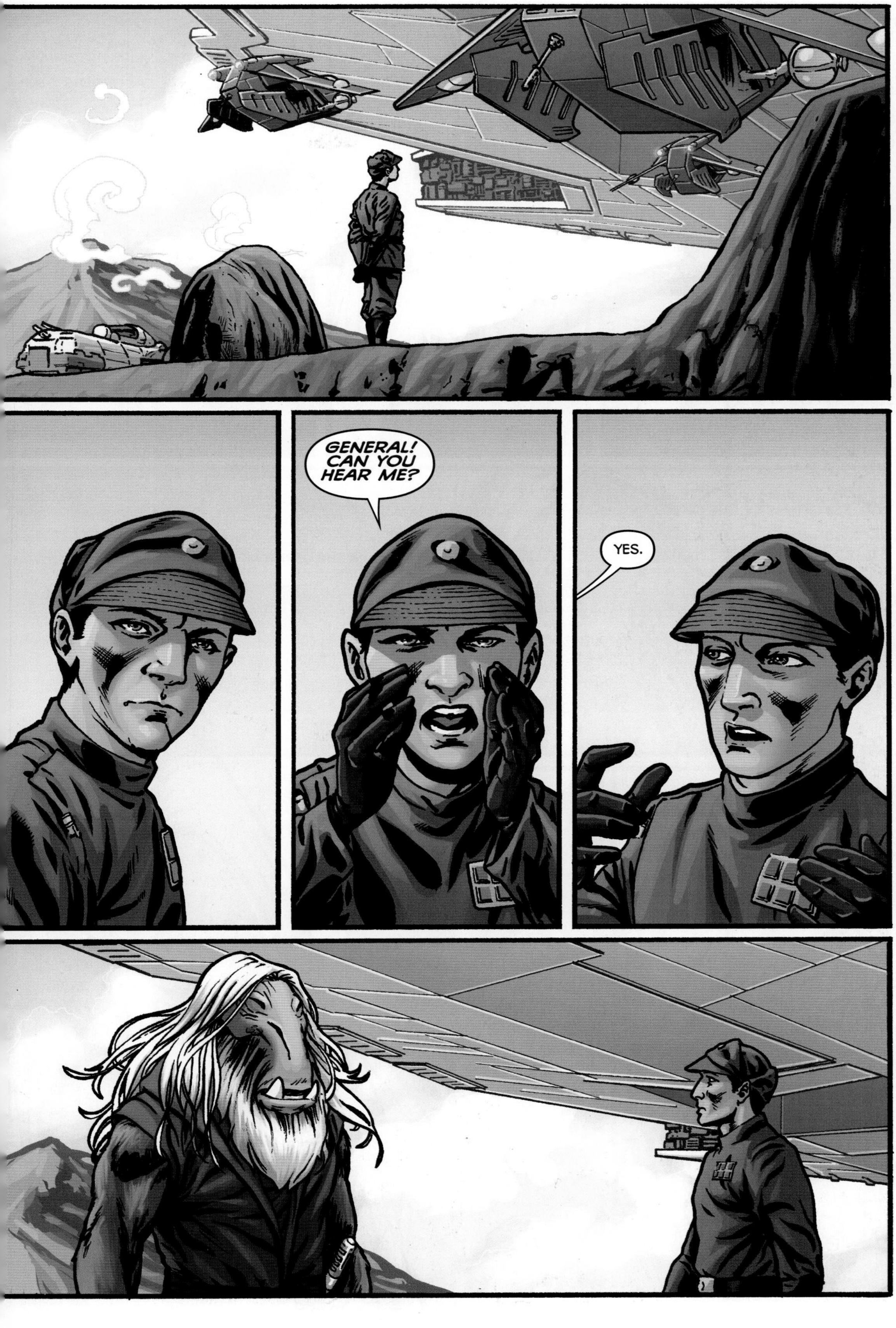
GENERAL! CAN YOU HEAR ME?
YES.

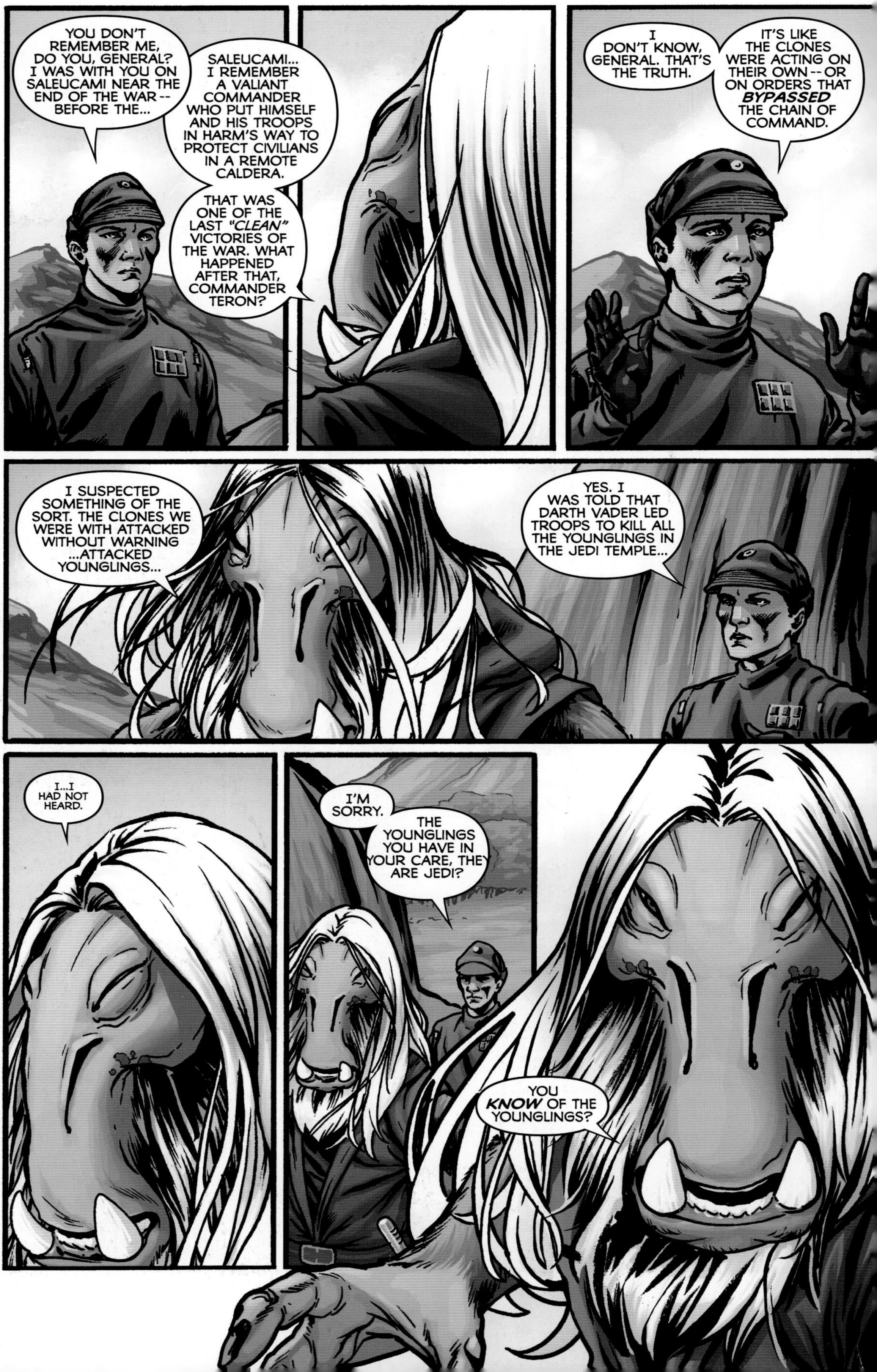
YOU DON'T REMEMBER ME, DO YOU, GENERAL? I WAS WITH YOU ON SALEUCAMI NEAR THE END OF THE WAR -- BEFORE THE...
SALEUCAMI... I REMEMBER A VALIANT COMMANDER WHO PUT HIMSELF AND HIS TROOPS IN HARM'S WAY TO PROTECT CIVILIANS IN A REMOTE CALDERA.
THAT WAS ONE OF THE LAST "CLEAN" VICTORIES OF THE WAR. WHAT HAPPENED AFTER THAT, COMMANDER TERON?
I DON'T KNOW, GENERAL. THAT'S THE TRUTH.
IT'S LIKE THE CLONES WERE ACTING ON THEIR OWN -- OR ON ORDERS THAT BYPASSED THE CHAIN OF COMMAND.
I SUSPECTED SOMETHING OF THE SORT. THE CLONES WE WERE WITH ATTACKED WITHOUT WARNING ...ATTACKED YOUNGLINGS...
YES. I WAS TOLD THAT DARTH VADER LED TROOPS TO KILL ALL THE YOUNGLINGS IN THE JEDI TEMPLE...
I...I HAD NOT HEARD.
I'M SORRY.
THE YOUNGLINGS YOU HAVE IN YOUR CARE, THEY ARE JEDI?
YOU KNOW OF THE YOUNGLINGS?

I NOTED THEM AT THE CAMP. BUT, GENERAL, BELIEVE ME, I WOULD NEVER DO *ANYTHING* TO JEOPARDIZE YOUR SAFETY -- OR THAT OF THE YOUNGLINGS!

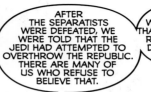

AFTER THE SEPARATISTS WERE DEFEATED, WE WERE TOLD THAT THE JEDI HAD ATTEMPTED TO OVERTHROW THE REPUBLIC. THERE ARE MANY OF US WHO REFUSE TO BELIEVE THAT.

WE KNOW IT WAS THE *EMPIRE* THAT OVERTHREW THE REPUBLIC. BUT WE DARE NOT SPEAK OUT --

-- BECAUSE THOSE WHO DO ARE IMMEDIATELY ARRESTED AND NEVER HEARD FROM AGAIN. BUT SOME OF US -- LIKE MY FRIEND COMMANDING THE *TENACIOUS* -- REMEMBER THE GOOD THE JEDI DID.

THE FACT THAT YOU HAVE JEDI YOUNGLINGS WITH YOU GIVES ME HOPE FOR THE FUTURE.

AND YOU AND YOUR FRIENDS GIVE ME HOPE, AS WELL, TERON.

MY INCOME AS A COMMANDER IS NOT GREAT, BUT IT EXCEEDS MY NEEDS. I WILL SPEND WHAT I CAN AFFORD ON THINGS YOU MIGHT NEED TO START A NEW LIFE HERE --

-- POWER UNITS, SEEDS, FARMING EQUIPMENT. I WILL RETURN HERE EVERY YEAR ON THE FIRST DAY OF LOCAL SPRING WITH SUPPLIES FOR YOU.

I WILL ACCEPT YOUR GENEROUS OFFER, COMMANDER. THANK YOU. AND MAY THE FORCE BE WITH YOU.

GOOD LUCK TO YOU, SIR.

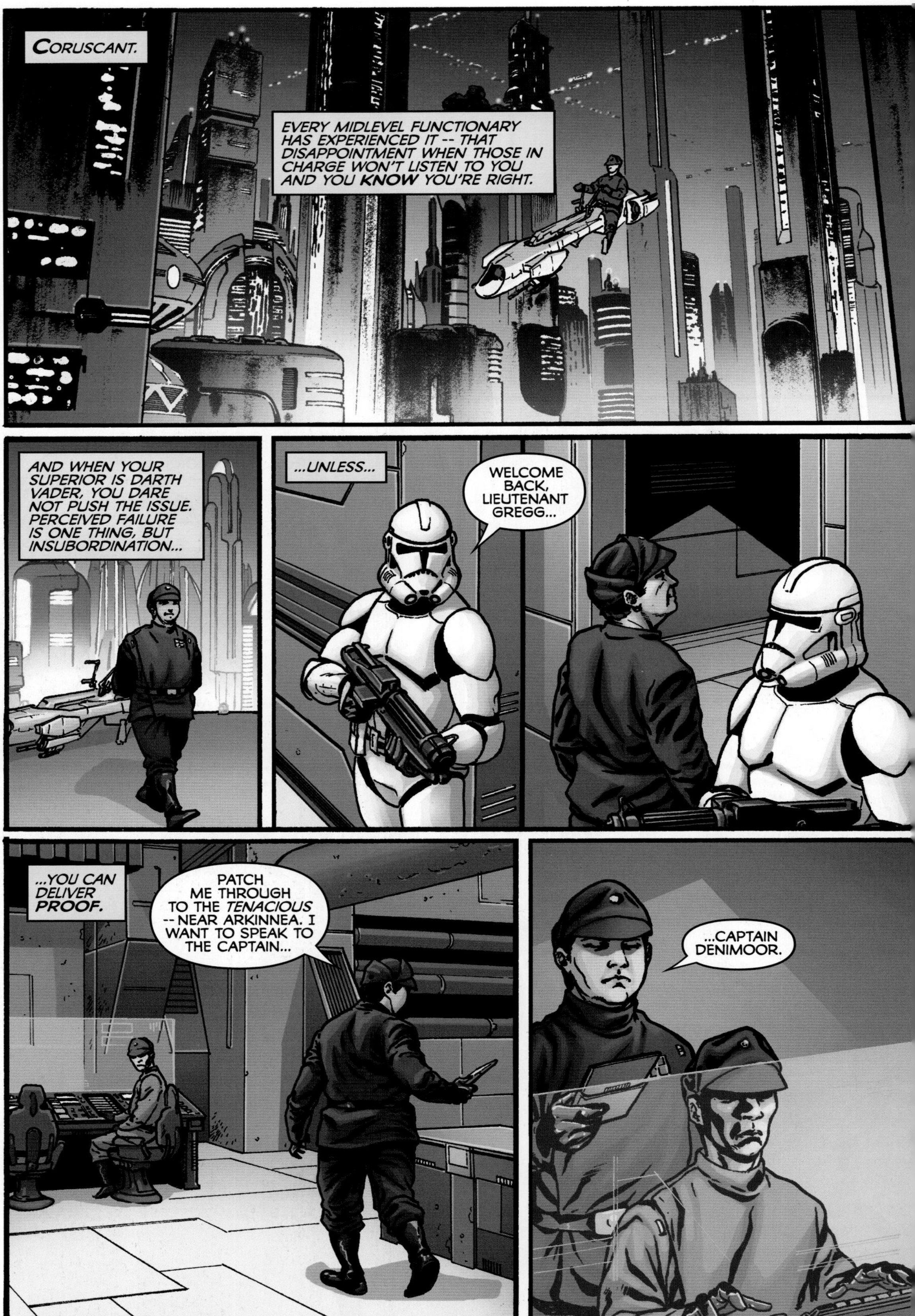
CORUSCANT.
EVERY MIDLEVEL FUNCTIONARY HAS EXPERIENCED IT -- THAT DISAPPOINTMENT WHEN THOSE IN CHARGE WON'T LISTEN TO YOU AND YOU KNOW YOU'RE RIGHT.
AND WHEN YOUR SUPERIOR IS DARTH VADER, YOU DARE NOT PUSH THE ISSUE. PERCEIVED FAILURE IS ONE THING, BUT INSUBORDINATION...
...UNLESS...
WELCOME BACK, LIEUTENANT GREGG...
...YOU CAN DELIVER PROOF.
PATCH ME THROUGH TO THE TENACIOUS -- NEAR ARKINNEA. I WANT TO SPEAK TO THE CAPTAIN...
...CAPTAIN DENIMOOR.

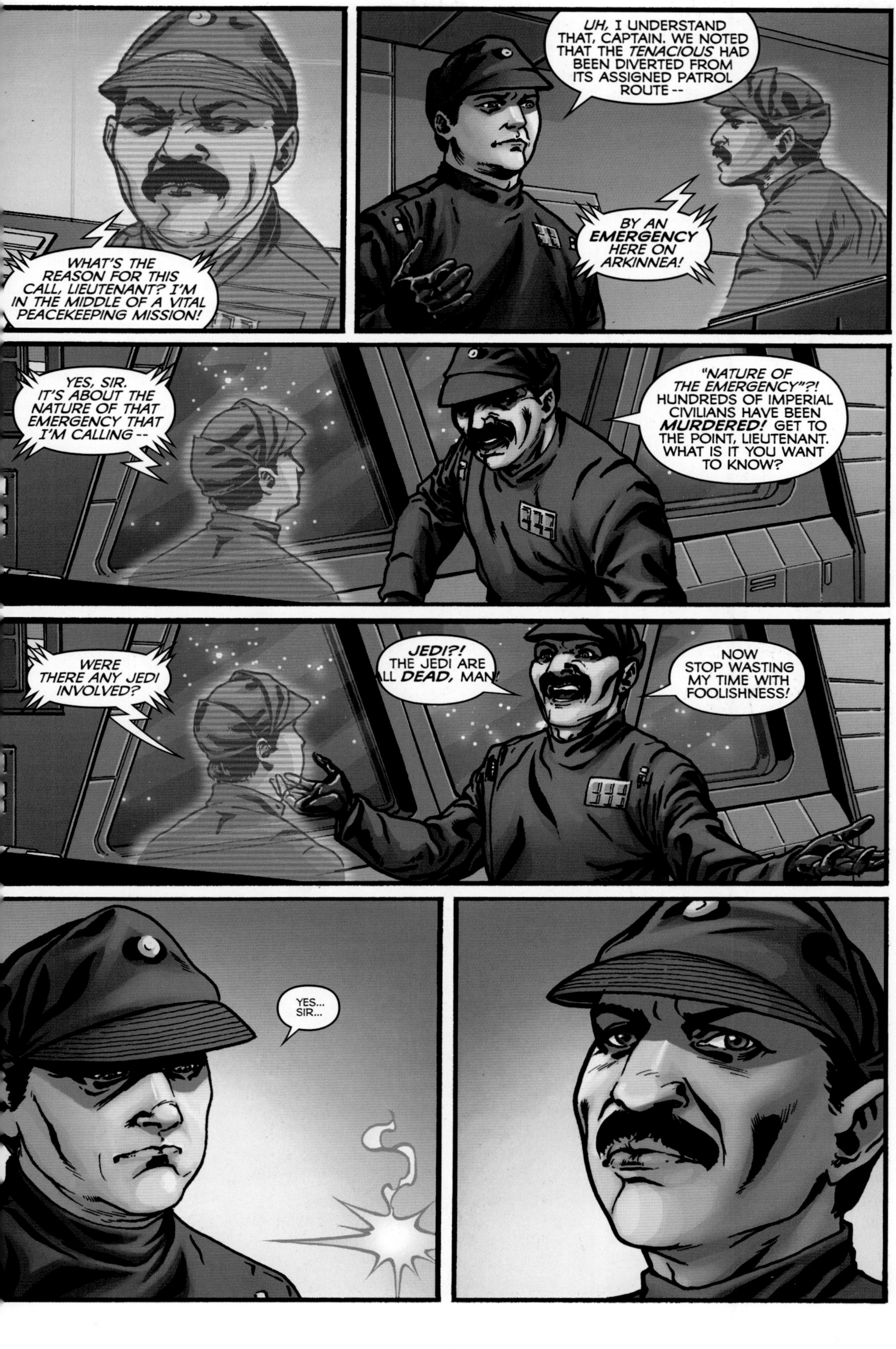
WHAT'S THE REASON FOR THIS CALL, LIEUTENANT? I'M IN THE MIDDLE OF A VITAL PEACEKEEPING MISSION!
UH, I UNDERSTAND THAT, CAPTAIN. WE NOTED THAT THE TENACIOUS HAD BEEN DIVERTED FROM ITS ASSIGNED PATROL ROUTE --
BY AN EMERGENCY HERE ON ARKINNEA!
YES, SIR. IT'S ABOUT THE NATURE OF THAT EMERGENCY THAT I'M CALLING --
"NATURE OF THE EMERGENCY"?! HUNDREDS OF IMPERIAL CIVILIANS HAVE BEEN MURDERED! GET TO THE POINT, LIEUTENANT. WHAT IS IT YOU WANT TO KNOW?
WERE THERE ANY JEDI INVOLVED?
JEDI?! THE JEDI ARE ALL DEAD, MAN!
NOW STOP WASTING MY TIME WITH FOOLISHNESS!
YES... SIR...

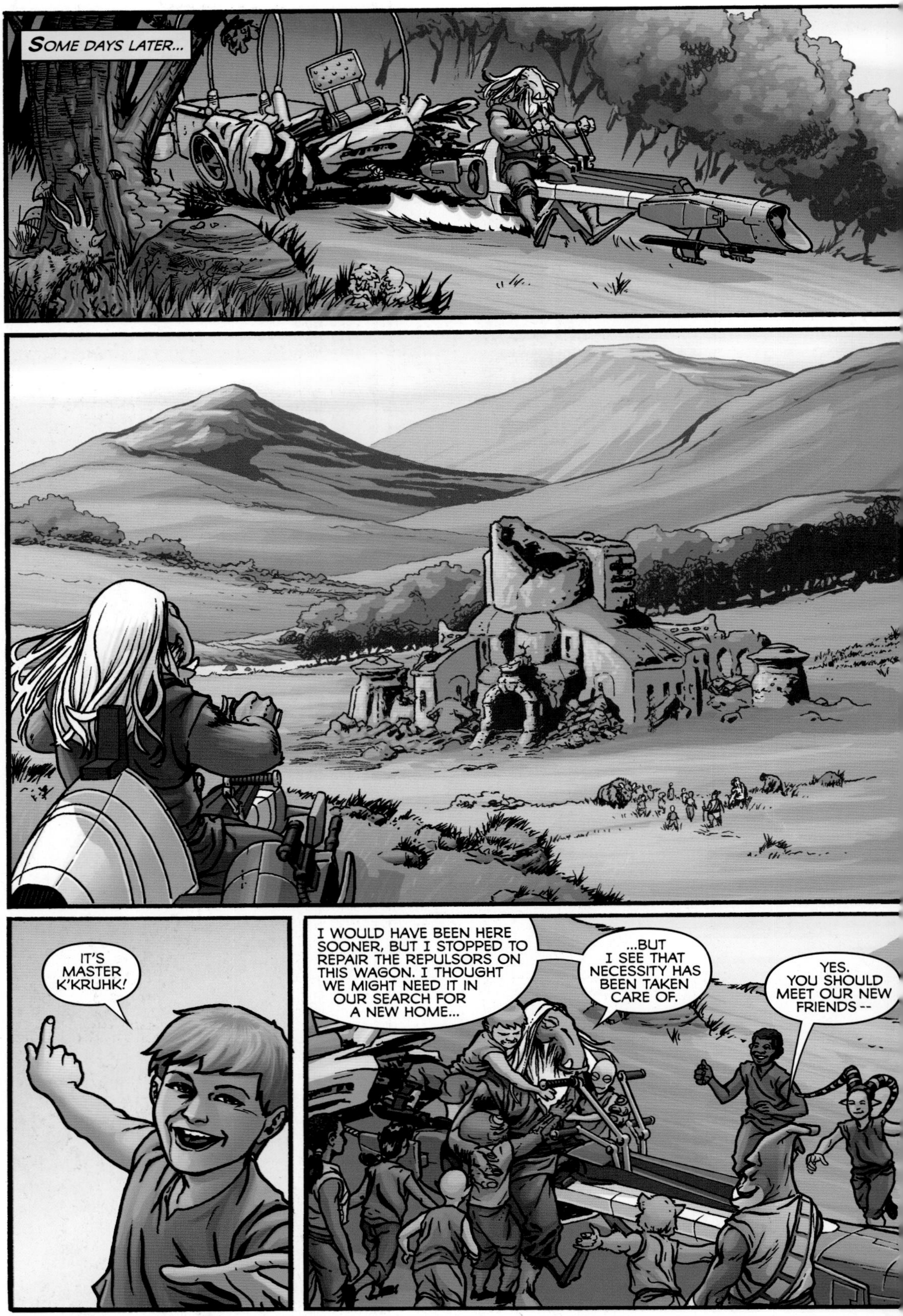
SOME DAYS LATER...
IT'S MASTER K'KRUHK!
I WOULD HAVE BEEN HERE SOONER, BUT I STOPPED TO REPAIR THE REPULSORS ON THIS WAGON. I THOUGHT WE MIGHT NEED IT IN OUR SEARCH FOR A NEW HOME...
...BUT I SEE THAT NECESSITY HAS BEEN TAKEN CARE OF.
YES. YOU SHOULD MEET OUR NEW FRIENDS --

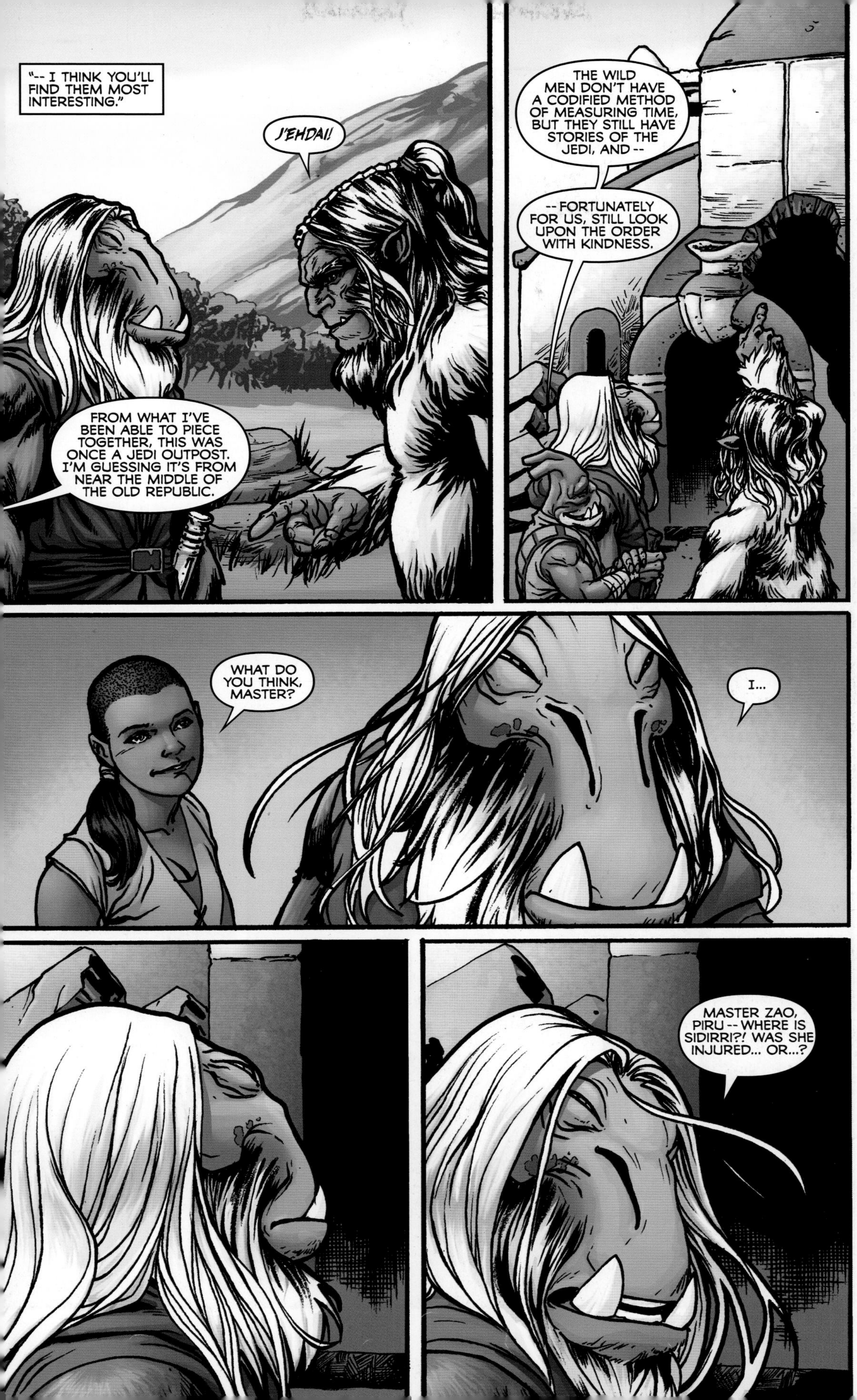
"-- I THINK YOU'LL FIND THEM MOST INTERESTING."
J'EHDAI!
FROM WHAT I'VE BEEN ABLE TO PIECE TOGETHER, THIS WAS ONCE A JEDI OUTPOST. I'M GUESSING IT'S FROM NEAR THE MIDDLE OF THE OLD REPUBLIC.
THE WILD MEN DON'T HAVE A CODIFIED METHOD OF MEASURING TIME, BUT THEY STILL HAVE STORIES OF THE JEDI, AND --
-- FORTUNATELY FOR US, STILL LOOK UPON THE ORDER WITH KINDNESS.
WHAT DO YOU THINK, MASTER?
I...
MASTER ZAO, PIRU -- WHERE IS SIDIRRI?! WAS SHE INJURED... OR...?

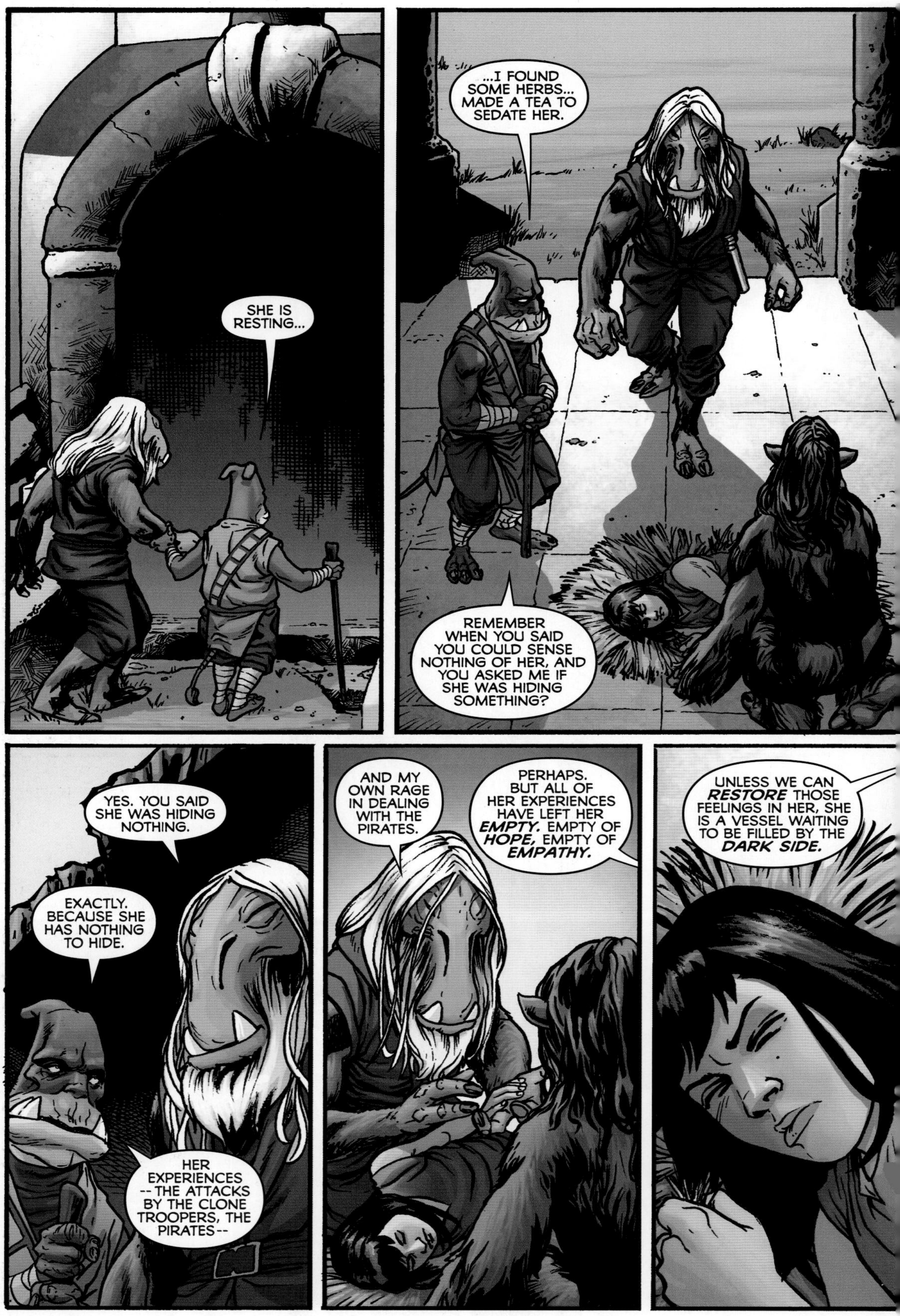
SHE IS RESTING...
...I FOUND SOME HERBS... MADE A TEA TO SEDATE HER.
REMEMBER WHEN YOU SAID YOU COULD SENSE NOTHING OF HER, AND YOU ASKED ME IF SHE WAS HIDING SOMETHING?
YES. YOU SAID SHE WAS HIDING NOTHING.
EXACTLY. BECAUSE SHE HAS NOTHING TO HIDE.
HER EXPERIENCES --THE ATTACKS BY THE CLONE TROOPERS, THE PIRATES--
AND MY OWN RAGE IN DEALING WITH THE PIRATES.
PERHAPS. BUT ALL OF HER EXPERIENCES HAVE LEFT HER *EMPTY.* EMPTY OF *HOPE,* EMPTY OF *EMPATHY.*
UNLESS WE CAN *RESTORE* THOSE FEELINGS IN HER, SHE IS A VESSEL WAITING TO BE FILLED BY THE *DARK SIDE.*

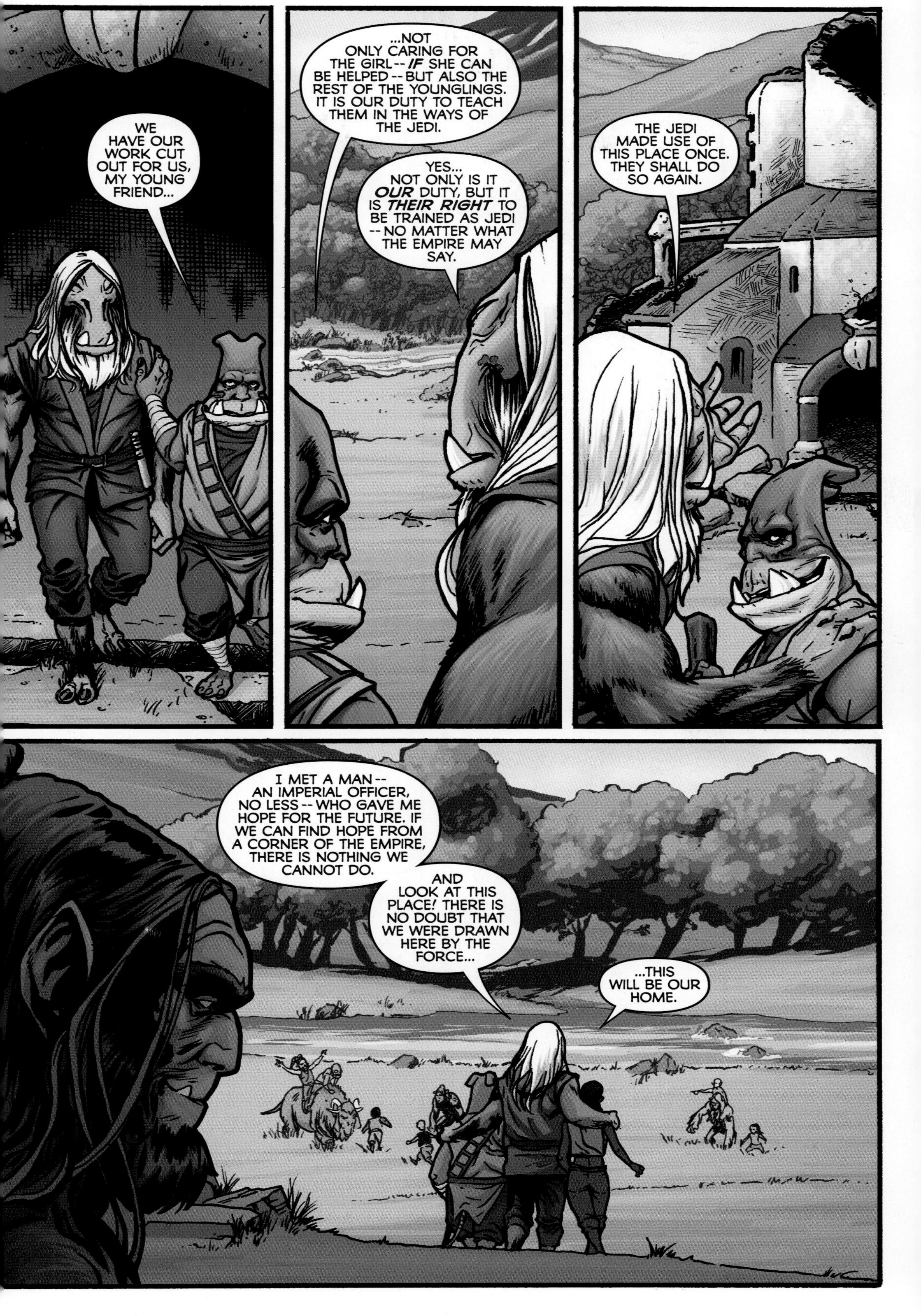
WE HAVE OUR WORK CUT OUT FOR US, MY YOUNG FRIEND...
...NOT ONLY CARING FOR THE GIRL -- *IF* SHE CAN BE HELPED -- BUT ALSO THE REST OF THE YOUNGLINGS. IT IS OUR DUTY TO TEACH THEM IN THE WAYS OF THE JEDI.
YES... NOT ONLY IS IT ***OUR*** DUTY, BUT IT IS ***THEIR RIGHT*** TO BE TRAINED AS JEDI -- NO MATTER WHAT THE EMPIRE MAY SAY.
THE JEDI MADE USE OF THIS PLACE ONCE. THEY SHALL DO SO AGAIN.
I MET A MAN -- AN IMPERIAL OFFICER, NO LESS -- WHO GAVE ME HOPE FOR THE FUTURE. IF WE CAN FIND HOPE FROM A CORNER OF THE EMPIRE, THERE IS NOTHING WE CANNOT DO.
AND LOOK AT THIS PLACE! THERE IS NO DOUBT THAT WE WERE DRAWN HERE BY THE FORCE...
...THIS WILL BE OUR HOME.

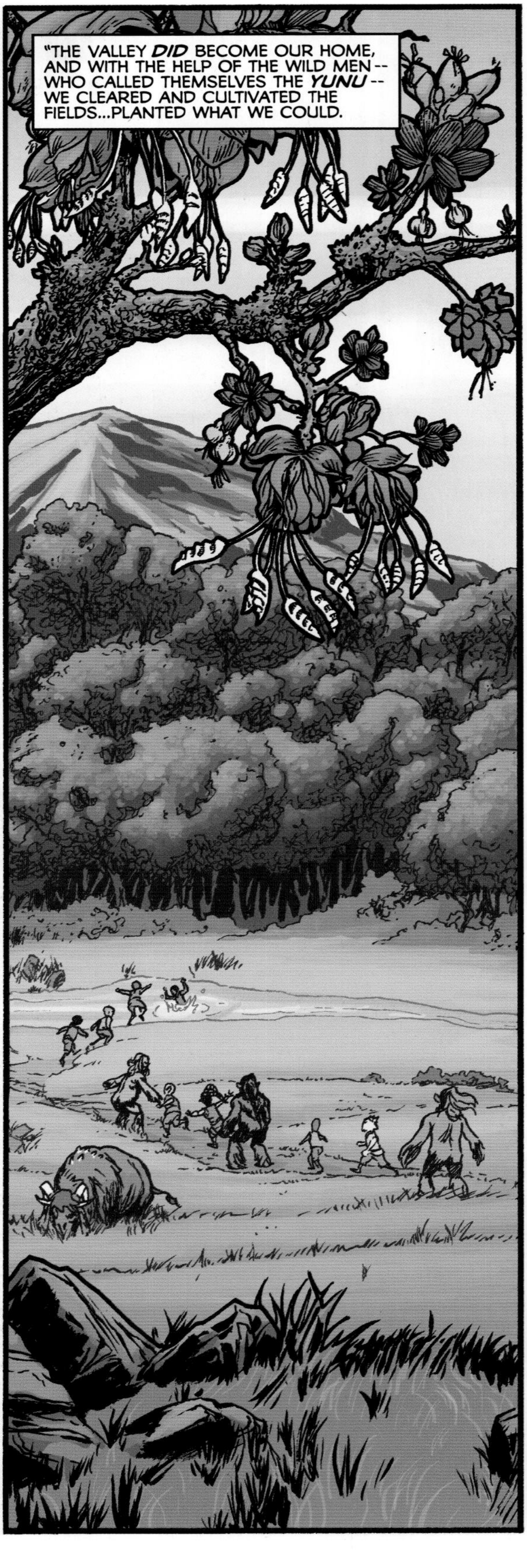
"THE VALLEY DID BECOME OUR HOME, AND WITH THE HELP OF THE WILD MEN -- WHO CALLED THEMSELVES THE YUNU -- WE CLEARED AND CULTIVATED THE FIELDS...PLANTED WHAT WE COULD.

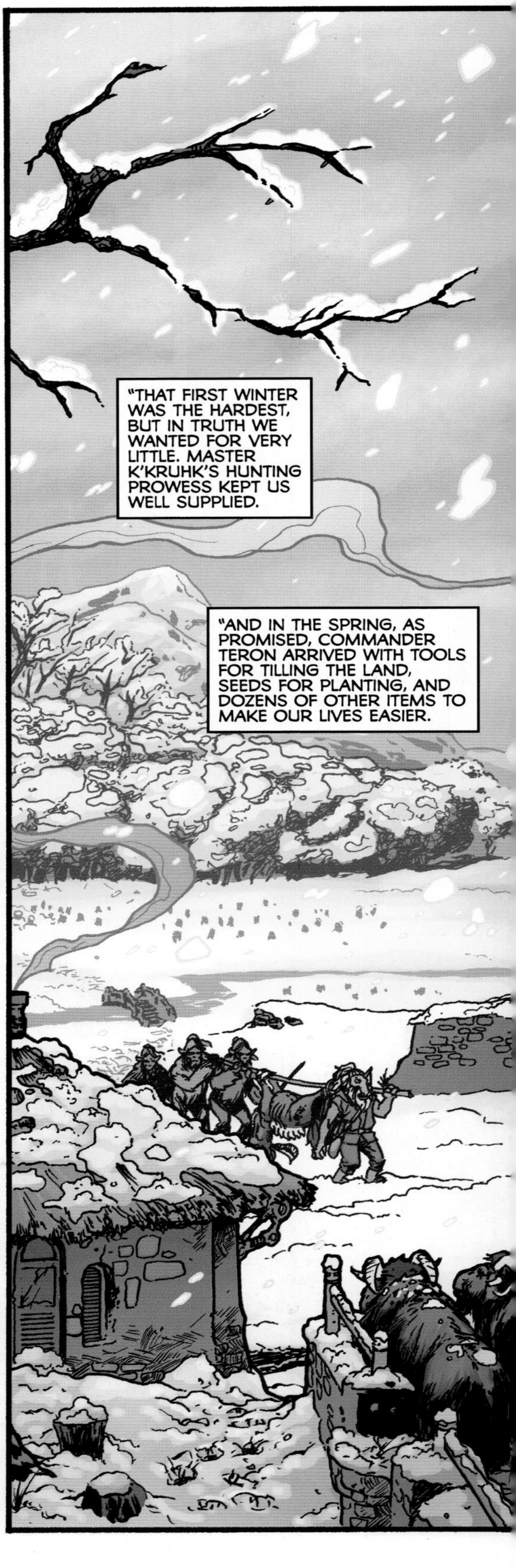
"THAT FIRST WINTER WAS THE HARDEST, BUT IN TRUTH WE WANTED FOR VERY LITTLE. MASTER K'KRUHK'S HUNTING PROWESS KEPT US WELL SUPPLIED.
"AND IN THE SPRING, AS PROMISED, COMMANDER TERON ARRIVED WITH TOOLS FOR TILLING THE LAND, SEEDS FOR PLANTING, AND DOZENS OF OTHER ITEMS TO MAKE OUR LIVES EASIER.

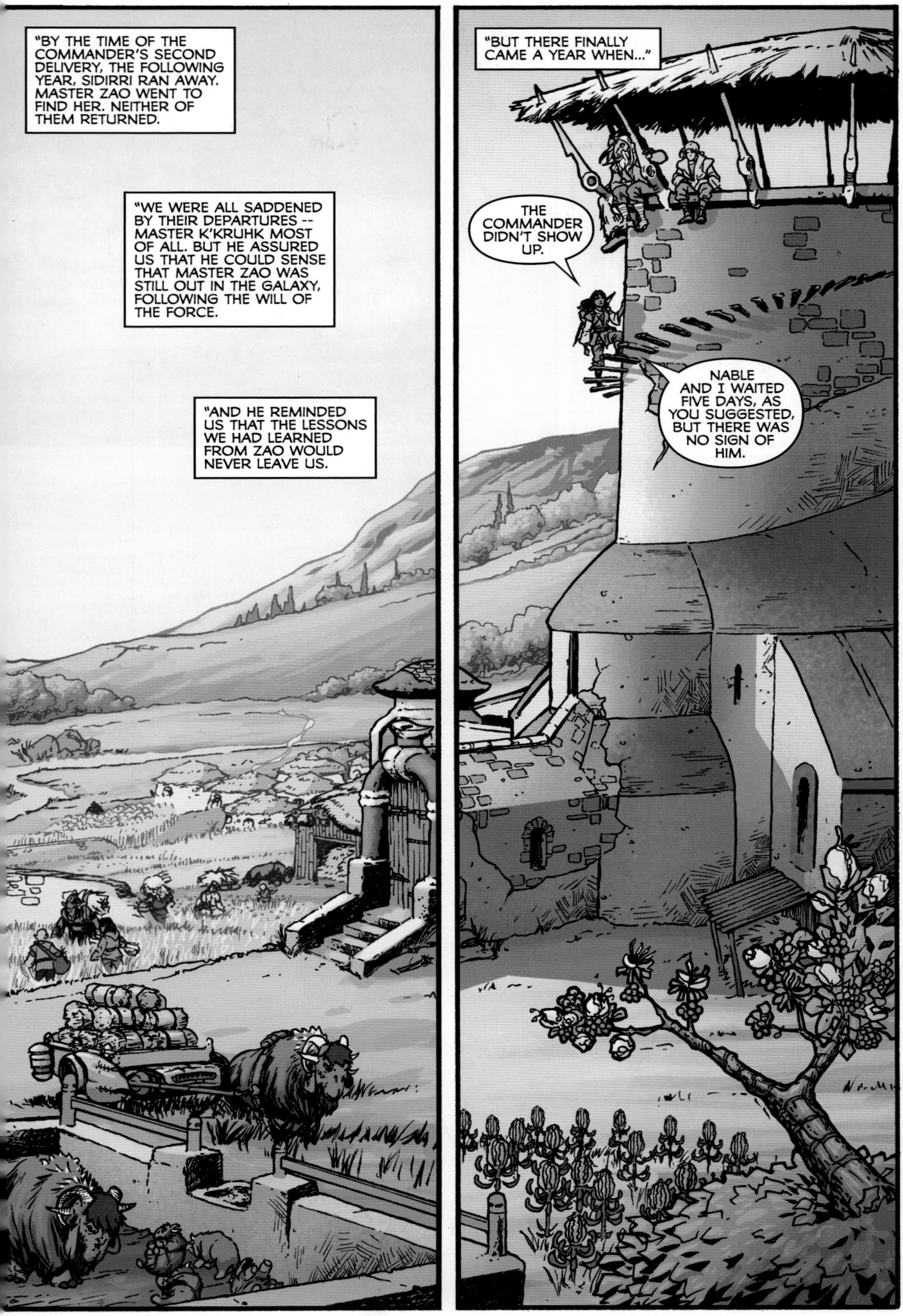
"BY THE TIME OF THE COMMANDER'S SECOND DELIVERY, THE FOLLOWING YEAR, SIDIRRI RAN AWAY. MASTER ZAO WENT TO FIND HER. NEITHER OF THEM RETURNED.
"WE WERE ALL SADDENED BY THEIR DEPARTURES -- MASTER K'KRUHK MOST OF ALL. BUT HE ASSURED US THAT HE COULD SENSE THAT MASTER ZAO WAS STILL OUT IN THE GALAXY, FOLLOWING THE WILL OF THE FORCE.
"AND HE REMINDED US THAT THE LESSONS WE HAD LEARNED FROM ZAO WOULD NEVER LEAVE US.
"BUT THERE FINALLY CAME A YEAR WHEN..."
THE COMMANDER DIDN'T SHOW UP.
NABLE AND I WAITED FIVE DAYS, AS YOU SUGGESTED, BUT THERE WAS NO SIGN OF HIM.

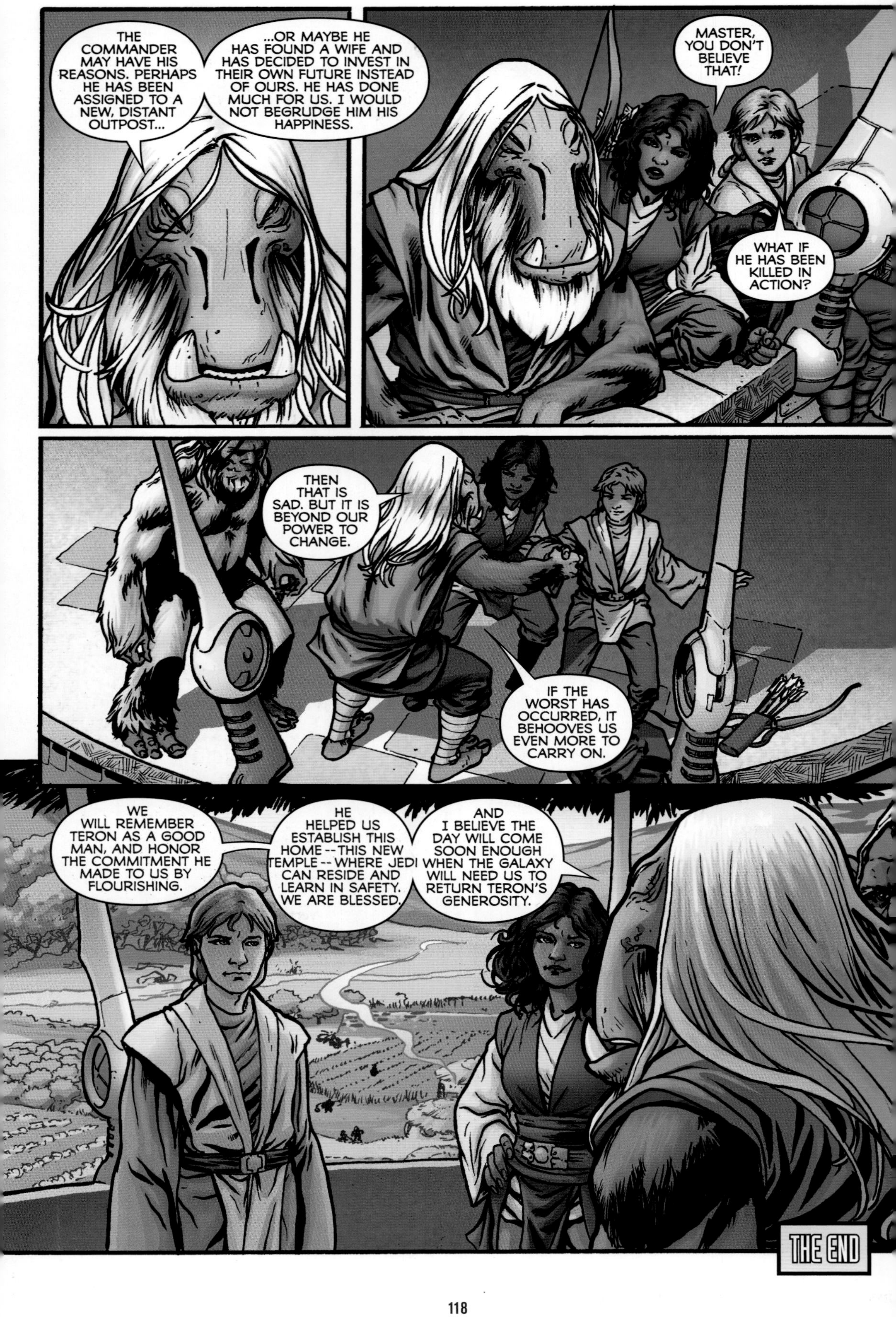
THE COMMANDER MAY HAVE HIS REASONS. PERHAPS HE HAS BEEN ASSIGNED TO A NEW, DISTANT OUTPOST...
...OR MAYBE HE HAS FOUND A WIFE AND HAS DECIDED TO INVEST IN THEIR OWN FUTURE INSTEAD OF OURS. HE HAS DONE MUCH FOR US. I WOULD NOT BEGRUDGE HIM HIS HAPPINESS.
MASTER, YOU DON'T BELIEVE THAT!
WHAT IF HE HAS BEEN KILLED IN ACTION?
THEN THAT IS SAD. BUT IT IS BEYOND OUR POWER TO CHANGE.
IF THE WORST HAS OCCURRED, IT BEHOOVES US EVEN MORE TO CARRY ON.
WE WILL REMEMBER TERON AS A GOOD MAN, AND HONOR THE COMMITMENT HE MADE TO US BY FLOURISHING.
HE HELPED US ESTABLISH THIS HOME -- THIS NEW TEMPLE -- WHERE JEDI CAN RESIDE AND LEARN IN SAFETY. WE ARE BLESSED.
AND I BELIEVE THE DAY WILL COME SOON ENOUGH WHEN THE GALAXY WILL NEED US TO RETURN TERON'S GENEROSITY.
THE END

STAR WARS GRAPHIC NOVEL TIMELINE (IN YEARS)

Dawn of the Jedi—36,000 BSW4
Omnibus: Tales of the Jedi—5,000–3,986 BSW4
Knights of the Old Republic—3,964–3,963 BSW4
The Old Republic—3678, 3653, 3600 BSW4
Lost Tribe of the Sith—2974 BSW4
Knight Errant—1,032 BSW4
Jedi vs. Sith—1,000 BSW4
Jedi: The Dark Side—53 BSW4
Omnibus: Rise of the Sith—33 BSW4
Episode I: The Phantom Menace—32 BSW4
Omnibus: Emissaries and Assassins—32 BSW4
Omnibus: Quinlan Vos—Jedi in Darkness—31–30 BSW4
Omnibus: Menace Revealed—31–22 BSW4
Honor and Duty—22 BSW4
Blood Ties—22 BSW4
Episode II: Attack of the Clones—22 BSW4
Clone Wars—22–19 BSW4
Omnibus: Clone Wars—22–19 BSW4
Clone Wars Adventures—22–19 BSW4
Darth Maul: Death Sentence—20 BSW4
Episode III: Revenge of the Sith—19 BSW4
Purge—19 BSW4
Dark Times—19 BSW4
Omnibus: Droids—5.5 BSW4
Omnibus: Boba Fett—3 BSW4–10 ASW4
Agent of the Empire—3 BSW4
The Force Unleashed—2 BSW4
Omnibus: At War with the Empire—1 BSW4
Episode IV: A New Hope—SW4
Star Wars—0 ASW4
Classic Star Wars—0–3 ASW4
Omnibus: A Long Time Ago. . . .—0–4 ASW4
Empire—0 ASW4
Omnibus: The Other Sons of Tatooine—0 ASW4
Omnibus: Early Victories—0–3 ASW4
Jabba the Hutt: The Art of the Deal—1 ASW4
Episode V: The Empire Strikes Back—3 ASW4
Omnibus: Shadows of the Empire—3.5–4.5 ASW4
Episode VI: Return of the Jedi—4 ASW4
Omnibus: X-Wing Rogue Squadron—4–5 ASW4
The Thrawn Trilogy—9 ASW4
Dark Empire—10 ASW4
Crimson Empire—11 ASW4
Jedi Academy: Leviathan—12 ASW4
Union—19 ASW4
Chewbacca—25 ASW4
Invasion—25 ASW4
Legacy—130–138 ASW4

Dawn of the Jedi
36,000 years before
Star Wars: A New Hope

Old Republic Era
25,000–1000 years before
Star Wars: A New Hope

Rise of the Empire Era
1000–0 years before Star
Wars: A New Hope

Rebellion Era
0–5 years after
Star Wars: A New Hope

New Republic Era
5–25 years after
Star Wars: A New Hope

New Jedi Order Era
25+ years after
Star Wars: A New Hope

Legacy Era
130+ years after
Star Wars: A New Hope

Vector
Crosses four eras in timeline

Volume 1 contains:
Knights of the Old Republic Volume 5
Dark Times Volume 3

Volume 2 contains:
Rebellion Volume 4
Legacy Volume 6

Infinities
Does not apply to timeline

Sergio Aragones Stomps Star Wars
Star Wars Tales
Omnibus: Infinities
Tag and Bink
Star Wars Visionaries

BSW4 = before *Episode IV: A New Hope*. ASW4 = after *Episode IV: A New Hope*.

STAR WARS®
DARK TIMES

In the wake of the Clone Wars and the destruction of the Jedi Order, the dark times have begun; this is the beginning of the era of Darth Vader and Emperor Palpatine. The future is grim, evil is on the rise, and there are no more safe places in the galaxy.

Dark Times Volume 1:
The Path to Nowhere
ISBN 978-1-59307-792-1 | $17.99

Dark Times Volume 2:
Parallels
ISBN 978-1-59307-945-1 | $17.95

Dark Times Volume 3:
Vector Volume 1
ISBN 978-1-59582-226-0 | $17.99

Dark Times Volume 4:
Blue Harvest
ISBN 978-1-59582-264-2 | $17.99

Dark Times Volume 5:
Out of the Wilderness
ISBN 978-1-59582-926-9 | $17.99

AVAILABLE AT YOUR LOCAL COMICS SHOP OR BOOKSTORE

To find a comics shop in your area, call 1-888-266-4226. For more information or to order direct visit DarkHorse.com or call 1-800-862-0052. Mon.–Fri. 9 a.m. to 5 p.m. Pacific Time.

DARK
HORSE
BOOKS
DarkHorse.com